CITY OF REFUGEES

CITY OF REFUGEES

THE STORY OF THREE NEWCOMERS
WHO BREATHED LIFE
INTO A DYING AMERICAN TOWN

SUSAN HARTMAN

BEACON PRESS
Boston

BEACON PRESS
Boston, Massachusetts
www.beacon.org

Beacon Press books
are published under the auspices of
the Unitarian Universalist Association of Congregations.

25 24 23 22   8 7 6 5 4 3 2 1

This book is printed on acid-free paper that meets the uncoated
paper ANSI/NISO specifications for permanence as revised in 1992.

Text design by Michael Starkman at
Wilsted & Taylor Publishing Services

LCCN: 2022003001
ISBN: 978-080702467-6

for Ben

CONTENTS

Part III NEW AMERICANS

AUTHOR'S NOTE

In 2013, I got a call from a stranger. It was a Hamilton College economics professor, Erol Balkan, who knew I often wrote about immigrant communities. He said, "Did you know Utica has become a city of refugees?"

Utica is an old manufacturing town on the Mohawk River, about 100 miles northwest of Albany, New York. It might seem an unexpected spot for refugees fleeing persecution and war to put down new roots.

Four days later, I was in Professor Balkan's car.

He drove me through streets once filled with abandoned houses. Piles of sneakers now sat on the porches of homes where Somali Bantu families live. We ate at a tiny restaurant owned by a Burmese brother and sister. We passed a large Bosnian mosque, carved out of an abandoned Methodist church.

In the seventies, when I was a student at Kirkland College—Hamilton's coordinate school—I was intrigued by Utica, 15 minutes away. It seemed under a spell, like Sleeping Beauty. Its downtown—only 12 blocks long—was filled with empty storefronts and dark brick Victorian mansions that had seen better days. Social service organizations and food pantries had moved into many buildings.

Fascinated by how Utica had changed, I kept returning, and in 2014 I wrote a story about the city's revitalization for the *New York Times*.

But instead of moving on, I kept going back.

My first week reporting, I met three remarkable newcomers. Sadia, a bright, rebellious 15-year-old, answered the door. I'd come to see her mother, who had 11 children and worked at Chobani, the yogurt factory. "Will you save me?" Sadia said, laughing, as she pulled me inside. She'd recently been suspended from high school for getting into a fight with another Somali Bantu girl.

And I was drawn to Ali, an Iraqi interpreter with large reserves of feeling. He worked in Utica's courts and hospitals but seemed shadowed by war. Mersiha—a Bosnian refugee who ran a bakery out of her home—was a kind of visionary. Her head was buzzing with entrepreneurial ideas.

I didn't expect to follow my subjects for eight years. But their lives were changing so rapidly—and I kept wanting to see what was next.

Utica was not the only struggling city sparked to life by newcomers: Dayton, Chicago, Cleveland, Columbus, and Detroit, among others, were developing strategies to attract immigrants. They needed an economic boost—but also hoped that by becoming more culturally diverse, they would draw young professionals.

Sadia, Ali, and Mersiha were finding their way in a city that needed them. This was true for thousands of recent immigrants and refugees across the country.

In 2015, the world shifted.

More than 65 million people were on the run. It was the largest wave of displaced people since World War II.

Climate change helped trigger this migration: Extreme weather over the years had eroded people's ability to sustain themselves on small plots of land. People were fleeing ISIS in Iraq, and conflicts in Syria, Afghanistan, and South Sudan. The great hope was to get to the United States, Germany, or Italy. All through 2015, tragic accidents were reported: Over 3,770 people died trying to cross the Mediterranean.

An age-old nationalism started rising in Europe, and borders began to close. Donald J. Trump, running for president, held enormous anti-immigration rallies and called for building a wall.

In Utica that same year, more than 10,000 refugees were busy working and raising children. Sadia, a young Somali Bantu girl, was starting to break her clan's rules.

CITY OF REFUGEES

PART I   **LANDINGS**

1. DESIRE

LEAVES COVERED the yard of a formerly grand house on Rutger Street in Utica, New York. Inside, Sadia Ambure—wearing a fleece jacket and a long zebra-striped skirt—walked around her living room, holding her newborn sister, Rahama.

The baby had a thick crop of dark hair and wore a striped onesie. Sadia had hardly put the baby down all week.

"You know who's my best friend in the house?" Sadia asked her 19-year-old sister, Mana. "The baby! She won't tell anyone my secrets."

Mana, rail thin, with dark circles under her eyes, said, "Rahama brings charm to our family."

"She loves me way better," Sadia said.

"But you don't want kids."

"I don't."

"It will be sad if you don't have any," said Mana, the eldest of their mother's 11 children. "I want a lot. I'm used to them."

"I'll have *one* kid," Sadia, 15, said. "A son." There were only two boys in their family.

A total of 19 family members—including her grandparents, aunts, and uncles—lived in the house her grandmother, Halima, bought for $55,000 in 2011.

Halima, then 49, painted the walls sky blue, lavender, and deep purple. She ordered red brocade couches from a Saudi Arabian catalog, and hung long drapes, which are always kept closed.

The elegant, but run-down house—with 13 bedrooms and 2 large parlors—has been owned by a succession of families since the 1920s: native Uticans, Italian immigrants, then Bosnian immigrants, reflecting the changing makeup of East Utica. It was used as a drug rehabilitation center in the 1990s.

"Boys are easier to handle," Sadia said. "They'll sit down and watch anything on TV. Girls are harder—we fight."

Her uncle, Yusuf—a small, handsome man—crossed the room, heading out to the Turning Stone Resort Casino, where he worked as a cook.

"You never in your life cook for us!" Sadia called out.

"If you had something interesting in the house, I'd cook it," he said. "Your grandmother is very conservative—she only likes African food. I cook Italian and a little French."

It hit Sadia that she was hungry: "I love steak with mushrooms and onions," she said. But what she really craved was a Subway sandwich. They were forbidden by her mother—and had to be hidden in the refrigerator. It drove her crazy that she had to ask her mother's permission for everything—even to go to the store.

"Can you get me Subway?" Sadia asked Mana.

"Today is not the day."

"The kids get pizza when they're good."

"Not today," Mana said. "You hear them?" she asked, looking up at the ceiling. There was the thudding sound of children running. "I told them to be quiet."

Sadia lay Rahama on the deep-blue rug and drew her tiny sneakered feet into the air. The name Rahama translates as mercy or compassion from Allah. But to Sadia, it means unexpected gift from God.

Sadia buried her face in the baby's belly.

Her anxiety from the past tumultuous months drained away. She felt hopeful.

It was late October 2013; she wanted to get things back on track. Stop fighting with other girls at school. Concentrate on her classes. And most difficult of all—get along with her formidable mother, who was raising her kids by herself.

Sadia was filled with desires: "I want to be a writer," she said. "But it's hard for me, a foreigner." Her family—members of the Somali Bantu tribe—arrived in the United States from a Kenyan refugee camp in 2004. Still in ESL classes—though at the top level—she worried she did not speak or write as well as native-born students.

But school bored her—and she did not want to put in the effort regular classes would take.

She was obsessed with the television show *Game of Thrones*. "That writer has the wildest imagination," she said. "How could somebody be so good?" Someday, she hoped to create her own TV show. "I want somebody to remember me."

She had other desires: "I want to be a model, but my family won't let me," she said. "I want to go away to school, but my family won't let me."

Holding the baby, she drew aside the drapes: Across the street stood two large brick Victorian houses.

"I don't want to go to MVCC," Sadia said, referring to Mohawk Valley Community College in Utica. "I want something big."

———

Late at night, Ali Sarhan, 45, an Iraqi interpreter—who formerly worked for ABC News in Baghdad—feels pulled back home.

It is quiet on South Street—only three blocks over from Sadia's family's house—where he lives in an apartment with his girlfriend, Heidi Bakert, a Utica native. But he cannot sleep.

"Ninety percent of my problems in the world are that my sisters aren't married," he explained.

His sisters are single by choice: Retaj, 39, and Hawra, 32, both linguists, work for the Iraqi government. They live with their mother—who, before retiring, also worked for the government—in the family's home in Baghdad. There are six bedrooms and two kitchens. "My sisters have everything they need," Ali said. "The house, cars, money."

It was spring 2016; security in Baghdad had gotten better. "Things feel normal," he said. Always very social, his mother and sisters come and go—working, visiting friends, and attending cultural events.

But Ali, the only son—nearly 6,000 miles away—is the head of the household: He worries about his mother suddenly falling ill. And about his sisters—so independent now—growing old, alone. "There will be nobody to protect them," he said.

"Until I die, they are my responsibility."

He had a brother.

He tries not to think about Saif, who was two years older. Like Ali, he was almost six feet tall, but sunnier, and more traditional. He was different in another way: "He didn't judge people," Ali said. "Everybody loved him like crazy."

Ali cannot imagine his mother and sisters moving to Utica: "They have a beautiful life," he said. "They would not come here, go to the refugee center, and find work. For them, Utica would be a place to visit for maybe two or three days."

And he cannot go home: He left in 2008, after receiving death threats because of his work as an interpreter for Peter Jennings and other American journalists.

To quiet his mind, Ali thinks about the Salmon River, an hour outside Utica. Large and majestic, it flows 44 miles west, before emptying into eastern Lake Ontario. Ali always liked to fish, but rarely had a chance to in Iraq. In those days, he loved to watch men grill steelhead in large, open pits in Baghdad's markets. He would get one wrapped in newspaper to take home.

Some winter weekends, Ali heads to the river with four Palestinian friends, who also lived in Iraq. They all grew up in 110-degree summer heat but stand happily in freezing water, in a spot where the dark silver, speckled trout gather—especially at daybreak and at the end of a rainy day.

Ali is surprised: Over the past year, the small upstate city has sneaked up on him. He loves Heidi, who is warm and high-spirited. They have a circle of close friends. He joined a mosque.

"But if security gets better for me," he said about Baghdad, "I'll be the first one back."

———

Utica has no skyline. No grand boulevard.

But at 2 a.m., Mersiha Omeragic, 40, saw the sprinkling of neon lights on North Genesee Street—Delmonico's Italian Steakhouse, Best Western, McDonald's—and felt the same thrill she did arriving as a 19-year-old refugee.

She was returning from a trip to Paris.

Driving into the darkened downtown with her husband and four kids, past the low brick and brownstone buildings—some vacant—and the old Stanley Theatre, she does not see a down-and-out city.

Mersiha—who runs a bakery from her home—sees potential.

She dreams of opening a café and serving her cakes and Bosnian pastries to native Uticans—and to the newcomers: Bosnians, Burmese, and Sudanese.

"We have a lot of youth," she tells her husband, Hajrudin, 45, referring to the students at MVCC and Utica College. "A lot of diversity."

Hajrudin is more cautious, less optimistic; he spent time in a concentration camp during the Bosnian War. He reminds her that most new restaurants fail.

"We need to attract young and old," she says.

They pulled up to their house on Blandina Street. It is five blocks away from Ali's apartment.

Fifteen years ago, Mersiha and Hajrudin, newly engaged, were walking down Blandina Street when they saw a For Sale sign. The house had old siding, but it was big, with a porch and a long driveway leading to a two-car garage. The elderly owner was clipping bushes in his front yard and greeted the young couple. "Richard was Italian—his wife too," Mersiha said. "He invited us in. He said, 'I heard a lot of good things about Bosnians.'"

The two couples spoke all afternoon. "Richard told us, 'I can see you living in this house for years. You remind me of us.'"

Going in the side door, Mersiha entered the darkened kitchen. The air was humid; it was late August 2015. Her husband carried their youngest son, Elhan, 4, who was asleep. Her three older kids trailed behind. She and her husband had renovated the house themselves: putting in a new kitchen and two new bathrooms, and building rooms for the children in the attic.

She did not stop, heading upstairs. She tucked Elhan and her daughter, Ajla, 9, into bed. She steered Ismar, 16, and Faris, 14, toward their bunk beds.

Back downstairs, she told Hajrudin, who is thin with a lined face, "I need you to go to Walmart for the eggs, milk, butter."

Then she made herself a cup of thick Turkish coffee.

She had a rough night ahead. It was Wednesday. Saturday, she was catering a large wedding. She needed to produce a four-tier wedding cake and a dessert table for 250 people.

And in six hours, she needed to be at the Mohawk Valley Resource Center for Refugees for her full-time job teaching English as a second language.

She headed downstairs to the bakery. "I always work, work, work!" she said.

It was well lit, with walls the color of eggplants. Scores of bottled spices and homemade preserves filled the glass-covered cabinets. Sacks of flour, sugar, and nuts lined the counters.

Tying a bandana over her short, dark hair, she turned the light on in the next room; it looked like an artist's studio in Provence. There was an olive-colored love seat, small tables, and a hand-painted cabinet.

Strewn everywhere were pastries. Pistachio macarons were piled in a decanter. There was a stack of brownies under glass; two logs of strudel stuffed with Bosnian plums; and seeded rolls under a cloth napkin.

There was a luxuriant carelessness to the display. She looked around, happily; this is where she holds wedding tastings and does photo shoots.

Then, putting on her pink baker's smock, *Chef Mersiha* on the breast pocket, she brought a heavy bag of flour to the kitchen worktable. Always next to her is a framed photograph of her mother—a serious, dark-eyed young woman.

"My wrists and arms hurt," Mersiha said about the toll baking has taken on her body. "I had to have back surgery on my two discs."

"I should have used a pad," she added, about the hard linoleum floor. She recently tossed her flip-flops for supportive sneakers.

It was 2:30 a.m.: Rolling up her sleeves, she began assembling her bowls, spoons, and knives.

2. FIRE

F OR DECADES—starting in the 1970s—Utica was a city on fire.
There were church fires, store fires, apartment fires. But mostly there were fires in the abandoned homes around Cornhill, which had been a middle-class neighborhood of Welsh, Polish, Italian, and Irish—and in lower East Utica, which was predominately Italian.

As white people started fleeing Cornhill in the 1970s, Utica's small Black community, which had been limited to public housing projects downtown, began moving in.

"Fire was a huge issue for the city," said Scott Ingersoll, fire chief of the Utica Fire Department. At the height of the crisis, in the mid-1990s, there were over 300 fires a year. "Sometimes guys came in and worked three, four fires a day."

Just walking around the city, "you couldn't help but smell the smoke," said Nancy Ford, a photographer, who grew up in Cornhill and covered fires during the mid-1990s for the local paper, the *Observer-Dispatch*. Every night before going to sleep, she laid out her clothes and keys—just as the firefighters did—so she could quickly get out the door. "You could hear the sirens—Utica's not a big city."

Fire trucks raced down Genesee Street. They headed toward streets—Rutger, Bleecker, Blandina, South—where vacant frame houses had been set ablaze.

These fires did not spring up overnight: A vibrant industrial town in the 1950s, Utica was home to General Electric; the UNIVAC division of the Sperry Rand Corporation, a computer manufacturer; and Chicago Pneumatic, a power tools manufacturer. Griffiss Air Force Base was in nearby Rome.

These companies—and Griffiss—provided thousands of good jobs.

Then in the 1960s, things began to change: "We started to hear about dads being laid off," said John Zogby, a national pollster and former history professor, who grew up in Utica. His father, a Lebanese immigrant, owned a grocery store, but his friends' fathers worked at GE and Univac, which were downsizing.

Mr. Zogby, 72, recalled a day in elementary school when boys were supposed to bring in a dollar for a basketball T-shirt. Instead, kids told teachers, "Here's a note from my mother."

In a narrative unfolding in old manufacturing towns across the country—in Cleveland, Detroit, Dayton, Chicago, and St. Louis—plants began to close. General Electric pulled out of Utica in the early 1990s. Griffiss Air Force Base closed in 1995.

Genesee, the city's gracious main street—lined with a canopy of elms, before they got wiped out by Dutch elm disease in the 1960s—was a commercial hub: It had a large Woolworth Co.; Wicks & Greenman, a fine men's store; and the Boston Store, a nearly block-long department store. The Imperial Restaurant, a beloved, New York City–style steakhouse, was nearby.

But as Utica's population, which stood at about 100,000 in 1960, started to plunge, Genesee began to fill with empty storefronts.

"You had a city laid out for 150,000," Mr. Zogby said, "anticipating that the population would grow." Within years, "you have a lot of deteriorating buildings with no hope someone will buy them, fix them up."

Uticans had been proud of their town. And they had a gallows sense of humor about their notoriously corrupt politicians—and their volatile mayor, Ed Hanna, a wealthy businessman, who served in the 1970s and was twice elected in the 1990s. In a CBS interview taped in 1999, Mayor Hanna walked around a rubble-filled lot, looking disgusted.

Laughing, he told the interviewer he had a nightmare: "I dreamed I was the mayor of the city of Utica."

Now out of work and demoralized, residents turned against their city.

"You started seeing a funk," Mr. Zogby said. "People said to each other, 'I told you this place is no good. The politics are dirty. I hate to tell you this—I don't want you to go. But you gotta get out of here.'"

Many houses were now worth less than their annual taxes; it had been decades since there had been a property reassessment. A house in Cornhill worth about $10,000 in 1947 was now worth about $1,000.

"People just walked away," Mr. Zogby said. "They left their stuff" behind—furniture, rugs, and other possessions. Many moved to North and South Carolina, Ohio, and Oklahoma, following their companies, or looking for similar work.

Some residents still remember the bumper sticker: "Last one out of Utica, please turn out the lights."

Absentee landlords bought houses at auction—then hired people to burn them so they could collect the insurance money. And some owners torched their own homes.

"Arson rates just skyrocketed," Chief Ingersoll said. In the mid-nineties, 45 percent of all structure fires were ruled arson, twice the national average, and three times the New York state average.

The arsonists were relentless: "We'd put out a fire in a vacant building," said Lieutenant Phil Fasolo, who joined the fire department in 1990. "Then a few hours later, we'd be called back to the same burning building."

His older brother, Acting Deputy Chief Michael Fasolo, was fighting a fire on Neilson Street when he looked to his left: Another fire was burning on the same side of the street.

Firefighters could see the signs: Milk containers filled with gas at the top of stairs. Balloons filled with gas. Gas thrown down sinks and spilled along hallways.

At a third-floor fire on the corner of Columbia and Fay, Captain Anthony Zumpano, then a firefighter, opened his hose, accidentally dislodging a big container. "Fire just exploded, curled around us," he said. It was only afterward, standing outside, that he realized he was covered with liquid gas.

Arson was difficult to prosecute, partly because the investigative process was cumbersome. The morning after a fire, a fire marshal would start investigating. By the time a fire was determined to be arson, witnesses, occupants, homeowners, and landlords may have disappeared.

"You've lost a lot of time; you've lost the potential to secure evidence," said Lieutenant Fasolo, who became a fire marshal in 1994. There was rarely closure: Investigations into about 350 suspected arsons in Utica from 1988 to 1993 produced only a handful of convictions.

The police lost control of neighborhoods: Drug dealers and gang members from New York City started moving onto blocks that had been extremely close-knit.

"At one time, everyone knew everyone else on the block," said Sergeant Robert Di Pena, a veteran Utica police officer who investigated arsons, in an interview with the *Observer-Dispatch* in 1998. "Now you have a neighborhood of strangers. Anyone can walk into a neighborhood and commit a crime, and no one knows if he belongs there or not."

Instead of using guns to settle turf wars, drug dealers often set fires. And drug users accidentally set fires, trying to keep warm as they crashed in abandoned houses.

Just walking around could be dangerous: Azira Tabucic, 26, a Bosnian refugee—on her way to an English class—was crossing South Street when a pack of dogs ran out of an abandoned garage. One hung on to her leg, biting it, before they all ran off.

Other Rust Belt cities had a similarly bleak landscape.

Buffalo lost over half its population between 1950 and 2010—and gangs, squatters, and young people frustrated by the lack of opportunity burned down hundreds of houses a year. On virtually every block in East Buffalo, there were boarded-up and burned-out buildings. By 2000, there were vast stretches of no-man's land—about 8,000 abandoned structures and about 10,000 vacant lots.

In Youngstown, Ohio, which had been a steel giant, everything changed on September 19, 1977, known as Black Monday: Youngstown Sheet and Tube abruptly laid off 5,000 workers. Within 10 years, 40,000 manufacturing jobs were gone. In the 1960s, the city bustled with about 170,000 people. By 1997, the population had declined to about 70,000, and many neighborhoods burned.

———

Uticans are tough and used to taking blows. Yet when the Kanatenah—a once-elegant, historic apartment building on Genesee Street—went up in flames in 1994, the city was stunned.

It was the magnitude of the loss: An enormous seven-story Victorian building of dark red brick, the Kanatenah was a reminder of what Utica had been in the 1890s, when it was built.

It was designed by Richard George, a German-born architect and builder, along with local developers Milton Northrup and Seymour Dewitt Latcher, as townhouses for Utica's wealthy doctors, lawyers, and merchants. In recent decades, it had fallen into disrepair; its tenants were mostly working class and poor.

"It was one of the biggest fires of that era," said Peter Caruso, then deputy chief of the department. Starting within the walls of the second floor, flames quickly shot to the seventh through the building's hollow walls and shafts. Ten fire trucks and 50 firefighters arrived, every resource the department had.

At 2 a.m. on an icy March morning, firefighters banged on 93 apartment doors. For hours, people streamed from the lit-up building. "There were squatters, guests, transients," said Lieutenant Fasolo, then a 24-year-old firefighter on duty. "Nobody knew how many actually lived there."

People fought their way out of exits and fire escapes taped with sheeting to keep out the cold. Smoke detectors had failed. Some emergency exit doors had been nailed shut.

Many had already survived fires: Sherman Green had moved to the Kanatenah the previous year, after being burned out of his apartment on South Street. Grover Smith, asleep in front of the TV when he heard sirens, had recently been burned out of his James Street apartment.

Hundreds lined up to watch. "People came from all over the city," said Ms. Ford, who covered the fire for the *Observer-Dispatch*.

On the fifth floor she spotted a man, poking out from a window, wearing a Panama hat. "He was teetering on his stomach," she said, as smoke billowed behind him. "I thought he was going to jump."

She pointed him out to Deputy Chief David Paul, who said they had to wait for the next ladder truck.

"The guy pulled himself over the ledge, still wearing his hat," she said. As soon as the ladder reached him, he started climbing down, head-first.

Lieutenant Fasolo was below. "We climbed up and grabbed him," he said.

Lieutenant Fasolo heard that an elderly woman was trapped on the seventh floor. "There was an orange glow coming from that area," he said. He carried the fragile, 90-year-old woman out like a baby, wrapped in a flowered bedsheet.

When the Kanatenah collapsed, its seven floors toppled to the ground floor. And the city began to absorb the loss: About 150 residents—now homeless—were taken in by various social service agencies around the city. Three were hospitalized for smoke inhalation, including Bill Knief, a stocky, gray-haired man known as Bill the Poet, who handed out his poems downtown.

Later that night, Ms. Ford saw the man in the Panama hat. He was taken to the hospital but had returned.

He was leaning against a car repair garage across the street, just staring at the burning building.

"It was as if nothing had happened," she said. "He looked unaffected. But his nostrils were smoke stained."

3. THE FIGHT

SADIA had stitched together an American and Somali Bantu identity. She kept Steve Madden boots in her locker, which she wore under long skirts ordered from Somali Bantu catalogs. Her young aunt Sofia, 19—her best friend—provided many of the accessories of her American life: a cell phone, scarves, shoes.

Obsessed with food, she loved her mother's goat stew.

But she had grown up in Utica—and took pride in the food Utica claims as its own: half-moon cookies, chicken riggies, and tomato pie.

She had her own way of making chicken riggies, the city's signature dish, mixing chopped chicken and pasta, then dumping in a can of alfredo sauce.

Hearing that tomato pie—a focaccia-like pie—is hard to find in New York City, she said, delighted: "You mean we're better than New York?"

Then in 10th grade, Sadia had a fight with another Somali Bantu girl. It began as a hostile post on Facebook, like a thousand other high school taunts.

But it escalated—kicking off a shift in her relationship with school, with her mother, and with her clan that has reverberated through the years.

"We never even talked," Sadia said about the girl. But they had been in a class together, and their mothers had once been friends. "She's the one who always gets the answers right."

Sadia—like all her siblings—had always been defensive of her mother. Everyone in the Somali Bantu community knew Zahara was unmarried and had children with several different men. She was a rule breaker; she went her own way. But she was respected for being hardworking and raising good kids. Also, she was devout; she prayed five times a day and attended mosque when she could.

And then one afternoon after school, Sadia opened her computer and saw the girl's post: *Your mom's a slut.*

Sadia just sat there—her heart pounding. Her mouth went completely dry. Every curse word she knew sprang into her head.

Sadia attacked. So did the girl. Then Sadia. Then the girl.

Sadia wrote, *I'm going to get you, you stupid little bitch.*

The next day, the principal of Thomas R. Proctor High School called Sadia and her mother into his office. The other girl and her mother were not there.

Zahara, 37, in a jilbab that covered her head and chest and a long dress, was distressed to have been summoned.

Sadia listened, amazed. The principal talked about the threatening message Sadia had sent, but he did not know the other girl had instigated the fight. That girl had deleted her own words, but she had screenshot Sadia's.

"The principal said I was *cyber-bullying*," Sadia recalled. She had sat there, embarrassed. She did not say a word about the other girl's messages.

"I'm not a bad kid," she told me. It bothered her that her mother did not say a word in her defense. "She never sticks up for me."

Later that night, Sadia told her mother what had happened.

Her dark eyes on her daughter, Zahara said, "Don't listen to what anyone says! They're saying it about *me*, not you. You don't have to defend me."

"Of course, I do!" Sadia said.

Deeply upset that her daughter had caused such trouble, Zahara did not speak to her for a week.

The principal suspended Sadia for three days. Then he placed her temporarily at BOCES, an alternative public school serving students with disciplinary problems and special needs that supports several school districts in the area.

Sadia loved BOCES. At Proctor, she was used to sitting, dazed, in large ESL classes. "I don't like sitting in class," she said. "It's the teenage hormone thing."

"At BOCES, there were only three kids in my class, with a teacher and an assistant. You learn there so fast."

Many students stay at BOCES for short stints, so they do not really get to know each other. But there is an upside to this, Sadia said: "The kids are divided. Everybody minds their own business. They only fight on the bus. They're not drama queens—so the teachers can teach."

"At Proctor, my average was 70," she added. "At BOCES, it was 100. I never missed a day."

After a few weeks, the principal called Sadia into his office. He talked to her about self-control. About managing her anger. And about doing well in school out of respect for her mother.

"He's the one who made me understand," Sadia said. "Nobody's ever going to love you more than your mom. No one's better. Your mom is your best friend."

He was bringing her back to Proctor.

She was determined to take things more easily. She would ignore anyone who baited her: "If you don't like me, that's OK. Don't look at me. Don't stare at me. Don't touch me."

"We can pass through each other. It's a big school."

First day back, Sadia slipped into class. She was surprised: No one turned around to look at her. There was no sign of interest or curiosity.

"Nobody even knew I was missing," she said, amazed. "I'm quiet in class. Some classes I don't even talk. But I've been at that school since 9th grade!"

Even her Global Studies teacher—who was her favorite—did not know she had left school. "She thought I got transferred to another class."

It did not seem to bother Sadia that the other girl was not punished.

"She's living her life," she said, shrugging.

Sadia admired how savvy the girl had been in manipulating the fight. For a moment, Sadia imagined the girl's future: "She's up there in life—successful. She's smart, talks well. She'll be on TV."

Sadia added wryly, "While I'll be inside with my kid, suffering."

4. TRUCE

FOR A WHILE, things got better between Sadia and her mother: Sadia passed all her classes. Both were relieved that a crisis had passed. On a sunny afternoon in January, they bantered, as Rahama—full cheeked and breathing softly—slept on the couch:

"I have a secret boyfriend," Sadia said.

"Shame on you!" Zahara said.

In many Somali Bantu families, dating is not allowed unless a girl is engaged. And though Zahara felt free to break rules, she was strict with her daughters. "*Here*, girls can have a boyfriend. But *we* don't do boyfriend."

Later, it was Zahara's turn to tease: "Sadia's fat," she said, pinching her daughter's arm.

"I'm not," Sadia said, brushing away her mother's hand.

"Here—and here!" Zahara said, touching Sadia's butt and belly. "No good for a young girl."

Zahara was worried about the weight she had gained during pregnancy—and had started drinking a "weight-loss tea."

Sadia was the rare teenage girl, confident about her looks. She did not compare herself to the thin girls in American magazines. She knew she was as pretty as the models in the Somali Bantu fashion catalogs she and her sisters pored over.

She fantasized about being a model. Recently, without telling her mother, she had a friend take some headshots. Then she sent them to a man she had connected with online, who said he ran a Somali Bantu modeling agency. But when he talked about meeting her, she got scared.

"When I was young, I was skinny," Zahara told her.

"That's because you were starving in Africa!"

Sadia picked up Rahama, who had just awakened. "Did you think I'd forgotten about you?" she asked the baby.

Sadia and her sisters were proud of their mother. Before giving birth to Rahama, she worked at the Chobani yogurt factory in New Berlin, rising at 4 a.m. and returning home at 3 p.m. Zahara's mother, Halima, took care of the younger kids when she was gone.

Zahara relished the work, the paycheck—and the camaraderie. "We had our Chobani family," she said. "And our home family."

At lunch, coworkers—from Nepal, Burma, Cambodia—shared home-cooked meals. "Tomorrow, can you bring me food?" Zahara would ask if she saw something good. And she would bring in spicy beans and rice for them.

She appreciated the small prayer room set up for Muslim employees. And she liked the managers: "When we feel bored, they say, 'Are you OK?'"

"We felt rich," Sadia said about her mother's year at Chobani. "We had everything we needed." For six years before that, Zahara worked as a caregiver at a nursing home.

Sadia admired her mother's independence. "*She* was the one who divorced her husbands," Sadia said. Some irritated Zahara. Some did not want to be around so many kids. She would say, "If you can't handle us, you don't have to be here."

Zahara is proud to have 11 kids. "The ideal is to have about a dozen," said Dr. Kathryn Stam, a professor of anthropology at SUNY Polytechnic Institute and codirector of the Midtown Utica Community Center, where she works with young refugees. "For Somali Bantu parents, children are a family's legacy, their silver and gold—and their honor in the community."

In the past, there were practical reasons for having many children, Dr. Stam added: Mothers lost a third of their children to malnutrition and disease. Parents needed extra hands for farming and tending animals. And having lots of kids ensured that a mother would be taken care of in her old age.

———

Sadia was surprised by how happy she felt to be back at Proctor. It was as if the school had suddenly opened its doors to her.

"I love running," she said. She had just started running track at school. "I'm African—track is life."

In Global Studies, she was absorbed by stories about Greece and

Rome, the Middle East and Islam. She was touched that her teacher had given her a book by Chinua Achebe, the Nigerian writer. And she was excited about next year's courses: "I want to take Photography!"

The outside world beckoned: "I want to get used to some other cultures," she told her mother. She had never traveled, except to family weddings.

"I want to go to California. If we lived in a big city, there'd be a lot of *stores.*" All the women in their family loved fashion.

"I don't like a big city," Zahara said. Utica's quiet streets felt like a haven to her. She belongs to the Mudey clan, and over a hundred extended family members live within blocks of one another.

Zahara did not like St. Louis, where she and her kids were first resettled. She was relieved when she joined her mother in Utica.

"Don't you want to settle down and have kids?" she asked Sadia.

"No."

Sadia was hungry to travel, but the logistics seemed overwhelming: "You have to get your plane tickets, your hotel reservation, your food," she told her mother.

Zahara did not say anything. She peeled an apple and let the long peel fall in her lap.

At 14, Zahara had been fleeing civil war, running toward the Kenyan border. She was two months pregnant with Mana.

Sadia and her younger sisters only knew bits about their life in the refugee camp: "We slept on the floor," Zahara told them. Ten people, including her parents and siblings, lived in a one-room mud hut. They cooked outdoors in an oven built of mud and stones. They had three kerosene lamps.

Rations were meager: "Dried corn, beans—no rice—and a little oil," Zahara said. Armed members of the Turkana, a seminomadic Kenyan tribe, often stole their food and clothing at night. Women going into the forest alone for firewood risked being raped.

Zahara's mother, Halima, graceful in a head scarf and long skirt, crossed the living room and headed toward the kitchen. She did not look at Zahara or Sadia.

"I don't talk to her," Sadia said, glancing at her grandmother. "She's ignorant! I have a problem with Somalis. You're killing your people for no reason! You can't kill a girl for losing her virginity or getting raped."

"You can't bury girls alive."

In the kitchen, Halima started cutting vegetables for a stew.

"What my grandmother has gone through," Sadia said, slowly, "is way harder than what I've gone through."

5. THE GREEN ONION

ALI was at a loss, arriving in Utica.

Though he was 39, he had never lived on his own. "I didn't have that much experience," he said. He had never done laundry. Or cleaned. "My mom and my sisters didn't allow it."

He did not enjoy the whiff of freedom.

His mother ran a lively household, with extended family and friends dropping by. Suddenly, he was in a small efficiency apartment in North Utica, which his friend Einas, also an interpreter, had found. She had encouraged him to move to Utica; she said she would help him find work.

He was grateful: She stocked the furnished studio with toothbrushes and soap, and pots and pans from the Family Dollar store. But the place was forlorn: a kitchen table and a bed.

Einas put him in touch with the refugee center, which housed a translation service that needed interpreters. While there, he started chatting with a Middle Eastern refugee, who was very friendly. Hearing that Ali had recently arrived, the man mentioned a nearby pub, the Green Onion. "He said it's a small bar, very nice," Ali said. "He knows people there."

Ali does not drink—and rarely goes to bars. But he had been in Utica a couple of weeks without meeting anyone, and he was lonely.

He has a protocol when in a pub: "I order a juice," he said, "so I don't make people nervous."

That evening, Heidi—a small, sturdily built woman with blue eyes—was sitting alone in a booth at the Green Onion, feeling as if she was unraveling. She was in the process of leaving her husband of 20 years, the father of her three children.

"This is not something women do every day," she said, wryly. "It's usually something the man does."

She was the one moving out. Her kids—two teenage boys and a 10-year-old girl—whom she loved, would remain with their dad. She would see them every day, going back to help with homework and to cook dinner. She knew there were good reasons for her decision to leave.

But that evening, she sat there, worrying: Was she an evil person?

And what was she even doing in a bar?

"For months, I'd been acting like a fool," she said, as she coped with the trauma of leaving and with feelings of shame.

But that evening, Heidi—who works in the claims department of a large pharmacy—decided to grab another beer and try to shake these thoughts.

Approaching the bar, she saw a tall man walk in. He had dark eyes and thick eyebrows—and wore a skull cap over his bald head.

He looked lost.

Heidi, 41, decided to somehow engage. She was on home turf: She had known the owners for years, college friends who had wanted to open a neighborhood bar. The man with the thick eyebrows was from somewhere else.

Out of her mouth sprang an odd question: "Do you want to arm wrestle?"

Ali's face lit up.

Without waiting for an answer, she said, "Come on," and led him back to her booth. Rolling up her sleeve, she bent her arm, held out her hand, and waited.

Ali stared at her. Then, grinning, he rolled up his sleeve, grabbed her hand, and clenched it in a tight grip.

She felt a jolt of clarity.

Then came a rush of adrenaline. For a moment, Heidi—who is strong—held her own against Ali, who is powerfully built.

But then he brought her arm down gently. On his forearm, she noticed a tattoo with Arabic writing. Their hands still connected across the table, she asked him what it said.

" 'God is great.' "

Tears welled in Heidi's eyes. "Yes," she said.

———

The next day, Ali stood at an ATM in a panic. The machine had rejected his credit card.

He had not realized it had expired. It was Saturday, and the bank was closed. But his rent was due.

It hit him: He was a newcomer in a city where he knew no one except for Einas. And he would never ask her for help. She had a husband and kids, and was not well off.

Yet, he would not have asked even a close friend for a favor. "I would lend money to someone," he said. "But for me to take money would not be acceptable."

Later that day—out of the blue—he got a text from Heidi: *How are you doing?*

He quickly texted her what had happened.

She wrote back, *Don't worry!*

"That day, she paid my rent—$650," Ali said, shaking his head. "Of course, I paid it back right away. But I was shocked."

"Why was she doing this? In Iraq if you need anything—if you are hungry—people will help. You don't have to return anything. But here?"

"I was a stranger," he added, marveling. "What made her think I'd give it back?"

6. VOWS

A COUPLE OF MONTHS after he met Heidi, Ali moved into a studio apartment on Rutger Street. And soon Heidi joined him.

She knew this seemed rash to those who knew her—and she was still in turmoil about her divorce—but she was happy with Ali.

Ali felt the same way. "Heidi is nice, she is kind," he said quietly.

But the old brick building—across from Sadia's family's house—turned out to be poorly maintained. The hallways were dirty. And then one afternoon, in the elevator, they saw bedbugs.

"We were like crazy people," Heidi said.

They ran to get insecticide—a huge 10-gallon drum. They wrapped the bed in a plastic tarp. They caulked every chink in the walls.

"We only saw one or two bedbugs in the apartment," Heidi said.

But at night, Ali—worried Heidi would be bitten—refused to sleep. He sat in a rocking chair, watching over her. "I'd wake up in the middle of the night," Heidi said, laughing, "and he'd just be staring at me."

Ali had gotten a job as an interpreter in Utica's hospitals and schools, which he liked. He slept during the day, between appointments.

After a couple of months, Heidi found a clean one-bedroom apartment on South Street, just a few blocks away.

Ali bought a comfortable recliner, his first piece of American furniture. After work, he would relax next to Heidi, smoking his hookah filled with applewood tobacco.

They exchanged vows in private. "We did it a Muslim way," Ali said, "between me, Heidi, and God."

"She respects my religion as if it were her own," he added. It did not bother him that Heidi is Christian. He has never brought up the idea of her converting—and she has no interest in it.

Heidi—after a miserable marriage—was not interested in a legal ceremony. "I don't need it," she said about a marriage license. "My marriage ended—so what did that paper mean?"

Heidi quickly adapted to living with an observant Muslim. "I kind of roll with things," she said. Ali fasts during Ramadan; she is attuned to his needs that month but does not fast. There is no pork in their house; all their meat is halal.

"Ali is really strict about no alcohol," Heidi said. "Sometimes, I work around that," she added, smiling. "I'll say, 'My doctor said my good cholesterol is low—a glass of wine would help.'"

In some ways, their backgrounds are similar: "Both sides of my family are very warm and welcoming," Heidi said. Her mother's family is from Italy, her father's is from Germany.

"Iraqis are simple," Ali said. "They knock on your door—they help. They forgive even when you hurt them."

But they do not always forgive, he added: "Revenge is very bad. It is only for when a big thing happens. A killing in the family. Or when someone attacks a group of people. Then you will defend."

———

Heidi liked having her stereotypes about Muslims broken: She found Ali's friends to be unusually tolerant.

Her best friend, Karen, who is 4' 4"—"a little person," Heidi calls her—has dwarfism.

"My whole life I've watched people react to Karen," Heidi said. "There's always that one half-second people take to process what they're seeing. Most people don't even know they're doing it."

"I've yet to see that reaction from anyone in the Muslim community. If someone's different—disfigured—there's no being taken aback, no looking away."

When Ali first met Karen, he went up to her, got down on his knees because he is so tall, hugged her, and then kissed her on both cheeks.

Karen—a pretty woman with dark-brown cropped hair—was so flattered she kissed the top of his hand.

"Please never do that!" Ali said. "In my country that means someone's far above you. It would be like meeting a god!"

Heidi had assumed Muslim women were modest and submissive. So, she was amazed to hear about Ali's household: that his mother held an important government job. That Retaj, his older sister, who speaks Russian, has written several books about the arts. "Retaj isn't shy around men," Heidi said. "She has collaborated with men on projects."

Ali's sisters revere him. They told Heidi, "We will never find a man like our brother."

When she repeated this to Ali, he laughed: "Who said that? I'm a bad guy. I do horrible things!"

Heidi knows Ali will return home if he is needed. There are no assurances their relationship will last. "We're just taking it one day at a time," she said. "We want to enjoy each other."

Recently, Heidi got a glimpse of Iraqi culture that surprised her.

At a wedding reception in Utica, Heidi followed the women into one room; Ali went off with the men. "At that point, the women were dressed very modestly," she said. But head wraps and shawls quickly disappeared. Long, shiny hair emerged. Everyone wore tight, brightly colored dresses and high heels.

Elaborately painted nails flashed as women danced with each other. "It was a bunch of Kardashians out there," she said, laughing.

When everyone came back together, the wives had put their head wraps back on, and covered their dresses with black shawls. Some had removed their false eyelashes. "Everyone still looked fabulous," Heidi said, "but toned down."

Ali intensely enjoys the male camaraderie at the Islamic Center, though he does not go often. It is a small, informal Utica mosque, where most members are Shiites from Iraq and Iran. Women rarely attend.

Heidi likes that he has found this connection. "But I just don't get the separation between sexes."

The center is where Ali celebrated one of the most important moments of his life—becoming an American citizen. "When something good happens, you want to say, 'Thank you, I've been blessed,'" he said.

After his naturalization ceremony in 2013, he bought a sheep from a local Bosnian farmer, who slaughtered it. Ali went from house to house, dropping off bags of cut-up meat to friends.

Then he asked a longtime friend, who had been a chef for CNN in Baghdad, to cook an enormous meal and bring it to the mosque.

Huge pots of rice and meat arrived—so heavy that two men had to carry each one.

"Fifty men—maybe more—came," Ali recalled, happily. "I invited everybody!"

"I wasn't there," Heidi said drily.

7. THE GIFT

MERSIHA was still a teenager when she got to Utica.
  She was still thinking about the things stolen from her by the Bosnian War: Her high school graduation. Her prom. She had looked forward to parading down the main street of Travnik with her classmates, wearing a short black dress, as townspeople clapped.

"I became an adult in like 48 hours," she said, laughing. Suddenly, she was the one translating for her mother, Ismeta, 44, and her sister, Melissa, 17.

She was overjoyed to be reunited with her mother, who raised her daughters by herself. They were separated for 18 months during the war. To keep them safe, Ismeta sent the two girls to Croatia with her sister.

"I'm never letting go of you again. Never!" Mersiha said, hugging her mother in their rental apartment.

When the girls were growing up, their mother was a perfectionist.

She baked buttery cakes, which she placed in a row, the swirls in the frosting facing the same direction.

"She ironed everything—even underwear," Mersiha said, laughing. "She smoked, but you couldn't smell it, because she cleaned everything with bleach."

Soon there was no time to dwell on anything.

The three of them got jobs at a curtain factory. Her mother worked as a seamstress. Mersiha and Melissa were baggers. Young and strong, the sisters threw themselves into the work.

"I bagged 3,500 curtains in 8 hours," Mersiha said, proudly. She was lightning quick—grabbing folded curtains off a machine, then throwing them into a bagging machine. "I would break that machine constantly. My sister was the best bagger in the place."

The sisters hoped that if they worked hard, they would get a raise.

"How dumb we were!" Mersiha said, laughing. They stayed at minimum wage. Yet they did not slow down.

Their coworkers thought they were crazy: "The Americans said, 'My God, what are you guys doing?'"

But their mother showed signs of exhaustion. She said her legs hurt. Her skin became bruised.

The day she was to go to the hospital for tests, she put on a red blouse and a black pencil skirt. She was living with Mersiha and Hajrudin, who had recently married. Waiting for Melissa to pick her up, she smoked a cigarette on the stairway.

"This might be my last one," she said.

That evening, Melissa returned, alone, carrying their mother's clothes. She was being held overnight at the hospital.

Mersiha just stared at the red blouse.

For the next two years, their mother fought leukemia. The disease and its treatment initially mystified and frightened the family. "We didn't know—what is cancer, what is chemo?" Mersiha said.

The doctors started their mother on an aggressive course of chemotherapy. "She had every side effect; she lost her hair. She was not able to walk."

At the end, their mother was hospitalized. "But she was never alone," Mersiha said.

When the sisters saw her for the last time—a small, still figure in the hospital bed—they both lost consciousness.

A nurse administered shots of adrenaline to the two young women.

———

Mersiha had an American friend, Elaine. She was a high school teacher, who befriended many young Bosnian refugees; she often checked on Mersiha after her mother's death.

Elaine encouraged her.

"Maybe this is the time you should start college," she told Mersiha. "It would make your mother happy. This is what she wanted for you."

It was true: Mersiha had promised her mother she would go to college. Elaine said she would help her apply to schools—and she did.

She told Mersiha, "I can't see anything stopping you!"

Mersiha received an associate degree at a community college. Then she completed an online bachelor's degree through SUNY Empire State College—and got a job as a teacher's aide at a middle school.

But every few days, she baked Bosnian pastries, her mother's way: Hungarian Girl, palm-sized rectangles of chocolate and hazelnut. Peachies, cookies that look like two cheeks pressed together.

As a child, she watched her mother expertly roll out dough for an apple cake, spooning chunks of fruit onto it, before lifting the dough into the pan. "When I tried, the dough would break," she said.

Mersiha's baking delighted Hajrudin. "I didn't think I had any talent," she said.

Then one afternoon, Hajrudin, who worked at Utica Metal Products, slipped on the wet factory floor, damaging his spinal cord. And this accident—which could have paralyzed him—sent them spiraling into new lives.

At home, recovering, Hajrudin was struck by how much Mersiha did for their family.

"I thought, 'How can I help her?'" he recalled. "I felt so sorry for her—and honestly, for myself, too," he added, laughing.

He started baking bread. Every day.

He was not just trying to be helpful: "She's the brain for everything," he said admiringly about his wife. "I wanted to impress her."

Mersiha thought his bread was good. That he had potential.

"Why don't you take some classes?" she said. She knew there was a culinary arts program at MVCC and thought he could use a career change.

The class's first assignment was baking baklava. But when Hajrudin brought the dessert home, Mersiha was appalled.

"You call that baklava?" she said. The pastry was dried out, crackly. Her baklava was rich with ground walnuts; the phyllo was feathery.

Hajrudin was not offended: "You make some, and I'll bring it to the teacher."

That night, Mersiha stayed up late, baking.

She was amazed when the professor called her the next day.

"She ordered a sheet of baklava," Mersiha said. "Oh, my God! I felt very honored."

She started to see herself differently.

She remembered her eighth-grade art teacher telling her she could not draw: "You'll never have any artistic talent."

"That's not true," she told me, laughing. "I can't draw, but I have these things in my head. I can make things with my hands."

When her niece went to law school, she made a cake that looked like a pile of colorful law books. For a friend's wedding, she baked a cake topped by a fancy edible shoe.

She posted her photos on Facebook.

"People started asking me, 'Can you make this? I can pay you.'"

8. THE CAKE BOSS

WHEN MERSIHA opened her home bakery in 2011, the orders flew in. She made Porsche cakes, soccer cakes, flag cakes. Vegan and gluten-free cakes. Her customers said her cakes tasted different than any bakery-bought cake. "In Bosnia, we use more butter, and also Nutella," Mersiha explained. "American cakes are sweeter."

She soon had 6,000 followers on Instagram.

She and Hajrudin worked as a team. He baked the cakes; she covered them with fondant, a smooth, thick paste made of sugar and water. Then she decorated them.

Her mind would spin: "I think about product, product," she said.

She started following different pastry chefs online. She liked Buddy Valastro, the star of *Cake Boss,* the reality TV series. He had taken over Carlo's Bakery, his father's Hoboken shop, before starting a food empire.

"But he tries to appeal to everyone," she said. On his videos, he made Christmas cookies, rolled out a cake that looked like a Las Vegas casino, and gave tours of his home. "He's not a perfectionist like me."

Her favorite was Ron Ben Israel, an Israeli-American pastry chef based in Manhattan; she admired his elegant, whimsical cakes. One of his cakes resembled a pile of Chanel and Hermès boxes. A wedding cake had a cluster of white peonies.

"He's the king of cakes," Mersiha said. "That's how I fell in love with cakes."

But she and Hajrudin were not making any money. Materials were expensive, and since they were just beginning, they kept their prices low, afraid people would not pay more. They were overly generous: If a customer ordered a cake for 125 people, they delivered one that served 150.

"I'm just making change," Mersiha said, matter-of-factly. "I make more teaching my ESL classes."

"But we're trying to make our names. That's all that matters for now."

Her customers' delighted response—and emails sent by guests at events she catered—excited her. "When I see that smile . . . ," she said.

By the end of her first year in business, her confidence had grown. She stopped watching videos of the Cake Boss and of Ron Ben-Israel.

"I saw I can do it."

9. IN BLOOM

UTICA became a refugee magnet by accident.

In the 1970s, Roberta Douglas, a local resident, became concerned about the mistreatment of Amerasian children in Vietnam. She helped one Amerasian resettle in Utica. Then along with Catholic Charities in Syracuse, she started resettling hundreds of Amerasians, and later, working with others, established the Mohawk Valley Resource Center for Refugees.

Over the next 40 years, there was a remarkable migration: Thousands of immigrants seeking sanctuary, including Vietnamese, Russians, and Burmese, have transformed this once-fading industrial town.

The newcomers make up about a quarter of Utica's population of 60,000, according to Shelly Callahan, executive director of the Center for Refugees, recently renamed The Center, a nonprofit group that helps to resettle refugees and assist others in the community. And they have been an economic engine for the city, starting small businesses, renovating down-at-the-heels houses, opening houses of worship—and injecting a sense of vitality to its streets.

"It was so much more than economics," John Zogby, the national pollster, said about the refugees' effect on the city. "A whole generation couldn't wait to get out. Then you had thousands of people who wanted to live here."

"Other people started feeling good. It was infectious."

———

The refugees came in waves: In the 1980s, people arrived from Vietnam, Cambodia, Laos, Poland, and the Soviet Union. Starting in the early 1990s, over 4,500 Bosnians fleeing the Balkan conflict became the largest group to be resettled.

In the 2000s, there was a surge of refugees from Burma—including the Karen, an ethnic minority persecuted by the Burmese military, who fled to camps in Thailand—and from Iraq, Nepal, Somalia, and Sudan. By 2019, more than 4,000 Karen and Burmese were resettled, becoming Utica's second-largest group.

"The refugees helped stem the decline," Ms. Callahan said. "They have a great work ethic and are willing to take jobs that native folks don't want."

The refugee center helps cushion the landing: It spends about $1,100—federal and state money—on each refugee. Newcomers are given a furnished apartment, with the basics to get started.

Every refugee initially accesses public assistance—but is supposed to take the first viable job offered. "Refugees don't come here to be on public assistance," Ms. Callahan said. "That's not the dream."

Many currently work as dishwashers, groundskeepers, janitors, cooks, housekeepers, and card dealers at Turning Stone Resort Casino in Verona, New York. Others are employed at Chobani, the yogurt factory in New Berlin, owned by Hamdi Ulukaya, a Turkish immigrant. Chobani estimates that approximately 30 percent of its manufacturing workforce in New Berlin are immigrants or refugees.

The Bosnians have been the most successful group.

Many arrived with educations and building skills. "All of us had everything," said Sefik Badnjevic, 62, a retired machinist, referring to the many middle-class lives uprooted by war. "We try to find here what we lost in Bosnia."

Mr. Badnjevic was offended when his new neighbors asked questions like: "Did you have stores in your country? Did you have a TV?"

He would show them a video of his home, which he shot before the war: "This is my apartment! This is my car!" he said.

The Bosnians quickly adapted, often working two jobs to get ahead.

Then in the late 1990s, there was a stunning confluence of events: The fires, which had been raging for decades, abated. The city tore down almost 200 vacant structures; the National Guard helped clear away the debris.

And the Bosnians bought hundreds of run-down houses in East Utica.

The stage was set for what amounted to a massive rebuilding project: Bosnian families—sometimes three generations—did the work themselves. They tore out and rebuilt kitchens; they put in extra bedrooms. They fixed up garages, built decks, and planted gardens.

Many chose two-family homes, living in one as they rebuilt the other. They often rented the second to parents or siblings.

Every Saturday, for seven years, Mr. Zogby gave a ride home to a Bosnian woman who worked for his family as a housekeeper; in Bosnia, she had been a police officer. One Saturday, she told him she had moved, and directed him to her new home.

"It was only a few blocks from where I had grown up," Mr. Zogby said. It had been a photo studio, in a two-family house that had declined.

He pulled up to her new residence: She, her husband, and two tall sons had transformed it into a one-family home with white pillars.

"Outside was a massive American flag," he recalled. "I knew what she was saying: 'I turned this into my palace.'"

The Bosnians have now been in the city for two generations. They are doctors, nurses, physical therapists, contractors, police officers, firefighters, restaurateurs, bar owners, and restaurant managers. They work in Utica's banks and at City Hall.

Many have stayed in their renovated homes—rather than move to New Hartford, an affluent suburb—even as new, struggling refugees have settled in their neighborhoods.

"If I sell my house, I'm selling my memories of my kids, my family," said Sakib Duracak, 56, a contractor, who is president of the Bosnian Islamic Association of Utica. "I can't remember seeing 'House for Sale' signs in Bosnia."

In 2008, the community purchased the old, abandoned Central United Methodist Church from the city for a thousand dollars. It would have been costly for the city to demolish. Over the next four years, they built a soaring mosque downtown, doing the labor themselves.

Two other refugee groups that have been in Utica for more than a generation have also done well: The Vietnamese initially opened restaurants and food stores; most are now fully integrated into the community. Russians, who escaped religious persecution in the former Soviet Union, opened furniture stores and car dealerships.

For more recent arrivals, coming from refugee camps, "the learning curve has been longer, slower," Ms. Callahan said. Yet the Karen, from the Karen state in southeastern Burma, have established a foothold, opening markets and buying homes.

The Somali Bantus—a community of about 2,000—have had a tougher time adapting.

In Somalia, the Bantus have long been persecuted. They are not seen as true Somalis, but as the descendants of slaves brought from other countries: In the 19th century, Arab slave traders brought Bantus to Somalia from southeast Africa to work on Somali plantations. Yet the largest group of Somali Bantus arrived thousands of years ago from West Africa, before the nomadic Somalis.

In recent years, the Somali Bantus worked small family farms, but they had little access to medical care, education, or jobs beyond manual labor.

They were powerless against armed Somalis: "If you were walking to a larger village, and met Somalis on the road, you could be taken and used to work their land," said Mohamed Ganiso, 41, a community leader and the former director of the Somali Bantu Association of Central New York in Utica.

Armed Somalis sometimes took over the Bantus' farms: Ahmed Mukonje, 46, who lives in Utica, was forced to be an unpaid laborer on his own land. "I was farming—but for them," he said. "Slavery stopped when I got to the refugee camp."

Clans provided an element of protection: "Everything is the clan," said Mr. Ganiso, who is Halima's nephew. "If a person in power was not in my clan, I didn't trust them." Disputes were brought before a community chief: "The chief decides what's fair."

For Somali Bantus, there was a deep sense of dislocation upon arrival in Utica. "The teachers sent home letters about the kids, but the parents couldn't read them," Mr. Ganiso said. "If they applied for a job they were told to go online, but they couldn't."

Uticans did not open their arms to the Somali Bantus, as they did for the Bosnians. "The Bosnians came with resources—and white skin," said Dr. Kathryn Stam, the anthropology professor. "The Somali Bantus came with black skin, no education, and centuries of persecution. They were seen as backward."

But in the last few years, there has been a sense of accomplishment and possibilities: Mr. Ganiso, who worked as a machinist at Chobani and now owns his own trucking company, estimated that unemployment in the Somali Bantu community, which was about 50 percent a decade ago, dropped to about 30 percent in 2019. That year, the unemployment rate in the Utica/Rome area was 4.7 percent.

More than half of Utica's Somali Bantus own their own homes. Dozens of their children are now enrolled at MVCC and other colleges.

"In the camps, we were almost not thinking," Mr. Ganiso said, describing the years Somali Bantus spent in limbo.

"Now everybody's thinking about the future."

———

Utica has always been a city of immigrants.

At the turn of the century, Italians, Germans, Poles, and Irish were drawn to Utica's factories and mills.

They helped produce boots, screws, tools, hot air furnaces, cast-iron pipe, and beds. They made broom handles from logs that had been floated down the West Canada Creek from the Adirondacks and cut into lumber.

Utica's large textile mills employed thousands of immigrants. The city was dubbed the Knit Goods Capital of the World. Women mostly worked in the woolen mills; men in the bleacheries. Utica Knitting Company, the city's largest mill, was said to produce 34,000 pieces of underwear every 24 hours.

When the Italians started arriving in the 1880s, they found steady work and established a close-knit community in East Utica. Many soon began small businesses: "My great-grandfather was the first gentleman to walk up and down the streets of Utica yelling, 'Lemon ice!'" said Anthony Amodio, 56, who works in the restaurant industry in Utica. Later, his grandfather opened a salumeria.

Lebanese and Syrian immigrants arrived around the same time, as part of peddling networks based in New York City and Boston; they sold linens and other dry goods. Many eventually opened grocery stores. By 1940, there were over 70 grocery stores owned by Syrians or Lebanese. Almost a quarter of the city's population was foreign born, a similar ratio to the city's refugee population today.

When Utica's textile mills closed in the 1950s and relocated in the South, it wasn't the tragedy it might have been. General Electric and other large manufacturing plants moved in. Picking up the slack, they replaced the 5,000 jobs immigrants had lost.

These jobs, too, would eventually vanish.

But in the 1960s, the city was still in bloom. And East Utica—to its immigrant families—was the center of the world.

"Houses were full, bursting!" said Mr. Zogby, who lived there for 36 years. "A family with four sons downstairs. Another with three sons upstairs."

"It was a tough, none-of-your-shit culture. But as much as there was bullying going on, people had your back."

Bleecker Street—a long, commercial strip—was the heart of the Italian community.

"There was everything here—you didn't have to leave the street," said Carmela Caruso, 62, a small, dark-haired woman who owns Caruso's Pastry Shoppe on Bleecker Street, which her parents opened in 1958. "You could get your hair cut, your shoes shined and fixed."

There were Italian restaurants and Syrian markets. A fish store served raw clams at sidewalk tables.

And there was a tradition: "Monday nights, that's when people flocked downtown," Ms. Caruso said.

All the stores stayed open late that night, and people strolled from Genesee Street down Bleecker. Starting in fourth grade, Ms. Caruso stayed up late, too. "I used to wait tables, make wedding favors, or do my homework, still wearing my Catholic school uniform."

At 10:30 p.m., her dad and the other shop owners locked up.

"Everybody walked home," she said. "That was normal. That was our life."

10. THE WEDDING

I WANTED to go," Sadia said about the wedding in Utica. She did not even know the girl. But dozens of her young cousins would be there.

Somali Bantu weddings are loosely put together affairs—a kind of family reunion, which can draw hundreds of clan members. These marriages are often arranged by the parents; a contract is signed, and the young woman's family receives a dowry.

There is not a huge stigma associated with divorce: If a woman leaves her marriage, her family generally absorbs her and her children back into the fold. She may marry again.

These weddings are the highlight of summer—a chance for people to swap news, arrange marriages, and find out about job opportunities and living conditions in the cities where others have settled. Sadia has maternal relatives across the country: in Syracuse, Buffalo, Rochester, Burlington, St. Louis, Louisville, Columbus, and Denver.

A family might attend three or four weddings a summer. Often, there is no formal invitation; word gets around.

"You just know—there's a wedding that weekend," Sadia said. "And you go."

Sadia's mother was skipping this one. So were her sisters. "But my grandma and aunts were leaving in the morning," Sadia said, "and asked if I wanted to go."

But when Sadia went into the kitchen to ask her mother's permission, Zahara hardly looked up.

Sadia knew her mother was angry with her. She had just finished her junior year—a lot of things had gone wrong.

She plunged in: "Ma, can I go to the wedding?"

"She gave me this *look*," Sadia recalled. "My mom's generous—she gives everybody something. But not me."

"She said, 'You can't go! *You never want to sit down in the house!*'"

Her mother's words struck Sadia like a slap. "That's like calling some-one a dog in our culture," she said.

She knew what her mother was saying: You are running around. You never help me. A good Somali Bantu girl stays home, takes care of the younger children, and helps with the housework.

That was unfair, Sadia told me: "I'm always home. I'm an inside girl! And I help my mom—I clean 24/7!"

There were other things that pained her mother: Many mornings, Sadia could hardly get out of bed. She did not come home straight after school. She did poorly in her classes.

Her mother suspected she was seeing boys. That she had sneaked a boy into the house.

"Not true!" Sadia said. "I'm not fascinated by boys, especially young ones. I have other things to worry about."

Anxious about school and her home life, she had lost a lot of weight, and looked hollow-cheeked. "Sometimes, I'd just get up and not eat all day," she said. "I'd just drink water."

"I was trying to smooth things down," she explained. "Do better in school. Just worry about myself, not anybody else."

But sometimes, she got irritated. "This one teacher, he'd just grab my phone as I'm talking to my friend. 'Oh, what's happening?'"

Her mother recently moved her kids into a new house she bought, not far from Rutger Street. They all liked the house. "But my mom only wants me *here*," Sadia said. "'Why do you want to go to your friend's house?' Even if I go visit my grandmother, she says, 'What's wrong with *your own house*?'"

Deeply stung, Sadia decided to stay at her grandmother's house for the weekend. Her house had become a refuge.

Her uncle Yusef's wife, Fartoum, 19, was staying there; she had recently given birth. "She didn't want to be alone that weekend," Sadia said. "She felt no one was helping her."

Sadia did not pack anything. She already had clothes, a toothbrush, and deodorant at her grandmother's.

Hearing Sadia's footsteps by the door, Zahara called out, "Make sure you don't go with them!"

"I'm not," Sadia said, and softly closed the door.

It was hot for upstate, and Sadia holed up in her grandmother's living room for the weekend, with the drapes closed and the fan on. She took care of Fartoum's month-old baby girl and watched one of her favorite shows, *Star*, a Fox TV musical drama about three young singers. "Two of them came from poverty," Sadia said.

Both teenage girls were in good spirits. "Fartoum got to shower, relax—she felt more peaceful."

Sadia quickly got over the incident with her mother, and assumed her mother had forgotten it, too.

Sadia got home late afternoon the next day. Her mother's car was not in the driveway. Sadia knocked loudly on the old front door; she had lost her key. Her sisters did not hear her: The TV was on too loud.

She waited on the front steps for her mother.

Zahara saw her as she pulled into the driveway. Still a bit heavy from Rahama's birth, she made her way past the tricycles and old balls. Approaching Sadia, she said, "I told you not to go."

"Ma, I didn't!" Sadia said, looking up at her. "Ask Fartoum!"

"I don't believe you. She's going to lie, too."

As Zahara passed her daughter, her long dress brushed the steps. "You can't come in my house," she said.

"What?" Sadia said, stunned. "What?" Her mother shut the door, then locked it.

"I just sat there," Sadia recalled. "I was like—wow. This is your kid. You made this child! Don't hold grudges!"

She thought her mother was having a fit—that soon she would open the door and say, "Come in."

But the sun went down. It got dark.

"I went crazy," Sadia said. "I thought, 'I'm gonna quit. I just don't want to argue with her anymore.'"

Sadia had no money with her. No clothes, except for the long printed skirt and jacket she was wearing.

As she stood up and started walking, the old block, with its two-story, slightly askew frame houses, was shuttered and quiet.

11. WITH STRANGERS

SADIA knew her relatives would not take her in; her mother would see it as meddling.

But she walked about a mile to her aunt's house near Mohawk Street—and knocked on the door. Her aunt, Bishara—who was 28 and had four kids—just looked at her.

"I was at the door for two minutes," Sadia recalled. "She said, 'I don't want nothing to do with your mom's stuff.'"

So, Sadia went two doors down, to a house that belonged to a Somali woman who had once been friends with her mom.

A single mother in her thirties, this woman had developed a bad reputation in the community: She smoked hookah, and took in runaway Somali Bantu girls, letting them stay with her in exchange for doing domestic work.

Sadia hoped she could stay there for a few days. But the woman immediately started putting her down. She kept looking at her and saying, "What's wrong with you?"

"She thought she was better than us," Sadia said, "because she is Somali, not Somali Bantu. But her house was dirty as shit. She said if I didn't work hard for her, she'd call my mom."

"She was like an evil stepmother. She was looking for a slave, for some drama."

For a couple of days—feeling miserable—Sadia swept and made beds. Then surreptitiously, when the woman was not looking, she called another former friend of her mother's.

Maggie was a young white woman, a convert to Islam, whom her mother had befriended at the mosque. "She was poor," Sadia said, explaining that Maggie lived in a housing project. "She'd lost her kids. I think she used to be a drug addict."

Recently she had stopped practicing Islam and cut ties with Zahara and others in the community. "I think she felt ashamed," Sadia said, "that people would judge her."

But Maggie was kind—and when Sadia called her, she immediately drove over to the Somali woman's house.

Spotting Maggie's car from a window, Sadia ran outside. The Somali woman followed her, yelling, "Don't get in the car!"

As Sadia jumped in, the Somali woman chased the car down the block.

———

Sadia was always uncomfortable in a stranger's home; she was so used to her own. Maggie kept asking if there was anything she could get her. Her apartment was neat and immaculate. "I think she had OCD," Sadia said. "She had to have everything clean."

It was a new experience for Sadia to be in an apartment without children.

Sadia could not understand why Maggie liked visiting her family. "We're so boring," she said about her mother's household. To Sadia, it was the norm: the dizzying number of little girls in jewel-colored jilbabs running around, her two younger brothers with their noses always dripping.

But Maggie—who wore long patterned skirts, and sometimes dyed her short hair green—seemed to enjoy the tumult.

Sadia did not want to worry Maggie: "I tried to make it seem like things with my mom were OK," she said. "Like we didn't have family problems. That I just needed a break."

She was too depressed to eat what Maggie cooked: fried zucchini. "I only took a bite," she said. "Later, I went to the store and got a bag of chips."

Over the next two days, Sadia's sense of hurt grew: "My mom didn't check up on me," she said. "Nobody did."

She made only one call—to her older sister Ralya.

Ralya—who worked in the bakery at Walmart—helped raise Sadia. A pretty, big-boned young woman, she was the one who attended parent/teacher conferences and school plays as their mother worked. She showed up with treats when Sadia was babysitting. "She spoiled me," Sadia said.

But when Ralya, usually so upbeat, heard Sadia's voice on the phone, she was brusque: "Go home," she said.

The next morning, Sadia checked Ralya's Facebook. Then Mana's. And Sofia's.

Sadia sat there, frozen.

"They blocked me on Facebook," she recalled. All her sisters. All her young aunts and cousins. "I cried. 'Why are they doing this?'"

But she knew: Somali Bantu families function as a group: "If one person—like my mom—gets mad, everybody else gets mad. None of them would talk to me."

But Sadia was tough, too. She immediately retaliated: "I blocked them off group chats."

She felt she needed to get out of Utica. And she started thinking about her father, whom she had not seen in years. He and her mother had broken up when they lived in the refugee camp. Sadia was their only child together.

"He lives with his own tribe in Lewiston, Maine," she explained. "He has a new wife, other kids."

She decided to buy a bus ticket with her babysitting money and go visit him.

———

Nothing went as Sadia had pictured.

Her father, in his forties, was extremely tall—about 6' 4"—and skinny.

"He looks like me," she said. He has the same large brown eyes and broad nose.

"But he wasn't interested in me," she added, matter-of-factly. "He didn't care."

It turned out he was not living with his wife and kids. He had left them and was staying with a friend. Sadia's stepmother let her stay with her for a few days. But she was busy with her own kids, and they began to get on each other's nerves. "She kicked me out," Sadia said.

The next two weeks were disorienting: "Every single day, I was at a different house."

Her family in Utica was still blocking her. "I was losing more and more weight."

Then she stayed with a friend's mother, who was very caring. "She would worry about me," Sadia said. " 'Oh, you're going to the store, do you have your phone?' She used to cook for me all the time."

Sadia heard a rumor that her mother was calling people: "My daughter is bad. She doesn't listen to me. Don't let her inside your house if she tries to come."

"That was like killing me," Sadia said. "If you don't have your family, you're cut off from everything." But she kept her feelings to herself, pretending she was fine, that she was enjoying her time away.

But the pressure was enormous. After a month, she took a bus back to Utica.

Sadia thought she could stay with Maggie for a while. But Maggie worried she could get into legal trouble—and told her to leave.

After that, "I was just homeless," Sadia said.

———

She entered a kind of shadow existence in East Utica, just a few blocks from her mother's house. A friend hid her in her bedroom; Sadia managed to go to school every morning.

But the girl's parents found out: Her friend took her to an old vacated apartment in the same building.

The place was torn apart; there was a refrigerator lying on the floor.

"I was so scared," Sadia said. "It was so quiet there." She worried a homeless person would show up. That she would see rats.

And then, when Sadia could hardly take it anymore, an acquaintance of Zahara's stepped in.

"A Rwandan woman called my mom, and said, 'Your daughter wants to come home.'"

12. SHADOW

SADDAM HUSSEIN cast a shadow over Ali's childhood.

The highway to Saddam International Airport in Baghdad ran right by his family's house. Standing in his front yard, Ali would watch the convoys of arriving world leaders on their way to see President Hussein. A few times, his teachers took their classes to the airport.

"They put us in a line, to welcome the presidents," Ali said. "There would be 50 motorcycles, then all the limousines. They would slow down, open the roofs. I remember seeing Tito," he added, referring to the former president of Yugoslavia.

It was brutally hot, standing outside in the sun. Afterward, Ali would invite his teachers and some classmates back to his house for "tea, water, and sometimes lunch."

His parents, Shiites, were educated and secular; only his mother prayed. His mother—who was Iranian but had Iraqi citizenship through her marriage—worked for the Ministry of the Interior, in an ID office. His father, who owned a photography studio, "was one of the best black-and-white cameramen in the Mideast," Ali said, proudly.

His father told Ali that as a child, he had lived in the same Baghdad neighborhood as Saddam, who was from a Sunni tribe.

"He thought he was a thug," Ali said. "Sometimes, my father would curse him, call him names. I used to freak out. I thought we'd be arrested."

But there was a larger source of anxiety for their family: Tensions with the Shiite-majority nation of Iran were always high, but in 1980 Saddam sent troops into Iran—initiating a devastating war that would last eight years. The government sent his father to the front lines to photograph battles.

This angered his father, Ali said. "But you cannot say no to Saddam."

The government began deporting tens of thousands of Iranians and people thought to be of Iranian descent.

"Kids came home from school, they couldn't find their parents," Ali said.

Ali hated the red mark on his mother's government-issued ID card that indicated she was Iranian. It was unnerving that she herself worked in an ID office. "It was a very sensitive place," Ali said. "She needed clearance to work there." He knew the building where she worked was filled with government security forces and police officers.

"I felt at any minute, they could take our mom."

In 1984, when he was 13, police showed up at his aunt's house in Baghdad. It was before dawn; her family was asleep. They were not allowed to change out of their night clothes; the police pushed them into a car.

"They took my aunt, her husband, and her child to the Iranian border, and said, 'OK, go!'"

After that, "we were afraid all the time," Ali said.

This changed in March 2003, when the United States and allied forces invaded Iraq; nine months later, they captured Saddam. He was tried by an Iraqi court and executed in December 2006. "It was one of the happiest days of my life," Ali said.

He regrets that his father—who died in 2000—missed seeing the dictator's downfall.

Ali's sense of unease has never left.

In Utica, he is careful: driving down Genesee Street, or walking to see a client.

"Ninety-five percent of Iraqis have cop phobia," he said, sitting in his comfortable living room on South Street.

It does not take much: If Ali sees a young cop slowly driving by his old car, his heart races and he is on high alert.

There are only about 300 Iraqis in Utica. "I wish the city would bring in more Arab refugees," Ali said. "The more, the better!"

He needs more Arab-speaking clients; many Iraqis who moved to Utica years ago now speak English. And their kids are fluent. Without an influx of refugees, he will be out of work.

But also—he longs to connect.

He treats his clients like family, visiting those who have left the hospital and no longer need his services; he attends the funerals of those who have died. A few weeks ago, he dropped off two trout fillets at the home of the Alsayfis, an Iraqi family he has known since they arrived 10 months ago.

On a clear September day in 2013, the Alsayfis' small apartment was a pressure cooker.

The father, Sabah, a handsome man with a lined face, is disabled because of a back injury. The mother, Khoulood, who has warm, expressive eyes, rarely leaves the apartment.

But Ali was immediately comfortable: He was wearing a suit and tie—and had brought baklava.

The father lit up—and apologized for being in a sweatshirt. He had just come back from the dentist. "Back home, if I'm going outside the house, I wear gloves and a jacket."

The mother pushed a plate of tangerines toward Ali and me. Her two sons, Anwar and Ehab—strapping young men—were worried about her. A third son, Suroor, was not home.

Ali leaned toward the mother.

"I have friends outside the family," Anwar, 21, said. "But my mother has no one her age she can talk to."

"She is just *here*," he said, indicating the apartment. No pictures were on the walls—but there were a few chairs, blue curtains on the windows, and a table.

"It is very hard," the mother said. Tears welled in her eyes.

"She could go to school," Ehab, 27, said. "But my father needs help."

"I have to take care of my husband," the mother said.

"She didn't go to school in Iraq," Ehab added. "She had to stop after the second grade."

The mother is focused on her boys: When they come home on their lunch break from ESL classes, she puts out potatoes, eggplant, tomato slices, rice, and yogurt. "Sometimes spinach soup," she said.

Ali listened, appreciatively.

"I wish good things for my sons," the mother said, smiling. "Maybe they will not be doctors, but . . ."

"She always says, 'I wish for you to get married, and start a family,'" Anwar said.

"As long as I still have strength in me," she said. "I want them to get married. Then I'm done!"

Ali smiled at this.

"I will choose!" Anwar told her. "I will choose."

Anwar works hard in his ESL classes and has made progress. When he talks about his teacher, Jennifer, he smiles: "Every day is something different. Sometimes Jennifer brings her iPad and we can use it; sometimes she takes us to computer class." His plan is to get his GED, attend college, then work in computer technology.

Ehab, the eldest, is less hopeful. For years, he was a waiter at a restaurant in Damascus that served Middle Eastern and Western food; he dreamed of one day opening a café. But he is frustrated by his limited English, despite seven months of classes, and feels cut off and lonely.

"I'm sorry!" he said, apologizing for being depressed. "But that's the truth. Most of the time, I stay home and watch Arabic TV shows."

In a city with thousands of Muslim refugees, they are one of the few Mandaeans, part of a religion that sprang up in the Middle East, probably in the first three centuries AD. Its followers revere John the Baptist.

There are only three families of their faith in Utica, Ehab said. "Each family worships by themselves."

Almost a decade ago, the Alsayfis fled Iraq for Syria because of religious persecution.

Initially, Damascus, where they lived and worked for eight years, felt safe. But in 2011, about two years before they left, Assad's government forces started battling insurgents. There were explosions, clashes in the street.

"There was no security," the mother said. She spoke for a long time to Ali, who listened intently.

Finally, Ali said: "One day, she was with her husband in a cab. They were going to get new residency cards —you have to do this every three months," he explained. But people in the cars around them—from the Syrian Army and the Free Syrian Army—started shooting at each other."

After they got their cards stamped, the couple got in another cab to go home. But the Syrian Army stopped them at a checkpoint.

"Then members of the opposition drove up," Ali said. "They pulled out their guns and started firing."

No one in the living room spoke for a minute.

Then the mother said, "Before coming to Utica, it was very scary. We couldn't go out."   ____

Later, Ali quietly drove past blocks of small porch houses that needed paint. I noticed that while his eyebrows and the small amount of hair on his head were black, his beard was stark white.

"Why is that?" I asked.

Ali did not take his eyes off the road.

"My brother and my two nephews were kidnapped by terrorists," he said.

He was silent for a minute.

"When I heard that, I died," he said. He had fallen into a deep, bottomless sleep.

"When I woke up," he said, touching his beard, "it had turned white."

13. IN BOSNIA

IN THE SUMMER of 2015, the Omeragics took their kids home to Bosnia—and being away from baking, Mersiha could feel her body start to heal.

It was four years since she had started her home bakery.

After just a few days of rest, her back and legs did not ache so much. Her wrists and arms—no longer rolling out fondant and gum paste to make flowers and cartoon characters—felt less stiff.

They stayed with her aunt, her mother's older sister, in Travnik. She kept jumping up to serve Mersiha, though she was 67. "She wouldn't even let me get a glass of water," Mersiha said. "I kept saying, 'Auntie, sit down!'"

She and Hajrudin put over 5,000 miles on the car, crisscrossing Bosnia and Croatia to see relatives and old friends. Ismar, 16, sitting in the back seat, marveled at how relaxed they seemed: "Mom, Dad—this is so cool. You're not on the computer. You're not in the bakery."

Mersiha and Hajrudin were struck by his comment. They began to talk about how they had been living: each of them working, day and night for 20 years.

"The kids never complained," Mersiha said. "That's why I didn't stop."

"But on the weekends they'd say, 'Can we go to the movies? Can we go to Barnes & Noble?' I'd say, 'Honey, when I finish the order,' and then the weekend would be over."

"The bakery was taking away a lot. The kids need attention. We need attention from each other."

Mersiha and Hajrudin decided to get away—just the two of them. They would go to Paris; Hajrudin's sister would watch the kids. They would take a pastry class together.

Mersiha had always wanted to learn more about macarons. "To make them perfect, to have that beautiful little foot," she said. "Not that ugly skirt."

On their first day, the teacher, a tall Texan named Jason, who had married a Parisian, stopped and watched Mersiha whip together the simple ingredients for macarons: almond flour, sugar, salt, egg whites, and vanilla extract. She did not overbeat or overfold.

"You have *more* than a little experience," he said.

She and Hajrudin had never been to Paris. When they asked the hotel's concierge to recommend some places to eat, she advised them, "Just get lost."

They found great bread. They drank wine over long dinners. They went to the top of the Eiffel Tower, even though Mersiha is afraid of heights; she could hardly breathe up there.

When they returned to Travnik, her aunt and grandmother drew her aside.

"You need to slow down," her aunt said, "to think about yourself, your health."

Her grandmother asked, "Do you really *need* the bakery?"

That question shook Mersiha. She thought of all the time she had missed with her kids. Soon Ismar, then Faris, would be going to college.

She thought of her mother, only 52 when she died. Sometimes, she would just close her eyes and feel connected to her. Her mother's red blouse—clean and pressed—hung in her closet.

Folding up her skirt, her aunt showed Mersiha her legs: They were distorted by large clumps of varicose veins, from a lifetime of being on her feet. She had worked in factories since she was 17; she had taken care of her family.

"It scared me," Mersiha said. "My aunt is just like me. We always work."

She was frightened her aunt would have a heart attack. She begged her to go see a doctor.

———

The Omeragics returned to Utica late on a Wednesday night. And Mersiha immediately went downstairs and began baking for a large wedding that weekend. After two hours' sleep, she headed to her ESL class.

That Friday, she got a call—her aunt had had a stroke.

Her aunt was hospitalized for two weeks. Then just as she was about to be released, she had a heart attack.

"My uncle's daughter sent me a message," Mersiha said. "'Auntie passed away.'"

Her grandmother—who had already lost three of her children—went into shock.

The next morning, Mersiha did not hesitate. Opening her computer, she posted a message on Facebook:

Our dear customers,
While we were away on our vacation, we made a very important
decision, and that's to temporarily close our little bakery. As of
today, we are not taking any other orders, but we will finish all the
ones we already have . . .

PART II **MY UTICA**

14. THE STRIKE FORCE

THE NIGHT SKIES of Utica are no longer filled with smoke: Renewal began in April 1997, when the small city—devastated by arson—punched back.

A team of 16 experienced police officers and fire investigators set up shop on the second floor of a firehouse, just a few blocks from the heart of Cornhill. Sealing themselves off, they began working around the clock to take back the city.

"We needed to be alone," said Mickey Maunz, a retired captain in the Utica Police Department's Criminal Investigations Division, who was one of the original team members. "To talk different cases and run our ideas together."

Utica was one of four cities across the country—all losing battles against arson—chosen by FEMA's National Arson Prevention Initiative to set up a strike force. It was a large-scale collaborative effort: The city's fire and police departments were assisted by the Oneida County Sheriff's Office; the Oneida County District Attorney's Office; the New York State Office of Fire Prevention and Control; the Bureau of Alcohol, Tobacco, and Firearms; the New York State Insurance Fraud Bureau; the US Marshals Service; and the New York State Police. The FBI and FEMA also provided aid.

The Utica fire and police departments had worked together, but never as closely. "There was a little animosity, distrust," Captain Maunz said, wryly. But that quickly went out the window: "It was established we needed them as much as they needed us. We learned to trust each other."

In a photo of the Strike Force, the men—in white shirts and ties—stand close together, outside a firehouse. The youngest, crouched and smiling, is Phil Fasolo, then a 27-year-old fire marshal. The eldest is his uncle, Captain Claude DeMetri, 56, the Strike Force's commander. A pale, reserved-looking man, he is almost hidden in the back.

The men revered him: "He was old school," Lieutenant Fasolo said about his uncle, who died in 2006. "He didn't micromanage us, but he guided us like a father at times."

Previously, the Utica Fire Department had only basic investigative tools: cameras and tape recorders. The Strike Force was given state-of-the-art equipment: body wires to tape people and video cameras. They had access to marked and unmarked cars, and dogs trained to sniff out arson. The Strike Force was also given funding to build a custom database and a local area network, so investigators could send and receive information from other agencies.

The Strike Force took an aggressive approach: As soon as an alarm sounded, police investigators and a fire marshal headed to the fire. As spectators stood around, mesmerized, the team videotaped them, then canvassed the neighborhood, looking for the building's owner, landlord, and occupants. If the fire marshal decided it was arson, the investigation simply continued.

Investigators were able to track arsonists who fled the state: They emailed high-resolution mug shots of suspects to other agencies. US Marshals, working with the Strike Force, captured fugitives in North Carolina, Arizona, and Florida.

The Strike Force got guilty pleas from two Utica brothers, John and Joseph Kaminski, who had recruited poor local men to burn down 18 of their properties.

One arsonist slipped away: Lieutenant Fasolo, tracking a suspect, found him lying in a hospital bed in Syracuse.

He was all bandaged up, covered with burns that matched an explosion on Niagara Street in Utica. So much gas was poured into a building, "the entire front wall of the house blew off and landed across the street," Lieutenant Fasolo said. "We were 100 percent sure it was him." But the man had an alibi; he said he survived a barbecue fire.

The rate of convictions—which had been 2 percent—jumped to 100 percent, Captain DeMetri said in an interview in 1998. Arson was cut in half.

Some blocks looked less desperate as the city began to remove abandoned buildings. In 2000, when the Strike Force disbanded, the Bosnians were already standing on ladders and roofs, rebuilding.

———

The refugees—arriving from over 35 different countries—helped keep fire at bay by bringing blocks back to life. But they also presented challenges: The fire department was unprepared for the newcomers, some of whom had never seen a stove, used indoor plumbing, or slept on a mattress.

Communication was the biggest problem: A mother whose apartment is on fire might not speak a word of English. The site itself might be more crowded and chaotic than normal: An apartment meant for 6 people could turn out to hold 12.

"You're trying to figure out where everybody is," Captain Zumpano said. "Who's in, who's out? You're getting varying information—and spending more time than usual searching for people."

There is no time to call for an on-site interpreter. Emergency responders can access a translation service on their cell phones, but it is cumbersome.

Often, firefighters turn to an English-speaking child of the refugee family. These children often do a good job answering questions. "But a child doesn't process information like an adult," Captain Zumpano said, "and in that situation may be too frightened to speak."

"We're asking rapid-fire questions, expecting rapid-fire answers."

There are cultural practices that are potentially hazardous: Bosnians have sometimes smoked sausages in attics. The Karen display national flags and hang cloth from doorways. The Somali Bantus, not used to mattresses, would place them against doors and windows, blocking exits. They covered walls with tapestries and velvety pictures of Mecca—and hung long drapes.

Drapes can be a serious problem, Captain Zumpano explained. "Fire can jump from a tapestry to cloth very quickly. It can light the place up."

Cultural practices often evolve out of necessity: In their country, the Somali Bantus live in dark dwellings, Dr. Stam said. "They're hiding from the sun."

In Utica, "they like having the drapes drawn to keep out the light," she added. "And they like the privacy. They don't want people knowing what they're up to."

In the camps, the Somali Bantus cooked outdoors, using firewood. Moving into their new apartments, they were mystified by gas stoves.

When Zahara arrived in St. Louis, a woman from the refugee agency showed her how to turn on the burner. "But I was too scared," Zahara said. The woman had cautioned her about how easily a fire can start. Instead, she cooked on a neighbor's electric stove. It was weeks before she became comfortable using her own stove. And she kept checking: Is it on or off?

Many Somali Bantus started cooking on small hibachis they placed on top of burners. This felt more familiar. And some used stoves to heat their apartments during the long winters.

The fire department started seeing a flare-up of serious fires.

The department had held a few safety workshops at the refugee center. "But I was coming at things from an American point of view," Chief Ingersoll said. "I didn't have a great understanding of the conditions the refugees were coming from. I just knew they were here."

Then in 2013, a fire almost killed a 4-year-old Somali Bantu girl.

On a winter day, Johara Abdi, a Somali Bantu mother who had been out shopping, returned to her apartment in Adrean Terrace, a public housing project in Utica. Smoke was billowing from her duplex. Eight of her children—ages 2 to 17—had escaped. But they had not been able to reach their sister, Halima, napping on the second floor.

Fred DeCarlo, a veteran firefighter, managed to make it up the stairs. "It was pitch-black; he had no visibility," said Chief Ingersoll, then fire captain, who was putting out the fire in the kitchen. It had sprung from a hibachi sitting atop the stove.

Minutes later, Mr. DeCarlo ran out of the building with Halima, limp in his arms, her head flopping with each of his steps.

Halima—who suffered lung damage from smoke inhalation—eventually recovered.

"It was a turning point for us," Chief Ingersoll said. "We had to refocus and start bridging that gap."

"We started getting involved."

The department began coordinating with the refugee center and the city's Municipal Housing Authority. The refugee center did multiple training sessions with the firefighters.

"We wanted them to know the reality of the refugees' experiences," Ms. Callahan said. "If people have been cooking on the ground, you can't just say, 'No, this is wrong, use the stove.' You have to really connect with people."

The fire department started going to community events and talking to people about fire safety. "The goal is to help them understand the things we take for granted—how to use a stove, how to use a smoke detector," Chef Ingersoll said. The firefighters give out free smoke detectors.

In 2014, the city received a $250,000 grant from FEMA to install almost 1,000 safety burners on stoves in Municipal Housing Authority apartments, where many refugees live. These flat, cast-iron elements were designed to prevent cooking fires. The refugee center received almost $100,000 to provide community education and outreach about fire safety.

There is progress: The use of hibachis seems to be waning, Chef Ingersoll said. The citywide number of fires is the lowest it has ever been: In 2019, there were only 26 structure fires.

———

The fire department—predominately Italian, Irish, and Polish men—is slowly starting to change.

In recent years, the department has been trying to recruit refugees and other minorities, to better reflect the community. Currently, 11 out of 124 members are from diverse backgrounds: a Russian, a Belarusian, a Bosnian, a Karen, two Ukrainians, and two Puerto Ricans. There are only two African Americans, and one firefighter of mixed race. Four firefighters are women.

Since 2017, Pathways to Justice Careers—part of a national job training network—has been helping Utica teenagers gain experience in the fields of criminal justice and emergency services. They go on ride-alongs, attend classes, and participate in a junior version of the police and fire academies. More than a third of the 276 young participants are African American; less than a third are Karen and Burmese refugees. So far, they are too young to take the civil service exam; you must be 21.

There are lots of barriers: "You have to fight and scratch to get it," Captain Zumpano said about getting hired. There are only two or three openings a year, and candidates must get high scores on the written test and pass an arduous physical endurance test.

Captain Zumpano is frank about the role of legacies: Fire and police departments function as clans. Jobs tend to stay within families that have served for generations. "A lot of people are grooming their kids from the start," he said. "I've seen 2-year-olds running around in fire department T-shirts and hats."

Cultural change needs to happen slowly, Dr. Stam said. And to be reinforced by community leaders and young people: "You don't go from 0 to 100." She was referring to how the Somali Bantus are adapting to city life. But it is also true for how the fire department—initially blind to the newcomers—is adapting to them.

Sometimes, even a small cultural change can take years: In many Somali Bantu homes, there is the constant beeping of a smoke alarm needing a new battery.

If you point this out, you get a perplexed look. Nobody had noticed; the beeping is just part of the background. Conversation continues.

15. GRADUATION

IT WAS CHAOTIC outside the Utica Memorial Auditorium.

Families—many carrying flowers and balloons—headed inside, toward the bleachers, to see their teenagers graduate. There were women in printed sundresses, their bare feet in thongs; men in T-shirts, shorts, and baseball caps; and hundreds of women in hijab and long, layered dresses in tangerine, fuchsia, lemon, cream, black, silver, and gold. Head wraps and shawls sparkled with tiny sequins.

Sadia—standing outside, surrounded by her sisters—was resplendent.

She had draped a tiara of crystals across her forehead and wrapped three leis around her neck. Under her graduation cap, she wore a bright red scarf. Her smile was wide: She had made it through the year. "I passed all my classes," she said.

Her sisters were aglow, too: Aisha, 6, was in a beaded hijab and a dress of white tulle that looked like a miniature wedding gown. Halima, 11, was in pink from head to toe, her hijab embroidered with a swirl of sequins.

Mana—her thin face framed by a head scarf—looked tired but happy. She had recently gotten married. Her mother and new stepfather had arranged it; before the wedding Mana had never met the man, a 34-year-old Somali Bantu.

Asked about married life, Mana said, "Sometimes good, sometimes bad. He's very good to me. But I'm not sure yet. I don't really know him."

Zahara was not there.

If Sadia was pained by this, she did not show it. She seemed content with her sisters, aunts, and cousins milling around her in the June sunshine.

She and her mother had hardly spoken the past year, since she had returned home.

Sadia was hurt by her mother's response when she walked in the door: "She wouldn't even hug me, or say, 'Where were you? Where did you go?'"

"She was just annoyed by me."

It was more complicated: "Of course, I was worried," Zahara said, softly, when I asked about that time. "She's my child."

But she could not get over her anger at Sadia's rebelliousness—and what she saw as her lack of respect. She felt Sadia had shamed her by running away.

Sadia went up to a woman holding a clipboard.

She returned, looking thunderstruck. "I don't have my card."

"What card?" one of her sisters asked.

"I don't know."

Sadia disappeared inside the auditorium, then came back, relieved, carrying a card with her name on it.

Her family streamed toward the bleachers, passing a mural depicting a giant-sized glass of Labatt beer; the auditorium is a sports and entertainment complex. They settled into a row toward the back, the youngest children sitting on laps.

Far below, the senior class of 2016—about 600 students—sat facing the stage. Students were seated in alphabetical order. Families strained to pick out their child.

Ambure. Sadia should have been toward the front. But even though the principal and students looked like toys, it was clear that Sadia—with her red head scarf—was not there.

The principal made his opening remarks, then introduced a couple of local dignitaries. But the sound system was not working well. Then the valedictorian, Kelly Fam, a young first-generation American woman, spoke; it was hard to hear her.

Suddenly, Sadia hurried onto the floor.

There was one chair open at the very back, and she took it: The principal called up each graduate, shook hands, then handed them a certificate. Sadia's family listened attentively through the hundreds of names.

Sadia's was the last to be called.

———

Afterward she stood, alone, near the parking lot. She was waiting to be picked up.

She was hazy about the glitch at the graduation ceremony. And she was vague about her plans—she thought she would probably babysit that summer and start MVCC in the fall.

One thing was certain: High school was over.

16. CONFESSIONS OF A TEACHER

S ADIA sat restlessly through four years of high school. She did not even know some of her teachers' names.

She would have been surprised to glimpse things from the other side of the teacher's desk.

Danielle Brain, a charismatic pro, has been teaching English at Proctor High School for roughly 30 years. She knows exactly how many days till her retirement: "Three hundred and sixty-two school days and 730 calendar days," she said on a clear June day in 2019, her last class before summer vacation.

She kept an eye on her students as they gathered backpacks and headed toward the door.

"'Bye, Brain," a tall, thin girl in a hijab said, affectionately.

Ms. Brain had a rough month: A fierce storm hurled a tree onto her house in nearby Rome. "It crushed the house and my leg," she said, rolling up her skirt after her students left, and showing a scar.

There is little that throws Ms. Brain.

Proctor is one of the most diverse schools in the country: Its 2,600 students speak over 40 languages. About 80 percent of the student population is economically disadvantaged.

In Ms. Brain's classroom, students come and go: A Karen girl, knowing little English, may arrive from a refugee camp in Thailand. A student may vanish into an alternative program, just as Sadia did. A girl may return to the Middle East to get married.

"I don't get a heads-up," Ms. Brain, 52, said about the changes on her roster. And she gets little information about her new students. Records are often incomplete or have been lost, she said, since her students have come from so many different countries. Classes are large—between 25 and 30 students—so she does not have time to go through background material.

Sometimes, she will do her own quick evaluation of a new student by saying, "Hello. We're doing 'Romeo and Juliet.'"

The student may look at her blankly. Or they may say, "I love Shakespeare."

Whatever their response, Ms. Brain says, "Come on in, and let's get going."

Her years at Proctor have been draining: "You'll never teach harder," she said. "If you can teach in Utica, you can teach anywhere."

"But you wouldn't want to! You're getting a different lens from these kids. You can't get that teaching in New Hartford."

Years ago, her friend Krista Pembroke, an art teacher at Proctor, told her about a student from a refugee camp in Thailand. She was determined to use a particular shade of green.

The girl was painting the Adirondack mountains.

"There's no such green in the world," Ms. Pembroke said, looking at the girl's painting.

The girl insisted there was.

"Then Krista went to Thailand on vacation," Ms. Brain said, smiling. Standing on a bridge, overlooking a grove of trees, she saw her student's vibrant, yellow-green.

———

When Bosnian students started showing up in the mid-1990s, it felt like an explosion of newcomers, Ms. Brain said: "What can you do with a population that changes by the hour?"

Proctor's teachers had no special training to deal with non–English-speaking children. Most refugee students were placed into one of three different levels of ESL classes.

Those who arrive as children, generally have caught up by high school, Ms. Brain said: "If a kid comes in at elementary age, by the time I get them, they're good to go."

But some—like Sadia, Mana, and Ralya—never completely catch up. Sadia's younger siblings, born in the United States, were put into regular classes from the start.

There are programs that offer help along the way: The Young Scholars Liberty Partnerships Program, a collaboration between the Utica school district and Utica College, identifies talented minority students in the sixth grade and provides academic and social support until graduation.

AIS—Academic Intervention Services—is a program designed to help students pass the New York State Regents Exams.

When refugees arrive as teenagers, there are tremendous hurdles.

"You've got a 14-year-old who's never held a pencil," Ms. Brain said. "A 19-year-old—who drives and has a job—is put in the ninth grade."

Yet, some teenage refugees have soared.

When Pri Paw, 15, arrived from a refugee camp on the Burmese/Thai border in 2009, she was 4' 10", extremely shy, and could not speak English.

"I'd never seen a computer. I didn't have an American friend," she said about her first day at Proctor. "The person next to me showed me where to go."

Yet, she graduated in the top 10 of her class, and received a BA from SUNY Polytechnic Institute, majoring in biology.

Around 2007, Proctor instituted a new unwritten policy: Refugees over 16 were not allowed to enroll.

Young people between the ages of 17 and 21 who appeared at Proctor, wanting to register, were told they were too old—and were directed toward alternative academic programs. These programs, like the newcomer program run by the refugee center, focused on teaching students English, but did not offer credit toward a high school degree or help prepare students for the high school equivalency exam.

And they did not provide many of the other things available to Proctor students: free transportation and lunch, art, music, gym, and after-school activities.

In 2015, the state attorney general, Eric T. Schneiderman, filed a lawsuit against the Utica school district, charging that turning away teenage refugees was part of an effort to keep immigrants out of the city's only public high school.

It cited 19-year-old twin sisters, refugees from Burma, who had tried to enroll at Proctor in the summer of 2013.

They were told the law prevented them from attending, because they would not have enough time to pass state exams and graduate before turning 21.

This was a violation of state and federal law, the suit stated: All New Yorkers under the age of 21 are entitled to attend public school, regardless of their national origin or English proficiency.

Proctor was hardly the only high school barring older students: Mamaroneck High School in Westchester County, New York, initially refused to enroll a 16-year-old Guatemalan student who had moved from New Rochelle, New York. It sent him back to his old high school.

McCaskey High School in Lancaster, Pennsylvania, barred six refugees, 17 to 21 years old, sending them instead to an alternative school run by a private company.

In 2016, the American Civil Liberties Union filed a lawsuit against the Lancaster district; that same year the New York Civil Liberties Union battled Mamaroneck. In 2015, the NYCLU had filed a class action lawsuit against Utica, on behalf of six refugee students.

But Schneiderman's lawsuit against the Utica district went farther than the others. It described a coordinated effort to cover up what it was doing: Multiple levels of administrators were told to keep out older immigrant students—but to leave no record of their refusals.

By doing so, "the District could claim that these individuals were unknown to it—effectively strangers to the District, who never sought to enroll," the lawsuit said.

Deborah L. Wilson-Allam, who headed Utica's districtwide ESL program from 2011 to 2014, saw up close the effect of turning students away.

"I was supposed to inform older students they couldn't go to Proctor," said Ms. Wilson-Allam, currently executive director of international education at Utica College. But when a 17-year-old Sudanese girl came in with her mother and an advocate in 2013, determined to enroll, Ms. Wilson-Allam hoped the administration would make an exception.

"She was not an uneducated person," said Ms. Wilson-Allam, who has worked with refugees in Egypt. "She completed eighth grade."

But the administration refused to enroll her. "A month later, she came back with an advocate, crying, saying 'I want to be a doctor.'" Disheartened, Ms. Wilson-Allam had to turn the girl away again, steering her to an alternative program.

Ms. Wilson-Allam said that in 2014, she complained to the New York Civil Liberties Union about the district's treatment of refugees, and later gave a deposition to the NYCLU in the federal class action lawsuit against Utica, which was settled in 2016.

The district also settled the state lawsuit in 2016. The school system had to comply with federal and state laws and offer compensatory schooling for those hurt by its practices.

Notices are now posted around Utica—at the refugee center and at ethnic markets—stating that all students 17–21 have the right to attend Proctor.

The court case divided the city: Many still feel bruised.

It was not a black-and-white matter, said Dr. Randall J. VanWagoner, president of Mohawk Valley Community College. "On one hand, you have refugee students denied access to a full educational experience. They were segregated."

"But it was a very challenging dynamic for the school district," Dr. VanWagoner added. "You have 16- and 17-year-olds showing up: Within six months to two years, they have to take the statewide Regents exams. The state wasn't giving the financial support that can mitigate things."

Utica is one of the most poorly funded districts in the state, he added.

The city spends $17,128 per student, according to its proposed 2020–2021 budget; well-off New Hartford spends $21,286.

———

It is left to the teachers to deal with the wide range of students' ages, abilities, and backgrounds. "You're just under pressure all the time," said Ms. Pembroke, who retired in 2017.

There were cultural clashes in her classroom: Two boys—a Bosnian and a Serb—got into a fistfight. Parents got involved; the principal was able to smooth things over.

"They stopped fighting," Ms. Pembroke said. "But I don't think the boys became friends."

She was faced with deep wounds she could not address: One winter, as it started to snow, she saw one of her Bosnian students standing outside. He was distraught.

"Can you tell me what's wrong?" she asked.

He had been struck by a memory: Skiing outside his village in Bosnia, he stumbled over a pile of dead bodies.

Later, when he returned to the classroom, she overheard another student, a troublemaker, ask him if he had ever carried a gun.

"Yes," he said, matter-of-factly, "and a knife in my boot."

"Then there was respect!" Ms. Pembroke said.

A group of boys—who had been in Thai refugee camps—showed her a clip from an old Rambo movie: Enemy soldiers surrounded a village as people slept, then they attacked. "That's what it was like," the boys said, referring to the Burmese military's raids.

"You've got generations who've faced trauma," Ms. Pembroke said. "You've got to have support in place."

To cope with students' needs, the school offers the support of guidance counselors, psychologists, in-house translators, social workers, and community liaisons.

There is a tight connection between teachers and support personnel, Ms. Brain said. But it's impossible to keep up with students' needs. "If you're a psychologist, you're on all the time. Running all the time. You're bombarded."

When students are in distress, a counselor is the first to be contacted. "They're great people," Ms. Pembroke said. "Their hearts break for kids—that's why they chose this career." But they are overwhelmed by caseloads.

At a suburban school, if a minor clash starts with another student—as happened with Sadia—she might run to a counselor.

"That couldn't happen here," Ms. Pembroke said.

Yet, despite their struggles, most refugee students appreciate being at Proctor. "There's a good chance they know their life was crap before they came here," Ms. Brain said, bluntly. "They know what school can do for them."

In 2019, Proctor's total graduation rate was 75 percent, about 8 percent lower than the state's graduation rates. Fifty-two percent of Proctor students graduated with a Regents' diploma. The graduation rate of those enrolled in ESL classes was 21 percent, with 13 percent receiving Regents' diplomas.

Kevin Marken, the Utica director of On Point for College, a program that helps refugees and nontraditional students from low-income backgrounds apply to schools, estimated that in Proctor's class of 2019, about 60 young refugees went on to college through his program.

Most attend MVCC. "We call it the 13th year of Proctor," Ms. Brain said, smiling. Almost 10 percent of MVCC's student body are refugees. The college also offers a one-year certificate program, for college credit, in ESL.

But over the years, Proctor's refugee students have also graduated from Mount Holyoke College, SUNY Polytechnic Institute, and Yale University.

———

"They didn't come in with any cultural capital," Ms. Brain said about her refugee students.

But when they leave Proctor, she wants them to be able to read the social cues around them—so they can successfully navigate the world.

That's why she teaches them American idioms and sayings. And she answers questions, like: What are your nursery rhymes? Why is it that no one here lives like they do on *Dallas*?

"I'm trying to explain away their misconceptions of American culture," she said.

Her refugee students are dealing with so much, she added: They are trying to find a place for themselves at school—and at home, they are translating for parents who cannot speak English.

Yet, once they start to feel comfortable, they discover something unexpected: They have a good deal in common with the other students, despite the differences in their socioeconomic backgrounds.

"A lot of my students are dealing with upheavals. *Everybody's* got stuff going on."

She sighed. "I'm so drained."

"To be honest, I just don't have the energy anymore. A teacher knows when it's time to leave."

"I'm tapped—and I'm tapping out."

17. ISMAR'S DREAM

MERSIHA posted a picture of her comeback cake on Instagram: a joyful baby elephant. She managed to stay away from her business for only 10 months.

She had enjoyed having more time with her family—especially in the summer, when her kids invited their friends over for barbecues, and she would bring out steaming bowls of corn on the cob.

"But I can't lie—I love this," she said about her bakery. "I missed the business."

It touched her that so many old customers kept asking when she would be back. She was nervous before catering her first event.

"I wondered if I lost my touch," she said. "But we got eight emails right after the baby shower."

She was determined to run her business differently, for now: "I have to go small," she said. Only one cake a week. And she would focus on wedding cakes for which she could charge more, "not the little birthday cakes that take over everything."

Still haunted by her aunt's death, she resolved to take better care of herself. She had a doctor check her legs. She bought a thick pad to stand on as she baked.

But she knew she had to guard against her own impulses: "I have to go slowly. I cannot let things get out of control. I am my own worst enemy."

Being back in business released a stream of pent-up desires: She and her husband decided they would open a café as soon as their two oldest kids were in college. They discussed one day opening a culinary school. She wanted to complete an online master's in education she had started years ago, so she could teach if the café did not work out.

Mersiha had no idea that Ismar, her quiet, eldest child—about to turn 18—had his own dream.

Like all her kids, Ismar—a short, good-looking boy with horn-rimmed glasses—was dutiful, a hard worker. After school, he and Faris worked as waiters in the large senior adult facility, where their dad cooked and supervised the kitchen. They also helped deliver their mom's cakes.

When he and Faris decided they wanted a car, they saved up $7,200 and bought a 2012 Nissan Rogue to share.

He had a close-knit group of offbeat, nerdy friends; most were the children of refugees. Mersiha adored them: "They are the nicest kids in the world!"

In Bosnia, a young person's 18th birthday is a major event.

"We don't celebrate 16," she explained. There are only three big occasions: "Your first birthday, your 18th, and your wedding."

Mersiha decided to throw what she called a "Hollywood red carpet party" for Ismar.

Ismar happily went along with her idea. He had one request: a 'Kinder cake,' which is named after an Italian chocolate bar, with a creamy filling.

The day before the party, Mersiha transformed her bakery: She rolled out a red carpet. She loaded a dessert table with scores of pastries and a beautiful Kinder cake made of German, Swiss, and Belgian chocolate.

She set up different rooms: for video games; for dancing; for taking photos. When the young people arrived, she made 'VIP cards'—taking photos of all 22 friends—then laminating them and attaching cords.

At the end of the night, the teenagers—VIP cards around their necks—walked the red carpet, striking poses.

A few weeks later, Ismar was offered a full scholarship to Utica College, plus spending money; Mersiha and Hajrudin were thrilled. He had graduated as the salutatorian of his class at the Utica Academy of Science, a charter high school in Frankfort, New York.

They hoped he would become a doctor or go into cybersecurity, which Hajrudin saw as an expanding and lucrative field.

As refugee parents, they never considered the idea of his going away; they wanted him close by.

But Ismar had his own plan.

He had never talked about it to his parents—but he had decided a couple of years ago he wanted to design video games, something that had interested him since he was a child. And he had gotten into a new computer game design program at SUNY Polytechnic Institute, which accepted only a small number of students. The school only offered him a $10,000 a year tuition scholarship—but he figured out that by working part time and summers he could manage.

When he discussed this with his parents, they were mystified: How could he reject a full scholarship? How could designing games be a career?

Mersiha was still unconvinced after he took her to an open house at the SUNY Poly campus in Marcy. It was only about 10 minutes away, but she had never been there. Utica College was familiar; she had driven by it many times. "Everybody says Utica is a very good college," Mersiha told him. "A lot of people want to get scholarships there."

Then Ismar threw his parents another curveball: He said that after graduating college, he was moving to the West Coast—to Los Angeles or Seattle—to get a graduate degree in business. The gaming companies he hoped to work for were out there.

For Mersiha and Hajrudin, it was as if the earth dropped open. They had survived a war—and had managed to escape to a city nearly 5,000 miles away.

They had created a new life.

Now their son was talking about leaving for a part of America they knew nothing about. "I was freaking out," Mersiha said.

She told him, "Convince us!"

———

Ismar did not take this lightly.

"Having refugee parents is a kind of challenge," he said, sighing. "None of my struggles can compare to theirs when they came here. I wish I could've helped them more."

He did not know all the details of his parents' experience in Bosnia. But since childhood, he had watched them struggle. If you arrive as an adult, everything is harder, he said: "The first thing you're thinking is fear. Everything seems completely foreign. Your potential starts to fade."

Yet, his parents always had an underlying confidence they could make it big, he said. They carefully built the structure for a middle-class life. "It was, 'American dream, here we come.'"

Ismar knows his mother is the family powerhouse. He said, admiringly, "She lights up a room."

To please her, when he was younger, he thought about becoming a doctor. "But that interest faded away in eighth grade," he said. He began to think he wanted to find a career he would really enjoy. That making money should not be all-important. "I thought, 'What's one thing I've cherished more than anything?'"

When he was two and a half, his grandmother got him his first video game. All through his teens, he thought about narratives: "I liked a story that was complex, emotional—or just weird and funny," he said. His favorite characters started out heroic, but then became vindictive and cutthroat.

It helped that his friends were also taking singular paths. One was going into fashion; another wanted to be a music producer; another hoped to go into sports medicine.

Ismar put together a PowerPoint presentation.

It included a history of gaming. Different genres of video games. Specific companies he would like to work for. And potential salaries.

He presented it to his father first. Sitting in the living room, Hajrudin listened quietly. "He was in awe, shocked," Ismar said. He had no idea a programmer's salary could start at $100,000, or that it is a profession with its own hierarchy.

Then Mersiha joined them.

She sat in the dark, wide-eyed.

At the end, both parents burst into applause. "We'll always be with you 100 percent," Mersiha said. "You can go for it."

But the whole idea of moving West was trickier, Ismar said: "They couldn't imagine their oldest child going on an adventure to somewhere they'd never been."

They spent the next two weeks talking. Ismar took pains to explain himself: He planned to work as he completed his master's. After graduating, he hoped to get a job at a top video game company, based outside Seattle.

Hajrudin was impressed by the strength of his son's desire. And by how confident he was that he could take care of himself.

But Mersiha was skeptical: She saw him as an idealist. Faris, though younger, seemed tougher, more practical. Better able to take care of himself.

"Ismar is very pure," she said.

But again, Mersiha thought about her aunt's stroke and heart attack. And about her mother's life cut short. She did not want to stop him.

Mersiha saw a strong link between herself and her firstborn: "Ismar has his dream, I have mine. He can do it; he's very persistent."

18. THE BAN

WHEN Donald Trump was elected president in 2016, Mersiha was distraught. "I couldn't sleep all night," she said. She lay in bed, worrying about the Muslim registry Trump talked about creating—a database of all Muslims in the United States. "Would my family be in it?"

She was frightened by his nationalistic talk: Her mind leaped back to when she was 17, and Muslims started being targeted by Serbs: "My God, do we have to go through this again? Do we have to get our passports, leave the country?"

The next morning, opening her classroom door at the refugee center, she saw a few students crying. She hugged them and told them not to worry, though she felt it was the worst day since she had arrived as a refugee.

"One of my students said, 'Teacher—I no green card. I go home?'"

Later, when Hajrudin came home from work, he comforted her: "Don't worry, honey, it's going to go away. It won't work."

Oneida County—like much of upstate New York—has long been conservative. In the 2016 presidential election, 56.5 percent voted for Donald J. Trump, and 37.1 percent voted for Hillary Clinton. The county has voted for Republican presidents in every election since it went for Bill Clinton in 1996.

But in 2016, East Utica and Cornhill—where many refugees live—voted Democrat.

Donald Trump's victory sent ripples through the refugee community. So did his executive order on January 27, 2017, that banned foreign nationals from seven predominately Muslim countries from visiting the United States for 90 days, suspended entry for Syrian refugees, and prohibited other refugees from coming into the country for 120 days.

Some families were crushed when they heard about the ban. They had been expecting relatives from the camps: A 17-year-old Nepali girl had been waiting seven years for her grandfather. He was only days away from boarding a plane when he was told there would be a delay.

A 22-year-old Somali Bantu student at MVCC had hoped her cousins would get refugee status. "They could have come here, made money, and sent it back to their mothers," she said.

But many refugees—working long hours and focused on their families—had little time to tune into the news. "They're here legally, so they feel safe for the most part," said Chris Sunderland, codirector of the Midtown Utica Community Center. "They're not really worried."

Refugee status is granted indefinitely once a refugee has arrived in the United States. And there is a path forward: After a year, refugees are required to apply for a green card, giving them permanent resident status. After five years in the country, they may apply for citizenship.

Some older refugees, getting their news from broadcast stations back home, were confused about the recent election: "They don't really know what Trump represents," Dr. Stam said. "They have a basic misunderstanding of how American politics works."

Zahara, for one, follows the news. She felt Trump had no power over her.

She is used to authoritarian leaders; she does not expect much from them. She puts all her faith in God.

"The first time Trump says I will take back immigration, I feel bad," Zahara told me. She was watching TV in her living room.

"And when he says bad things about Muslims, I feel bad." Then turning toward me, she said, "Only God decides."

"Five times a day, I pray," she explained. "I say, 'God, I don't know who is evil or who is good, please protect me. You are my bodyguard.'"

"You think a human is going to protect me?" she asked. "Donald Trump is a human being like me. He can't do nothing to me!"

"When *God* says go back to my country, I go back to my country."

Zahara has not yet applied for citizenship, so cannot vote. Mersiha and her husband voted for Hillary Clinton.

Ali voted for Donald Trump.

He was excited when Trump got elected: "I liked most of what he was saying about the economy—new jobs, bringing back jobs from Mexico and China." He shook his head. "Upstate, most people are struggling."

Ali had hoped Trump would eliminate terrorism: "I felt this will be a president who will do some real action."

But then Ali heard Iraq was one of the seven countries banned.

He took this personally; he had risked his life working for Americans. So had thousands of other Iraqis. "It's a huge slap in the face," he said, pained. "A big mistake!"

He was glad when the ban was quickly amended to allow emigration by the families of Iraqi interpreters who had worked for the US government and military forces. But it did not take away the sting.

"Iraqis have been fighting against ISIS every minute, every day. How could he include Iraq?"

———

Three months after Trump's inauguration, Ali glanced at the TV, which was turned to the local news.

"When Saddam came to power, nobody knew what was going on," he told Heidi and her daughter, Julia; they were all eating pizza in the dining room. There was a bowl of potato chips and some carrot sticks.

"All we saw was Saddam Hussein—eight hours nonstop on TV—receiving officers, giving medals!"

"During the war with Iran, whenever you'd turn on the TV, you'd see parts of Iranian soldiers torn apart," Ali said, picking up a slice of pizza.

He held it aloft: "This big!"

Julia, 16, looked at Ali in amazement.

She had only recently started visiting her mom's apartment when Ali was there. Heidi had wanted Julia to wait until her ex-husband felt less angry about the divorce.

Julia was just coming out of a difficult time; as her parents were battling, she had suffered from depression. She was homeschooled for a while. But she had just started at Proctor; had a best friend, an Indian girl named Kurrine; and was feeling a lot better.

She liked Ali—who was generally quiet—so different from her father, who was loud and impulsive. Her dad worked full time at his family's meat market.

Ali said he had good news: Trump removed Iraq from the list of banned countries.

"I had a feeling that was going to happen," he said. "You cannot thank Iraqis by banning them."

"The wrong was corrected. I don't think Trump is anti-Muslim. I think he's anti-terrorist."

"I'm not buying it," Heidi said, reaching for some carrot sticks.

"Ali lived through Saddam Hussein," she told Julia. "So, if you look at Donald Trump through his eyes, he's just a guy with a big mouth, who says extreme things."

"And that all the people who got stuck in airports were just inconvenienced," she added about those stranded because of the ban.

"They weren't dropped in vats of poison. They weren't beheaded. But they missed their flights and were sent back home—that's still horrible!"

She looked at Ali. "I guess when Trump talks about improving the economy and infrastructure—these things seem more important. But I'm saying, don't you hear it—the racism. Why aren't you angry?"

Julia, extremely shy, decided to leap in, "I think Trump talks like an old white guy. He sometimes reminds me of my dad. It's just blunt talk. And at least he's got people talking—we kind of need that."

Ali sighed. "He backed out of the ban on Iraqis," he said. "It was quick. He said, 'I was wrong.' That's a good thing. Hillary was trained to make decisions and stick to them. That's dangerous."

Julia chimed in again: "Hillary pandered to too many people. It's great that she's pro-gay—I mean I'm gay—but what about the economy?"

Ali and Heidi did not seem to hear Julia's revelation.

"Look, I'm not a fan," Ali told them. "I voted for him because I hoped he'd bring jobs here. But I don't know what he's going to do. Maybe he'll start World War III tomorrow. But we can hope for the best."

Getting up, Heidi started to clear the plates. This was a familiar discussion; she had been an avid Bernie Sanders supporter, but had voted for Hillary Clinton in the election. There was no animosity.

Ali went into the kitchen to make tea, the Iraqi way.

"I boil star anise in water," he told Julia, "then turn the burner off. I add cardamom tea and boil it again—it gets darker and darker. Then I let it sit."

He serves it sweet. "I love a little tea in my sugar."

19. THE DRONE

LATER THAT SPRING, Ali leaned over his second-floor porch as if he might fly over it.

"Pratik!" he called down to the thin young man, who had just parked his car. "You're late!" And then a minute later, "We've started without you!" he called to his friends Bob and Dana—native Uticans who had converted to Islam—getting out of the car with their three kids.

In his Pink Floyd tank top, shorts, and flip-flops, Ali ran downstairs to open the door.

Twice a week, he and Heidi have what they call "our crowd" over for dinner. These are friends they have made together, as well as a few of Heidi's college friends.

"Ali's happiest when people are over," Heidi, said, "especially if it's a diverse group, with lots of kids. It reminds him of home."

But that night, he was keyed up, especially eager to be with friends.

He was finishing up an application for a government contract that would send him back to the Middle East for a year, as an interpreter for the allied forces. He would hate to be away from Heidi. And he did not want to leave Utica, where he now felt settled.

But these jobs were lucrative: He would return in the spring of 2019 with enough money to make a down payment on a house.

Ali was tired of sitting around as his interpreting work dried up because of Trump's policies. "This is all I know," he said. "I can't work in a factory or a shop."

He felt things were only going to get worse: Next year, only about 200 refugees were expected to arrive in Utica.

Nationally, the drop in the number of refugees admitted was dramatic: In Trump's first fiscal year in office—October 1, 2017, to September 30, 2018—the United States admitted only about 22,500 refugees, whereas nearly 85,000 refugees were admitted in the last full fiscal year of the Obama administration, according to the Pew Research Center.

Recently, Ali was stunned when a friend of his, another Iraqi interpreter, stole a few of his clients while he was out of town.

He saw it as a betrayal, but then heard that the man was in dire financial need. There was so little work; it was as if people were fighting over grains of rice.

Ali kept pacing the living room, making sure everyone had fresh hummus, pita, and pomegranate juice. Then smiling broadly, he showed off a surprise from his sister: On the dining room wall was a large portrait of him, dressed in a black and gold traditional robe—a thawb—and a white kefiyah. It is what he wears to a traditional Iraqi wedding.

"It was supposed to be small—two feet max," Ali said about the painting. "I didn't know it would be so beautiful!"

Last to arrive was Heidi's friend Karen. Ali—very fond of her—bent down to embrace her.

There was another reason Ali was tightly wound: It was just before Ramadan.

In hundreds of Muslim households across East Utica, there was a sense of expectation. People were getting ready: Rugs were carried outside, beaten, washed, and hung to dry. Old machinery and piles of bottles were dislodged from garages, bagged, and driven to the dump. Houses were cleaned from top to bottom—a little each day.

Anyone walking into Walmart or Hannaford can see families searching the aisles for special, beloved foods to stock up on, especially fruit, to quench thirst after a long fast: mangoes, pineapples, coconuts, dates.

Outsiders might pity those who observe Ramadan—no food or drink is allowed between dawn and sundown for 30 days. But "it's the best month of the year," Ali said, sitting for a moment in his reclining chair near his hookah. "You feel what poor people without food go through. It's a good time to thank others for what you have."

"It puts some mercy in your heart."

And yet, he dreads Ramadan. "The closer it gets—I get sadder and sadder."

"It's not just me," he added. "It's the same for all Muslim refugees who a few years ago came to the United States. You compare—what it's like here. And what it's like there."

"You're away from your family."

He leaned forward in his chair, remembering: "When I was working for ABC News, the first night of Ramadan, I'd leave work and go to an outdoor market."

"I'd get a huge thing of kebabs," he continued. "You pick the meat—lamb, sometimes a little bit of beef. You wait as they cut it for you. Then I go to the best baklava place in Baghdad."

"Or my mom calls, and says, 'I'm cooking! Get home at 6:30!'"

In his bedroom, he would wash up and change his clothes. "When they're ready, they call me," he said. "My sisters, my mother . . ." He did not mention his brother, Saif.

Jumping up, Ali got his iPad and pulled over a chair for Julia. Clicking *Ramadan*, he showed her photos of crowds dancing joyously in the street; scores of families feasting outdoors under tiny blue lights; and a night sky filled with multicolored balloons. "This is how Ramadan is celebrated in the Mideast!" he said.

But then he added, not wanting to give her the wrong impression: "Well, this is Egypt, not Iraq. But it's amazing."

Julia, who is pale and sandy-haired, listened patiently. Recently, she had been in a state of mourning; her two old dogs had died. Depressed, she had skipped school for six days. Heidi was relieved when she finally emerged from her room, her hair washed, skin shining.

Spring was in the air: Ali opened the apartment windows. And as Heidi and her friends cleared platters that had held chicken and basmati rice, salads, and flatbreads, Ali picked up a carrying case holding his new drone.

He started ushering Pratik, who was a friend of Karen's; Julia and her friend, Kurrine; and Bob's three kids toward the door. Bob—an imposing-looking man in a full beard, skull cap, and long kurta—was packing up his own drone. A former musician, he got interested in Islam when a jazz musician he knew gave him a book about the religion.

"Ali and Bob had an adventure," Heidi said. "They were flying their drones by the big waterfall at Hinckley Reservoir." The reservoir supplies water to the Erie Canal and is the sole source of drinking water for many in the Utica area. "A week later, they got a call from the anti-terrorism task force."

Somebody had reported them. But Ali did not take offense. "They questioned us a long time, but ended up being very nice," he said about the task force. "By the end of the call, they wanted to take us out to dinner."

Proctor Park was deep green in the fading light. The girls had no interest in the drones, which the men were unpacking—and they began heading off. "We're going to the playground," Julia said, pointing to swings in the distance.

"Uh, uh, no," Bob said, sharply.

"You can go," he told his daughter Molly, a rail-thin 16-year-old with a blond crewcut. "Stay," he told Edith, his middle child, who was imploring him. "That's teenage stuff. I want to keep you 11." He put his arm around Oliver, his 7-year-old son.

Within seconds, Ali's large, blinking drone soared straight up—100 feet, 200 feet. "It can go up to 3 miles," he told Pratik, who looked on, amused. "But it's not legal to go more than 400 feet."

As if it had a life of its own, the drone flew across the field to the playground, then came back, hovering. Ali's sense of dread about Ramadan—and his other worries—seemed to lift as the drone took off again, swooping to film the far side of the park, which was lusher, denser.

He recalled being in a helicopter, flying over a village, when he worked for ABC News in Baghdad. It was exhilarating: "I took video—hanging out of the helicopter—my left arm holding on to a strap."

Bob's drone suddenly appeared high above Ali. Then it dropped out of the sky, crashing in the grass.

Bob—on a nearby hill with his kids—came running. His mouth hung open. "That's not supposed to happen!" he said. "It's new." He shook his head. "That's not supposed to happen."

"It's under warranty," Ali reassured him. "They'll replace it."

The park was quickly getting dark.

"Where are the girls?" Bob asked, packing up the broken drone. Looking startled, Ali started walking toward the playground.

There were a few streaks of green in the sky. Ali loved the park, with its long fields and trails; he knew every inch of it. He coached an Iraqi soccer team there. He, Heidi, and Julia picnicked there with Bob and his family.

"Julia!" Ali called.

Pratik was behind him. Bob and his kids quickly followed.

"Julia!" Ali called again.

He could dimly make out the girls on the swings, their legs pumping air as they went higher and higher.

"Julia!"

It was inconceivable they could not hear him. Their voices—giddy and rushed—floated across the park.

"Julia!" Ali yelled.

"That's a father's voice!" Pratik said, laughing.

Slipping off the swing, Julia landed first. In the fading light, the girls started walking toward Ali.

20. AUGUST

I T TURNED OUT Sadia had not graduated from high school.
She kept it a secret: She had failed math—and was supposed to retake it in the summer. But she was distracted that summer and failed it again.

Zahara was furious when she found out: Sadia should have studied, passed math, and gone to MVCC in the fall.

Her two older girls had *tried* when they were at Proctor.

"Mana was a B student," Ralya explained. "I was a C student. My mom never complained." Zahara was proud that Mana was a manager at Walmart, and that Ralya worked full time in the store's bakery.

"My mom has ambitions for Sadia," Ralya added. "She treats each kid different, the way they need to be treated."

Zahara saw Sadia—who was babysitting—as wasting her life. And Sadia, feeling shunned, was angry. Her face closed; she had a faraway look in her eyes. And she said little at home.

But she still felt passionately about her mother. "I'd do anything for my mom," she said. "If I had $50, I'd give her all of it."

Sadia heard about a young movie star who bought herself a house in LA but refused to help her mother, who lived in public housing. Sadia was genuinely shocked.

She had admired this actress. "Now I hate her," Sadia said. "If I saw her, I'd spit in her face."

On a hot August day, Sadia dragged a garbage can to the curb. Her mother had asked her to help clear out the yard. She was elegantly dressed for such a dirty task in a long, flowered skirt, a tight top with a shirt knotted over it, and a cream-colored head wrap.

Blue plastic gloves covered her hands and forearms.

She was trying to please her mom but looked daunted. She started pulling old, falling-apart cardboard boxes from the can. Her close friend

Ayuong, a tall, thin girl from Sudan, similarly dressed in a long skirt and head wrap, looked on.

Then Sadia tipped the can: Water bugs skittered out in a slosh of black water—and she caught the water in a garbage bag. It stank.

Hurrying out of the house, Zahara looked on, critically, "Why are you pouring that in a bag?"

She ignored Sadia's friend.

"I can't dump it in the backyard," Sadia said.

"You'll have to wash that out," Zahara said, indicating the can.

"I know," Sadia said, calmly. Pointing to the girl, she said, "Mom, this is my friend, Ayuong."

Looking suspicious, Zahara slowly shook the young woman's hand.

A few weeks later, Sadia moved into her grandmother's house. She did not ask her permission: Halima was used to her grandchildren showing up and staying for a while.

Sadia was not getting along with anyone in her immediate family. "Nobody was talking to me," she said. "My sisters were like, 'Just do it, if it's right for you.' Only my mom was mad that I moved out."

21. COMING HOME

SOON AFTER Sadia left, Mana came home to stay. She had quit her marriage after only a few months.

You could feel her sense of relief and joy.

"I'm back in my old room with my two brothers," she said as a younger sister brought her a small plate with a cut-up sandwich.

Ibrahim, her 6-year-old brother, fed her a piece, while Abdiwle, the 4-year-old, climbed along the sofa's bolster and hugged her from behind.

"I brought them up," she said about her brothers. "This one was my tail," she said, indicating the older one. "This one was my eyes," she said about the younger. "He would follow me everywhere. When I would clean, he would be on my back."

There were a dozen kids that afternoon in her mother's living room—siblings and a few cousins. Most of Zahara's children have different fathers, so there is a vast range of body types, complexions, and personalities.

Mana has a big presence, though she is so thin she can seem to disappear. The younger kids like to bask nearby.

Halima, a quiet, thoughtful girl, in an apricot-colored hijab, and her younger sister, Zamzam, in a sparkly white one, pored over an electronics catalog.

"I like the Ninja Pro Blender," Halima said. She pointed to a Fitbit. "This tells you your heart rate, your distance, how fast you go."

"I like the trampoline," Zamzam said, flipping through the pages.

Zahara came over and became absorbed in the catalog.

"I'm looking for a new TV for the living room," she said. "Sixty-five inches." She read aloud from the catalog: "$899."

"Think about the quality," Mana told her mother. "Don't think about the money. I bought a laptop, a Dell—it seemed cheap. But it fell on the ground—and never came up again. I buy HP now."

Mana does not second-guess her decisions: "If something happens, I see it. Come to a conclusion. Talk about it. Then after that, I'm good. I'm on my way."

She had decided she did not want to be married. "For me, love is my family," she said. "With a stranger, not so much. I'd never experienced a man before. And you know what? I'm OK with that."

There were issues in the marriage: She was perplexed by her husband's emotion. "He said he loved me all the time. I said, 'I love you, too.' But I had no feeling inside my heart about that."

Maybe, it was because she never knew her father, she said: "I never even saw his face."

It bothered her husband that Mana put her mother first. Her response was: "Of course, I do!"

There was another problem in her marriage: "He's old!"

Mana knows she has an exalted position in her family. "I'm the oldest of my mom's children," she said. "Manipulating!" she said, swinging her youngest brother around. "Controlling!" she said, as he laughed, his legs splaying out. "It works!"

She knew her mother would welcome her back.

Zahara did not ask a lot of questions when her daughter came home. Mana—along with Ralya—had done the lion's share of helping with the younger kids. She cooked and cleaned, and rarely complained. Zahara trusted her.

If Mana left her husband, she had her reasons.

On the other hand, she felt Mana was young, hot-tempered—and without the experience to handle a partner. But Zahara did not feel she could say anything.

"Teenagers now are 'Leave me alone—get out of my face,'" Zahara told me, though Mana was 23. "We have to be patient."

"When we were young, we were like that, too."

It was 6 p.m. Her brother-in-law was coming in a few minutes to pick up his kids. Mana, who worked the night shift at Walmart, was leaving for work in a few hours. Zahara went into the kitchen to get herself something to eat. She came back with a piece of fried fish.

"That looks good," Mana said. "Can you make me some?"

"I'm not the maid," Zahara said. "You sleep all day. You wake up now."

"But you make it so good," Mana said, laughing. "I like the way *you* make it. Fry the fish!"

"You fry the fish," Zahara said, raising her voice. "I'm not your slave!"

———

Mana loves the night shift—10 p.m. to 6 a.m.—when the enormous store is quiet.

She is as authoritative at Walmart as she is at home. But she is more relaxed—walking the aisles in her long traditional dress and bright yellow manager's vest—overseeing the clerks, a couple of whom are disabled, and helping customers.

She enjoys coming home at dawn and sleeping till midafternoon: She sleeps lightly, listening in case there are any problems with the kids. If they get too loud, she screams at them.

Mana sees herself as a protector of "the old ways."

She feels Somali Bantus know best how to discipline their children. "In my country, if a child does something bad, everybody's together about it," she said, her narrow frame tucked into a corner of the straw-colored couch. It is considered OK for children to be disciplined at home, in school, or by a neighbor.

"But over here, if a kid does something wrong, one parent says, 'Yes, she should be disciplined.' Another says, 'No, don't do this to my child!' A neighbor says, 'What kind of parent would punish a child?'"

Sadia was breaking rules—and Mana was angry with her.

She did not like Sadia living with their grandmother. "My grandma doesn't approve, but she looks the other way."

Sadia now goes to the mall with male and female friends. "Women are supposed to stay in," Mana said. "She could get hurt," she added, her face drawn. "Men can hurt you, rape you."

"Sometimes, when we have money, or are in a good mood, my sisters will go out," she added. "To a restaurant or movie. But we go *together*."

Mana pushed away a footstool.

"Sadia's Americanized. I can't tolerate it. Not a bit."

"But she's my sister," she added. "I love her."

Mana knows her own world is narrow: "I go to work, come back," she said, laughing. "I love Utica. It makes me feel safe. I could never move out of Utica."

Her clan feels the same way. Especially her mother.

Recently, Zahara drove to Columbus, Ohio, where she has relatives. She was appalled by the city. "Columbus is dangerous—a very bad place," she said. "There are diapers in the street. You can't walk with your phone, without hiding it."

Nearing home, she was euphoric: She rolled down her car window: "Oh, my God—air! New York is my state!"

In Somalia—and in the refugee camps—Zahara was often afraid. Since then, she has never worried: "Utica is my safety."

Yet, Utica has the same crime issues as other small cities. On a spring night in 2019, Oneida County police responded to 911 calls regarding domestic violence, sexual assaults, burglaries, larceny, property damage, assaults, hit and runs, weapon possession, fighting, and drug overdoses.

Utica's police department—of about 165 officers—struggles to keep up with the city's opioid crisis. Residents overdose in public places like McDonald's, in parking lots, and homes. It is not unusual for a police officer to see the same person overdose twice in one week. In 2018, there were 37 opioid-related deaths in Oneida County. While the crisis affects families of every socioeconomic group, the refugee population has not been significantly involved.   ____

Mana wants to keep the larger world at bay.

Sometimes, she thinks about Mohawk Valley Community College, where she took some classes. But "I'm afraid of school," she said. "If I learn something I shouldn't learn, it's going to affect my life, change it. I would see things differently."

She already has a wild imagination: "I like to think, 'What if this happens, that happens?' It's already blowing me apart."

She hugged a zebra-striped pillow. "You start to think about what's beyond—that's dangerous. You become obsessed. You want to learn and learn. You stop thinking about what's around you."

"Right now, I only have time for my family."

Yet, Mana left open the possibility of returning to school: "I loved my psychology teacher at MVCC. She taught us about the three stages of sleep."

But even this new information was disturbing.

She smiled. "At night, going to sleep I'd think, 'What stage am I in now?'"

22. THE NEW APARTMENT

SADIA'S stay at her grandmother's was difficult from the start; Mana got it wrong.

She was not the only young woman in the big house on Rutger: Her best friend, Sofia—her grandmother's second-youngest child—had come home with her baby girl after a short, unhappy marriage.

Sadia hoped she would have more freedom at her grandmother's house. That she could come and go as she pleased. But her grandmother did not turn a blind eye on her and Sofia.

In some ways, she was stricter and fiercer than Zahara.

"Every single day, my mom was kicking us out," said Sofia, a soft-spoken 22-year-old. "She was always yelling and busting down doors."

From Halima's perspective, she had two vulnerable young women under her roof, who every single day were breaking rules. She clashed with them constantly—about where they went and who they saw.

Within their extended family, Halima is deeply respected. "She has the last word on everything," Sofia said. "My dad is her number two."

Halima shepherded numerous children through an epic run from their village in Somalia to a refugee camp in Kenya. People still talk about it with awe.

She saw terrible things on that run.

She took care of her own kids and Zahara's in the camp. She helped smooth things during the family's refugee application process.

And though she cannot speak English—or read or write—she bought the enormous house on Rutger and opened its doors to relatives.

But she expected proper Somali Bantu behavior from her family, not American-style behavior.

When Sofia was in high school, a neighbor reported she had walked home with a boy. Furious, Halima threw Sofia's clothes onto the lawn.

This happened again. And again.

Recently, Halima has been angry that Sofia *chose* her own husband—and the marriage failed.

"We picked our own people for you!" she keeps telling Sofia. Halima married her first cousin—and she wanted Sofia to marry a cousin from their village. Many Somali Bantus believe such marriages strengthen family ties.

"You did this to yourself!" she flung at Sofia.

The new level of turmoil alarmed Sofia. She worried about how her baby and niece were being affected.

"I wanted to get Amrah and Sadia out."

So, she and Sadia did something rare for two young Somali Bantu women: They began looking on Craigslist for their own apartment.

———

The apartment on Dudley Avenue was large and airy. It was about a mile from Halima's house.

There was a long living room and dining room, and three bedrooms off to the side. A light-filled kitchen painted sky blue was at the back. There was no furniture. Just a couple of metal folding chairs.

On their second day as apartment dwellers, their refrigerator already contained bottles of water, a pineapple, a big cabbage, orange and yellow peppers, and a bunch of carrots.

The two young women had not only moved outside their family's sphere, they had formed a new family unit. Sofia was working as a certified nurse assistant at a nursing home, doing double shifts on the weekend. Sadia took care of 8-month-old Amrah, whom she loved.

Sadia hoped to get a part-time job that suited Amrah's schedule. But she was not sure what to apply for. She had been a cashier at Walmart and hated it. And she did not picture herself a CNA like Sofia. "She is really patient," Sadia said. "I get angry quick. If somebody forgets something . . ."

But so far, even without Sadia working, they were able to afford the $800 rent.

The baby's dad was not missed, Sadia said. It was late morning; she had just awakened and was in a long green nightgown and braids. She held Amrah as she tidied up the apartment.

"He went back home to Kentucky. He's useless. We don't need him."

This was not exactly true: Sofia had hoped he would be a father to Amrah. And it pained her that he did not seem interested. He had visited a couple of times. But he came empty-handed; she felt he was only interested in getting her back.

Sofia—who was five feet tall and petite—came into the living room with a prayer rug. She had only 10 minutes before heading out to work. Despite the hardship of her breakup—and the months of fighting with her mother—she looked clear-eyed and well.

"I've never felt so comfortable," Sofia said.

She laid out the rug, getting herself ready to pray.

As Sofia prostrated herself, Sadia said, "I've got to start praying, too."

A few minutes later, casting a quick look at Amrah in Sadia's arms, Sofia headed out.

Sadia's family was not surprised she moved out of her grandmother's house.

"I'm different," she said, carefully steering Amrah away from a bucket of bleach. "I'm not into what everybody else in the family is into—like Indian movies. My sisters can speak Hindi because they've been watching those movies since they were born."

But then her cell phone rang, and her face lit up: It was Ralya. She was at Walmart, about to take her break. What did Sadia want for lunch?

"Just get me the chicken, any kind," Sadia said, watching the baby padding around by the kitchen cabinets.

"You want the rice?"

"Yes."

"What else?"

"Macaroni and cheese."

"What else?"

"Just pick stuff."

Then Sadia heard *thud*. For a second, her eyes had left Amrah; the baby overturned the bucket of bleach. As she sat there, startled—and soaked—Sadia scooped her up.

She quickly stripped off Amrah's clothes and bathed her. Then she wrapped the chubby, squirming baby in a towel—and whistled what sounded like a bird call: *wher, wher . . .*

"She loves making a mess and hates being cleaned up," Sadia said, putting Amrah down for a nap.

Ralya came in, sumptuous in a flowing navy dress and hijab, her nails painted orange. She was carrying take-out food from Walmart. Happy to be on her break, she started talking about one of her favorite subjects: Who has the most power in the family?

"I'm the ruler of the house!" said Ralya, 21, the second-oldest child. "I make sure everybody gets something for their birthday. Make sure they get treated equal."

"Mana likes the boys in the family," Sadia said, eating chicken fried rice.

"Maybe she runs things with the two little boys," Ralya said. "I like the girls."

"I take the kids to school events," she went on. "I've never missed one parent meeting. Yesterday was Math Day. There was International Day."

"Mom was always working," she added. "I didn't want the kids to feel left out, like they were missing something."

Sadia listened silently.

"They're winning prizes," Ralya said, proudly, about her younger sisters. "Both Zamzam and Halima got awards for being the most kind."

"At home, they're no better," Sadia said.

"They are so good!" Ralya said. "They help sweep the house, wash the dishes."

"I'm full," Sadia said, putting the take-out container in the refrigerator. Then she began talking about Mana. "She spoils mom a lot. She does whatever mom wants."

"I show mom the reality," Ralya said. "Nobody's perfect. I don't do everything she says. I'm not a mommy person. I'm a sister person."

But she holds their mother in the highest regard: "I'm proud of her!" she said. "She always took good care of us, and of herself."

"She never made us feel like we needed a dad. I never looked at another girl and thought, 'I wish I could be like her.'"

And Zahara has never pressured her to marry: "Mom leaves it up to me."

Ralya has high expectations for her future spouse: "I am very spoiled," she said. "My mom spoils me. My sisters spoil me. I would expect my husband to put me first."

"To know my personality," she added. "To appreciate me and my family. They never said 'no' to me. I wouldn't want to disappoint them."

Sadia was listening closely.

Light shined in through the kitchen window, framing her still-sleepy face and two long braids.

"I kind of believe in soul mates," she said, quietly. "God gives you the person you're meant to be with."

23. LOFTS

IN JANUARY 2006, Laurie Volk, a residential marketing expert hired by the city, gave a talk to a packed room at the Hotel Utica, downtown's once-elegant old hotel.

Local developers and businesspeople listened closely to her Power-Point presentation as photos of Utica's abandoned factory buildings and renderings of new apartments flashed by.

Ms. Volk's message was upbeat: *Lofts.*

Her research showed that up to a thousand people—Uticans and those in the surrounding area—were interested in moving downtown. Many expressed a preference for renting lofts—large open spaces with hardwood floors and exposed brick walls—rather than traditional apartments.

Utica's factories, with their high ceilings and enormous windows, could be brought back to life.

An outsider might be skeptical: In 2006, Utica's population stood at about 58,400, a loss of about 2,000 residents since the 2000 census. Residents' real per capita income was $26,473, compared to a national real per capita income of $32,117. Who was interested in luxury lofts?

Young singles and couples, Ms. Volk said. But her data also showed demand among empty nesters and retirees. She saw a market for 108 new units a year for the next five years.

Utica's city planners were not surprised. Since the 1970s, a growing number of Rust Belt cities had been repurposing old factories, banks, schools, and warehouses.

"I'd seen the potential," said Brian Thomas, Utica's commissioner of urban and economic development, who was then director of urban planning. He felt young people could be drawn downtown. "We wanted to prove to developers there was a market."

He was not worried about gentrification: "The city was able to accommodate 100,000 people 80 years ago," he said. "There's a wealth of buildings throughout downtown that could be revitalized without moving anybody."

For decades, Utica has provided low- and middle-income housing downtown. There are about a dozen such buildings—including Kennedy Plaza Apartments and Genesee Tower Apartments—many of them run by the city's Municipal Housing Authority. "They're not going anywhere," Mr. Thomas said.

In 2006, Ms. Volk's firm, Zimmerman/Volk, did residential market studies for over a dozen struggling cities, including Buffalo, Lexington, Detroit, Belding, Fort Wayne, and Kalamazoo.

In Rust Belt cities, "we don't look at supply and demand," Ms. Volk said. "We look at migration."

"Who's moving in and out? How much money do they make? Would they prefer to be a renter or a homeowner?"

Her firm gathers detailed information about "the likes and dislikes" of those with household incomes of $60,000. "The way people make coffee is very telling," Ms. Volk said. "Do they use a coffee grinder? A French press?"

Robert Palmieri—Utica's mayor since 2011—was in the audience during Ms. Volk's presentation.

"You had a lot of naysayers," Mayor Palmieri recalled. "But some people were happy and excited—they really did see the vision."

The developers had a wait-and-see attitude, he added: " 'I'm not going to be the guinea pig.' "

———

Michael Pezzolanella, a local contractor, was the first to jump.

He read Ms. Volk's report—but he was already interested. "I saw a future in the city," said Mr. Pezzolanella, who grew up downtown. His company had been building drugstores, shopping centers; a little of everything. "I love the old buildings."

He and his son, Francis, bought 421 Broad Street, a former sewing factory with about 200 windows. They built five lofts, which quickly filled, as well as retail space.

"But it was a rough haul," Mr. Pezzolanella said about the project, started in 2008, during the Great Recession. "Banks didn't want to deal with it. We sold other properties and maxed out our credit cards."

Others followed: A developer started renovating the old Doyle Hardware building, which covers an entire block. An accountant bought the Winston Building on Genesee Street and began turning it into loft apartments.

It was as if somebody lit a fire under an old kettle: A few new bars and restaurants appeared.

And then the Landmarc Building—a three-story luxury loft building, with a rooftop restaurant—opened in 2015. It helped shift the way residents saw their city.

"The perception was that nothing good had happened in Utica in a very long time," Mayor Palmieri said. "The Landmarc showed there's hope."

The building—which once housed the marble-covered Marine Midland Bank—stood on a prominent corner of Genesee, near the Hotel Utica.

When the city took it over, its basement was filled with water and mold; copper wiring and pipes had been stripped by vandals. Squatters had moved in.

The city was going to tear it down and build a parking lot when Mr. Pezzolanella bought it for $1,000.

Uticans were impressed: The Landmarc had 32 spacious lofts, including a penthouse suite with a private elevator. The restaurant had floor-to-ceiling windows looking out over the bleak city.

Mersiha was following these changes with a sharp eye; they made her more anxious to start her café. She worried about real estate becoming too expensive.

"I wanted to see it," Mersiha said about the Landmarc's new restaurant, Ocean Blue, and she made a reservation for Valentine's Day.

She and Hajrudin were taken aback by how fancy it was—it had an oyster bar and spare, modern-style furniture. "The guy invested millions."

Mersiha is generally critical of restaurant food: "But it was good," she said, grudgingly. "For Utica, it was super pricey." The couple's dinner cost $130 plus tip.

———

Change was in the air: Utica now had its own professional ice hockey team, the Comets, based at the Utica Memorial Auditorium. In its second season, it dominated the Western Conference and made it to the playoffs.

"It's huge," Mr. Thomas said about the Comets coming to downtown Utica. "There's pride—you can see a change in attitude."

For decades, Uticans were pessimistic, frustrated by the city's stagnant economy. This attitude hurt development: "There was a feeling among community leaders that we were our own worst enemy."

Politicians were part of the problem, he added. "For the last 50, 60 years, people saw promises made—good ideas that fell through."

In 2011, when Governor Andrew Cuomo came into office, he promised to turn around upstate New York's economy.

He encouraged companies to move north and awarded nearly $2.4 billion to create or retain upstate jobs through the state's Regional Economic Development Councils. Buffalo received $875 million—the governor's "Buffalo Billion" grant—which included technology initiatives. He legalized more casinos and set up tax free zones around the state.

And yet many upstate plants continued to downsize or close, including those involved with nuclear energy and light metals manufacturing. The region's economic problems were not so easy to fix, although Buffalo and the capital region around Albany initially saw a rise in employment, due to construction jobs on large, new projects.

Utica started to see a windfall: The state gave millions of dollars to upgrade the city's infrastructure and to renovate and expand the Utica Memorial Auditorium.

In 2015, Governor Cuomo made an announcement that tugged at hearts: General Electric—which left town in 1993—would return.

The company had provided generations of Uticans with jobs making radio components. The new project—a power electronics facility—would be housed on the SUNY Poly campus, and would create hundreds of new jobs over five years.

But there was an even bigger promise: The governor announced that AMS, an Austrian company that manufactures sensors, was going to invest more than $2 billion—and create and retain over a thousand jobs—in a facility to be built at the Nano Utica site in nearby Marcy.

For years, there had been talk about Utica being a nanotech hub.

"If it happens, it will be the best news this area has had in a long time," said Chris Hubbell, 63, a slim, silver-haired man. It was 2013. He was looking out the window of Hop & Goblet, the craft beer store he had just opened on Genesee.

His son, Colin, co-owns the Green Onion, the neighborhood pub—where Ali met Heidi—directly across the street.

"Ten years ago, there was nothing here, except Café Domenico," Mr. Hubbell said, referring to a coffee shop that was the lone outpost on this stretch of South Utica.

It is easy for Mr. Hubbell to feel nostalgic: In the 1950s, when he was growing up, downtown was the sun, which the suburbs revolved around. He still savors the names of the city's long-gone restaurants: "Grimaldi's. The Imperial."

But he was feeling optimistic: "A lot of people are realizing that not having to get in your car and drive somewhere is easier. Downtown living is coming back."

Young people—who left—started coming home.

They returned from Fort Lauderdale, Syracuse, Rochester, New Haven, Providence, and New York City. They heard Utica was changing.

Carmela Caruso, owner of Caruso's Pastry Shoppe, was delighted when her niece Catherine Raymond, 28, returned from Raleigh, North Carolina, with her husband and new baby.

"She was tired of worrying about floods," Carmela said. "In Utica, you come home, your roof's on your house, your car's in your garage."

Her niece wanted to be near family, she added: "You put a baby in daycare, it's expensive. Your mother is here. Your aunts are here."

Jason Allen Leonard, 30, was living with his husband in a small, expensive apartment in Astoria, Queens, when they decided to move back to Utica. They rented a loft downtown.

Their families go way back; both had Italian immigrant great-grandfathers who worked in Utica's mills. The couple had missed small-city life: "You know where to get your car fixed," Jason said.

For years, there was only one place to get breakfast downtown—the tiny Triangle Coffee Shop. In 2015, the couple opened Bite, a brick-walled café, serving ricotta blueberry pancakes.

"We wanted to be part of the revival," Jason said. "We thought, 'Utica's definitely on the mend.'"

24. MERSIHA LEAPS

MERSIHA had been waiting for Faris to graduate high school before starting her business, but suddenly, she was more than ready. "Right now, I have all this energy," she said.

It was 2018: She now had a wider customer base—in Syracuse and Ithaca. "They keep pushing me, 'When are you going to open your café?' "

She felt that rolling the dice was the only way her family was going to get ahead. "Hajrudin recently got a 22 cent raise," she said, exasperated. "He's still not up to $15 an hour."

She felt they were running out of time: She was 43; Hajrudin was 50.

Like everybody in Utica, she had been excited about Governor Cuomo's plan to make Utica a nanotechnology hub. She thought it would be great for her café.

But the plan fell through: The Austrian chipmaker withdrew after a bid-rigging scheme was revealed. Alain E. Kaloyeros, the president of SUNY Poly, in charge of the nanotechnology program, was indicted for corruption and wire fraud.

Mersiha shrugged off her disappointment.

Other Uticans did, too: "The feeling was, 'Here we go again,'" Mayor Palmieri said. " 'Another missed opportunity. Only in Utica!' "

But something new was on the horizon: A $480 million hospital—with $300 million coming from New York State—was being planned for downtown. Utica's two old hospitals—St. Elizabeth in South Utica, and St. Luke's in New Hartford—were going to be consolidated by the Mohawk Valley Health System.

A modern glass and steel building—set on 25 acres—was going to rise in the middle of the old city.

It was as if a flaming torch were thrown into a crowd: People immediately divided over the hospital.

"It was hugely controversial," said Jason, co-owner of Bite. "At every table in the café, people were talking about it."

Supporters felt a state-of-the-art hospital was badly needed—and putting it downtown would make healthcare more accessible for residents, as well as those from the wider region.

They saw it as an economic boon.

The hospital would bring 2,000 daily employees downtown, round the clock, said Mr. Thomas, commissioner of urban and economic development. He saw new businesses springing up around it: pharmacies, medical offices, restaurants, and bars.

Robert Burmaster, a city councilman representing West Utica, a low-income neighborhood with many vacant buildings, was hopeful: "If downtown thrives, the surrounding communities will do well, too."

But many residents felt that instead of building a new hospital, St. Luke's, which had ample land, should be expanded. And many were disturbed by the fate of the dozens of small businesses that would be forced to make way for the new hospital. On the fringes, a small but very vocal No Hospital Downtown movement sprang up.

Katie Aiello, owner of Character Coffee, a downtown café, worried about preserving the character of Utica's small downtown: "It will change the vibe of the neighborhood," she said. "I don't want to be in a hospital district."

Everybody agreed on one thing: The rollout was badly done. Hospital administrators felt they did their part by meeting with the public. But the community felt there was no real consultation.

"Residents should have been more involved," Mayor Palmieri said. "You can't shove something down someone's throat, without letting them have a taste on their own."

Mersiha—busy with work and family—avoided the controversy. "I don't know much about it," she said. Like many residents—no matter which side they started on—she accepted the idea of the new hospital.

But Uticans have been burned before.

And some remained skeptical: "Where is this money coming from?" Mr. Zogby asked. "They're promised $300 million. Where's the other $180 million?"

"The hospital people consider it done. But what if the governor ends up needing that money?"

———

Mersiha was sitting at a desk in an empty classroom. Because of budget cuts, her ESL program had been downsized from 12 teachers to 3 and moved into a BOCES building, off Bleecker. She now taught six-week sessions, preparing her refugee students for jobs in the hospitality industry.

She unwrapped cheese, bread, and an apple. A monk in a sleeveless, saffron-colored robe passed by the doorway.

"My monk!" Mersiha called out. "You want candy?" The Burmese monk, who took ESL classes, liked the hard candies Mersiha kept on her desk.

A small man in his forties, he stood expectantly in the doorway, holding his backpack.

"May I have three?" he asked Mersiha.

"I can only give you one," she said, handing him a wrapped orange candy.

Thanking her, the monk left.

Things have changed, Mersiha told me.

For years, Hajrudin sat on the ledge: "He's not a striker," she explained. "He always plays defense: 'What if this—and that—happens?'"

Then suddenly—out of the blue—Hajrudin jumped.

"He promised me something," she said, eating her lunch. "In the next year, we can open a business, a *real* business, outside the home."

They quickly agreed on a plan: They would start looking for a building to buy. It made more sense than renting a storefront.

Hajrudin would quit his job, though Mersiha would keep hers, so they would have at least one paycheck and her health insurance.

And they would eventually sell their beloved house. They hoped to find a café space that had an apartment above it; they would live there. That way they could run upstairs to see their kids, instead of driving back and forth to Blandina Street.

They would use the profit from the house as a cushion.

First, they went to their local bank, where they had gotten their home mortgage. Mersiha loved the loan officer, an ambitious woman in her twenties, who gave them a lot of time. She estimated they would need at least a $250,000 loan for their business.

She steered them to Utica's small business bureau; gave them a list of lawyers; and told them to go to city hall to find out about grants for women and minorities. Before consulting anyone, Mersiha planned to do research. "We want to be able to ask good questions."

Mersiha knew that opening a business would involve financial sacrifices. She was not fazed: Laughing, she said, "We don't smoke. We don't drink. We cook at home. We have old cars."

"Our kids don't request things."

Ismar and Faris already said they would work at the café for free.

It was almost 1 p.m.: Mersiha packed up her crumbs and the cheese wrapping and went down the hall to her class.

———

When I first met Mersiha in 2013, she hurried past the signs at the refugee center: *This school is betel nut free. Nose picking is gross, use a tissue.*

And past the poster, put up after New York State won its court case against the Utica school district: *You have the right to an education! Do you live in Utica, NY? Are you younger than 21? Enroll in Proctor High School now!*

And past the world map that pinpointed the nations her students had fled.

For a moment, Mersiha stood looking into her classroom. Some of her students, tired, had put their heads down on their desks. All wore traditional clothing; they came from a dozen different countries.

"This is my Disney," she said. "My students are so appreciative. When I open that door, I'm in another world."

Then she entered: Almost 20 years ago, she had been in one of those seats.

Mersiha put on a doctor's white coat. Her students were delighted.

"Hello, are we ready?" Mersiha asked. Her goal was to familiarize them with the process of going to the doctor—and to sharpen their language skills.

They leaned forward. Some had never had a medical exam before applying for refugee status.

"Physicals are necessary!" she said. "We need to see a doctor at least once a year. And women—after a certain age, we need breast exams, Pap smears!"

She put four wooden chairs together to make an examination table.

"You know your body best. If you notice any changes in your body, speak up!"

Mersiha knows "speaking up" is difficult for refugees: Back home, calling attention to yourself meant asking for trouble. Keeping your head down kept you alive.

"If you don't tell the doctor, he can't help you," she warned them.

The students listened, riveted.

"Before I go, I write my questions on paper," Mersiha said. "I have headaches every day. But if I don't write them down, I forget to tell the doctor."

"Let's say, I'm drinking a lot of water," she added. "That may be a problem! I write it down. My doctor might do a blood test for diabetes."

Putting a stethoscope around her neck, she said, "The doctor works very quick. Five minutes—done!" She clapped her hands.

"I need a volunteer patient."

Ahmet, an intense-looking man in his forties wearing glasses, came forward, then sat on the pretend examination table. He faced the window. "Turn around," Mersiha said.

"Ahhh," he said, looking confused. Then he looked up at her.

"Raise your arm," she said. He looked puzzled until she touched his arm.

"Raise your left leg." Springing up, he stamped his right foot.

"You have a problem with left and right," Mersiha said. "We'll work on this!"

Then, putting the stethoscope against his chest, she told the class, "Everybody, breathe in—breathe out! This is so the doctor can check your heart."

There was a bit of chaos. Chairs were moved away from desks.

"Breathe in!" Mersiha said, taking a deep breath. "Breathe out!" And as her chest rose and fell, the whole class followed her.

There was silence, except for breathing.

"Turn your head!" she said.

"Move your right leg."

"Cough!" Students tried this; discreet coughs spread across the room.

"Cover your right eye." This was a favorite; students smiled at each other.

"Now bend over, touch your toes." There was a rustle of saris, long dresses, and caftans. "Come up, slow."

"Make a fist!" Mersiha said, clenching her right hand, strong from baking. "What do we do every day when you go home?"

She bumped fists with Ahmet.

"Teacher," a young woman raised her hand. "My daughter, no sleep."

"You give her milk, juice before going to bed?"

"No juice."

"You give her candy, sugar?"

The young woman seemed unsure.

"Call your doctor and schedule an appointment," Mersiha said. "But if you give your children a lot of sugar—no good!"

A young woman, her long hair in a bun, asked, "We have insurance?"

"Everybody here have insurance," Mersiha said, firmly. Refugees get short-term health insurance for up to eight months.

"You get one free appointment per year. They will charge you nothing for that."

She glanced at her watch, suddenly exhausted. She had been up till 6 a.m. baking.

"Ladies, always check yourself!" she said, touching her breast. "To-morrow, I will show you how it feels if you find a lump!"

25. BOMB THREAT

ONE DAY in March 2018, Mersiha was surprised when a school administrator she barely knew stopped her in the hall and said abruptly, "You Bosnian?"

"Yes."

"How do you feel?" the woman said. "You and your people—what are you thinking about it?"

Mersiha felt a chill; she knew exactly what the woman was referring to: The day before, Fahrudin Omerovic, a 23-year-old Utica College student, who said he was armed, called in multiple threats to the college. For six hours, the school was in lockdown. When Mr. Omerovic, a Bosnian-American, was arrested at his home, no weapon was found.

"What does that have to do with me?" Mersiha said, trying to stay calm. "I'm not his mother or his sister." Then she walked away.

After that, the woman ducked when she saw Mersiha. But every chance she could, Mersiha said cordially, "Good morning."

Months later, she was still fuming. "My blood pressure went through the roof," she said about the incident. It pained her that an educated person—whom she thought should know better—would speak so divisively.

"I don't go around saying an Italian, or a Pole, did that," Mersiha said. "Whoever makes a threat should be punished—even if it's my own son."

Over the years, Mersiha has had barbed comments tossed at her. But since President Trump was elected, things have gotten worse: "People think they can say anything: 'Go back to your friggin' home.'"

Mersiha has been in the United States 24 years. But when she is introduced to someone, she explained, it's never, "Where do you live? Where do you work? Where do you go to school?"

It's: "How long have you been here?"

"I know I have an accent!" Mersiha said. "I can't do anything about it. Maybe I'll put a sticker right here," she pointed to her chest. "*I'm Bosnian, Muslim.*"

"I've been here long enough," she added, shaking her head. "Don't ask me!"

———

Like many immigrants and refugees, Mersiha feels suspended between two worlds. When she and her family visit Bosnia during the summer, they are not seen as true Bosnians.

"They call us 'the diaspora,'" she said, meaning those who fled after the war. "They think for us, it's easy. We come back with money."

She wants to tell them, "Do you know how much we have to save for one trip? Would we do that if we didn't miss this country?"

They have no idea of our longing, she said. "We are so tied to the past. It's like a hole inside us."

Skyping helps—but it is also painful.

Azra, Mersiha's 24-year-old niece, who lives in Sarajevo and was studying to be a social worker, has bone cancer. "She's a fighter—and very angry," Mersiha said. She had her left leg amputated at 17; a tumor is now on her right leg. She postponed her wedding because of her illness, but recently told Mersiha as they skyped, "Why didn't I get married before I got sick?"

"When you beat this crap, we're going to have a huge wedding," Mersiha told her, trying not to cry. "Any cake you want! We're going to dance all night!"

"You just have to keep sending positive thoughts," Mersiha said, discouraged.

She knows Bosnians think 'the diaspora' do not understand what they go through.

"But we don't understand things in America either," she said. "Where do we belong? Where's our place?"

"Nowhere!" Mersiha said, laughing and shaking her head. "I'm a refugee, and always will be."

26. THE RUTGER RESTAURANT

A S MERSIHA DROVE around Utica delivering cakes, she kept an eye out for buildings for sale. She checked out a downtown warehouse that turned out to be too pricey. A restaurant in East Utica that needed a lot of work, and had no parking lot. And a decrepit lawyer's office.

She noticed small changes downtown: A few new ethnic restaurants.

And there were glints of color: Mosaic trash cans had replaced the old metal ones.

Around this time, I noticed something mysterious. A beautiful hand-made kite, with green feathers, was tucked in a grate by the new Delta Hotel. A cobalt blue and yellow fish kite leaned against the Utica clock. A few hours later, they were gone.

Mersiha heard that the Rutger Restaurant, an old restaurant and ca-tering hall where she and Hajrudin married 20 years ago, was on the market. In recent years, they had delivered cakes there for customers' weddings. It was far from what they had in mind, but they decided to take a look.

Mersiha's heart quickened as they turned onto Rutger, driving down the wide, venerable street, with its stately Victorian houses.

The restaurant was almost at the end, set among small frame houses, near Proctor Park. It looked incongruous—a sprawling 1950s-era build-ing with a big black and red sign.

The owner—a Bosnian who had been running the place for 12 years—did not waste any time: He was having health problems, he told the cou-ple; he had just had a stent put in and was anxious to sell.

Mersiha wandered around: The interior of the restaurant was dark and run-down—but enormous, over 10,000 square feet. There was a large bar area. A big, industrial kitchen. A small, neglected party room that could hold 80 people. The ballroom—where they had their recep-tion—was big enough for 300.

A new image began to replace the homey mom-and-pop café she had been picturing for 10 years.

"I realized the potential of the place," she said.

They could turn the bar area into a café. And they could renovate the party room quickly, so they could start catering baby showers and anniversary parties. Later—after they had made some money—they could tackle the ballroom.

Mersiha was not overwhelmed. "I felt we could do this because we're good at this."

Hajrudin also saw the possibilities; he was quiet, walking around.

Then Mersiha noticed something: "I smell mold," she told the owner.

"No!" he said laughing. "The place is just old—there's no mold!"

He wanted $245,000.

"I will give you everything," he said: A walk-in freezer, two pizza ovens, a 10-burner stove. Hundreds of plates, mugs, and cups. Also, there was an apartment—with a good tenant—above the restaurant. So, they would have an extra $800 a month income.

Mersiha and Hajrudin conferred: The restaurant was completely down-at-the-heels. They would need to redo the walls, change the flooring, add their own tables, chairs, and sofas. But they were both excited.

They came back the next day.

"How about $165,000?" Mersiha blurted out.

"That seems too low," Hajrudin said, taken aback. Mersiha shot him a dirty look.

"$225,000," the owner said.

They settled on $200,000.

The couple felt it was a good deal: If they took out a mortgage for $60,000, and collected $800 from the tenant, then their monthly mortgage would be only $800 a month. Eventually, they would renovate the apartment and move in.

Mersiha had taken a wild leap, just like her hero, the Cake Boss. And Hajrudin had followed. But over the next few weeks, he would wake up at night, his heart pounding.

He did not like change—and there would be plenty of it ahead. He would have to quit his job, which he loved. He thought of the dozens of things that could go wrong as he renovated the restaurant.

Mersiha, in contrast, felt unleashed: She pored over the websites of popular cafés in Europe and Japan, studying what they did with lighting, glassware, and furniture.

"All Utica cafes have wooden chairs and rustic things," Mersiha said. "I want my café to be different, to look like other parts of the world."

Always in the background was the couple's anxiety about getting their mortgage application approved. But their loan officer treated them like a relative.

Every day, Mersiha looked forward to 6 p.m., when she called her with an update.

27. NINETEEN

SADIA was on a mission: She wanted two black helium balloons, embossed with a 1 and a 9. Ayuong—now a freshman at SUNY Poly—was turning 19; Sadia and her friends were taking her to the Turning Stone buffet for lunch.

Inside the party store in New Hartford, Sadia looked like a young actress—her dark eyes were lined with silver; her eyelids were a glittery ice blue. She wore a head wrap, a belted shirtdress over her ripped jeans, and knee-high riding boots.

The young clerk, behind the balloon counter, was dazzled. But Sadia did not notice.

"Can I help you?"

The clerk searched different cubbyholes for the balloons. Then he got on a ladder and searched some more. Sadia checked her texts.

"I think we're out of black," he said.

Sadia was crushed. "I wanted black."

A mother and her little boy walked by with a shopping cart loaded with party supplies.

"Is there another color?" he asked.

"OK, silver."

He checked, then said, "Got it!" He went in the back—then returned with two enormous balloons.

"Thank you," Sadia said, turning away. He kept staring as she made her way toward the cashier. "I don't know why I'm so excited about Ayuong's birthday," she said. "I'm more excited about it than mine." Her 19th birthday was five months away.

"My other friends are too clingy. They want to take too much. Ayuong doesn't want anything."

Sadia admired how skillfully her friend was able to navigate the outside world. "She's smart, does great at school," Sadia said. Unlike most of the African girls she knew who went to college, Ayuong lived in a dorm.

As she stood in line to pay for the balloons, Sadia's cell phone rang. Looking down, her face softened then lit up. The young man on the screen was about 20; he had brown eyes and a wide smile.

"Wow—who you looking so pretty for?" he asked. "Why you dressed up, wearing makeup?"

"We're taking Ayuong out," Sadia said, looking embarrassed.

He said something in a low voice.

"Sshh," she said. "Just talk halal."

She muted the phone, put in earbuds, and talked to him softly. There was a radiance about her as she moved forward in line.

Distracted, Sadia paid $25 for the balloons.

She had been seeing Chol—Ayuong's cousin—for a year, she said, crossing the parking lot to the car.

He was studying engineering at a community college in Syracuse— and he came from a good family. A few times a week, he drove from Syracuse to see her. "Ralya, Sofia—they love him," Sadia said.

But their romance had a rocky start.

"I didn't trust him," she explained. "This girl pressed me—to ask him about other girls. People try to break you up. They come around to ruin your life."

And Sadia took the bait: "I said things to him that were cruel, things you shouldn't say."

Chol stopped responding to her on social media; he disappeared. But then a couple of months later, she was at a party and saw a pasta and meat casserole that reminded her of a Sudanese dish his mom cooks. "We used to eat it all the time," she said.

She texted Chol: "I've just eaten something you used to be obsessed with."

He did not answer. He had been waiting for her to calm down—but was also angry at how she had misunderstood him.

You can ignore me, she texted the boy she loved. *But do you got to be so mean?*

28. DESIGNING A HOUSE

ZAHARA heard the loud grrrr-ing sound of a lawn mower and opened her living room window.

It was a neighbor, who had decided to cut her grass as a favor. "Thank you!" Zahara called out.

She was delighted with her house on Steuben, which she had just renovated. The house had been neglected when she bought it, but she and her new husband, Mustafa, had patched walls and painted. Everything inside looked new.

"People come here, they think Mana and Ralya did this," Zahara said, pointing to the comfortable couch and salmon-colored walls. There was a framed picture of a lion. Green fluted bowls sat in a glass hutch, and silver pineapples rested above a large-screen TV.

"But everything I do myself. I like to design a house!"

She exulted in the new upstairs bathroom installed for $1,500. She had bought the materials at Home Depot. "The glass for the shower was $800," she said, amazed. The bathroom—sparkling with glass and chrome   had stoked her ambitions: "I want to do another bathroom. I want to design a kitchen."

"But money, money," she added, lamenting the high cost of renovating. She hoped to save enough to tackle a second bathroom next year.

This new house sprang from Zahara's feelings for Mustafa.

They met at Chobani: She filled yogurt cups; he was a machine operator. One afternoon, she was coming back from a lunch break. "You're late," teased Mustafa—a slim, quiet Sudanese man.

"Only five minutes," she shot back.

She and Mustafa started carpooling together with a few other people. They became friends.

"The older man and I, we were already separated," she added, referring to her ex-husband, Rahama's father.

One afternoon, she and Mustafa were taking a walk after work. He said he was thinking of buying a house, to rent out as an investment.

She felt a rush of warmth—and clarity.

"We buy together," she said.

She explained to him: They would find an inexpensive house. After they paid off the mortgage, she would buy out his half. He would then have enough money to purchase a house, which he could rent out.

Zahara has always had an entrepreneurial streak.

In the refugee camp, she made sambusas—pastries stuffed with vegetables and meat—which she then sold in the marketplace. In Utica, she owns a second house on Jay Street, which she rents out.

Her clan—like many immigrant and refugee families—functions as a kind of financial co-op. When a family member wants to buy a house, relatives pitch in.

The family gathers as big a down payment—in cash—as possible: When Halima bought her house on Rutger Street, she and her sister each put in $4,000.

The family buys directly from owners, rather than going through a bank. And they pay off their mortgages quickly.

Mustafa was amazed by Zahara's offer: "You'd do that for me?"

"Yes."

The following week, Zahara found the house on Steuben, about a dozen blocks from her mother's house. She told him, "I like. But I don't know if you like."

He said he did not even need to see it: "Whatever you like, I like."

They bought the house for $62,000. A month later, Zahara moved in with her children.

But soon she had another idea: There was an empty bedroom on the first floor. "Can you live in the downstairs room?" she asked him. "I'm worried in the new neighborhood."

He was taken aback. "Man and woman can't live together like that. They should be married."

She had already taken stock of him: She thought he was humble—and kind. In the years since he had arrived in America, he had worked nonstop.

"I already dreamed about that," she told him. "I already decided you're my man."

"Are you sure?"

"Yes. When can you move in?"

"Next week."

"That's too long!" she said. "I can't wait that long. I need you tomorrow."

———

Zahara was used to living with three generations: in her village, in the camp, and in her mother's rambling house on Rutger Street.

Now she savored the word: *privacy*.

"I want my *privacy*," she said, describing why she liked being in her own house with Mustafa and her kids.

Mustafa's friends felt she had too much influence over him: "They say Mustafa only listens to his wife," Zahara said. "They don't like him now," she added, and shrugged. But she seemed pleased.

Polygamy—a centuries-old practice in Africa—is common among the older generation of Somali Bantus in American cities. Zahara's father had other wives—for short periods—during his long marriage to Halima. And for a few years, Zahara was in a relationship with Rahama's father, who had another wife.

But Zahara ended up unhappy—and broke it off.

For many Somali Bantus, polygamy is an accepted holdover from village life, Dr. Stam said: It developed because of a scarcity of resources. "Families gained power, money, and prestige by bringing in brides' dowries."

Many men had two wives in the refugee camps, she added. If both wives got resettled, there was a dilemma: "One wife may have been resettled in Utica, another in Akron or Burlington. So, the husband had to make a choice."

Often, both relationships continued, with the husband visiting his other family on holidays. "As long as he brings money or gifts, and visits the kids, the wife may feel, 'Oh, whatever . . .'"

The children, too, are generally accepting, she added. "It's seen as a fact of life. 'Oh, dad has another family.'"

Sadia was accepting when her grandfather took another wife. "If it's someone else's decision, I can't do anything about it," she said.

But she worried—and felt protective of her mother when she was with Rahama's father, whom Sadia disliked. Yet she became close friends with one of his sons, who was in her class at Proctor.

"The younger generation doesn't do what our parents do," she said about polygamy. "I'm not accepting it. I'd walk out."

———

Zahara is proud of her arduous schedule, which helps foot the bills for her new home: She works 3 p.m. to midnight, caring for her sister's children, and is paid through New York State's Child Care Subsidy Program. Ralya takes over the household while she is away. Four days a week, from 9 a.m. to noon, Zahara attends BOCES, learning to read and write.

Mustafa leaves at 8:30 p.m. to work the night shift at Chobani.

"I like to make my *own* money," Zahara said. "I don't want to beg," she added, referring to public assistance.

"But I get Medicaid. And they give me food stamps—that's all."

Zahara was familiar with the phrase *the American Dream*. And she had a strong sense of what could be accomplished in America. That is why she could not get over her anger at Sadia; it kept bubbling to the surface.

"I told Sadia today, 'Get your high school diploma!'" Zahara said, staring at the TV. "'Go find your own job. To watch somebody's baby is not a job for you. You grew up in America!'"

"'Bring me that baby,'" she added, referring to Amrah, Sofia's daughter. "I watch that baby. Smart is not staying home. *Smart is going to school.*"

She heard children scuffling upstairs. Then a crash of something falling. Getting up with effort, Zahara made her way upstairs. She had just joined a gym to help her lose weight.

Ibrahim, her 7-year-old, was in the new bathroom, looking guilty, though everything seemed in order.

Zahara suddenly focused on a soap dish near the sink; there was something congealed in it.

Smelling it, she looked disgusted. "You make mess!" she told Ibrahim. "Coconut oil mess."

Zahara now had a dozen kids; she was used to disorder. It was a never-ending battle to keep the house clean.

She had wanted this new bathroom to stay pristine. Frustrated, she said to herself, "No! No more kids for me! I'm tired."

Then looking at Ibrahim's stricken face, she remembered what her older daughters had told her: Ibrahim had slid down the banister that morning, though he had been warned not to. He had fallen off and bumped his head, doing the same thing, last week.

"Why you not walk down stairs?" she demanded. "I said, 'Don't do that!'"

Then she saw Aisha—her thin 9-year-old—disappearing around a corner. Zahara called her back. "You do this, too?" she asked, showing her the gloppy soap dish.

"No, I didn't," Aisha said.

Zahara was not convinced. "Go get me the stick."

Her eyes widening, Aisha ran off.

Zahara settled herself back in front of the TV. Then a few minutes later, Aisha and Ibrahim hurried into the room. Casting her quick looks, they sat on the floor, close to the TV. Their backs looked tense.

After a few minutes, Zahara asked, "Aisha, you think I forgot?"

Aisha quickly jumped up and left the room. After a few minutes, she returned with a long-handled wooden spoon.

"This is all I could find," she said tersely.

"How many you want?" Zahara asked.

"Three," she said, and extended her small, upturned hand.

Her mother hit it deftly. Not too hard, but enough to sting.

Aisha's eyes welled slightly with tears. She quickly went back over to the TV.

"Ibrahim!" Zahara called.

Ibrahim tentatively went up to her.

"How many you want?"

"Two," he said, his eyes wide.

She quickly rapped his palm twice.

"Why you make noise?" his mother asked. "Why you go down banister? I give you a chance," she added, meaning there could be more punishment.

She pointed to the straw broom leaning in the hallway. "Go clean."

29. THE CROSSING

IN THEIR EARLY TWENTIES, Ali and his brother, Saif, could not have been more different. "He was a traditional Middle Eastern man," Ali said. "He used to pray—I didn't. He listened to Arab music—I didn't."

Saif was tolerant and enjoyed getting to know all kinds of people: poor people, rich people.

"Wherever I went, people knew I was his brother," Ali said. "They treated me in a special way."

Shaking his head at his younger self, Ali said, "I didn't like hanging out with just anybody. Only guys like me, who were Western-style and dressed nice."

He fell in love with Western culture when he was four: He heard a Beatles tape at a relative's house. "I thought, 'That's beautiful!'" he said. And taking the tape home, he listened to it over and over.

In his teens, he started listening to Madonna and Michael Jackson.

He taught break dancing to his friends. Like an American teenager, he turned his room into a sanctuary, plastering it with posters of rock bands, and Samantha Fox—a British model and singer—posing in a bikini.

"Nobody was allowed into my room," he recalled, laughing. But one day, when he got home from school, his sister said, "Hey, mama went into your room today." But his mother was not upset by what she saw on his walls. "She knew I wasn't doing anything bad."

"I was the *black duck*," he added, meaning the different one.

Saif's room was just the opposite: It was simple and spare, with a twin bed. And an antique cabinet, where he kept his books and cassettes; it had belonged to their mother when she was a teenager.

Both brothers started out working for ABC News. Saif took a job as a guide and driver with ABC News, then became a broadcaster at one of Iraq's main channels; he married and had a baby girl. Ali worked as an interpreter for American journalists, then did some interviewing in Arabic, as well as some shooting and reporting.

The camerawork delighted him, since it was a link to his father. It began with a gift: The office gave him a small camera when he was covering the news in Basra, in southern Iraq. "I started playing with the camera, getting footage," Ali said. The bureau chief told him he had a good eye and asked somebody to show him how to get better-quality photos—as well as how to protect himself in a situation such as a car bombing.

Ali started carrying his camera everywhere. "If I saw something I'd jump from my car, show my badge, and get permission."

One afternoon, he spotted something unusual: American forces were using a rowboat—remotely controlled from a bridge—to defuse an IED on a Baghdad street. When he asked permission to film, he was told no. "So, I drove my car far from them, and zoomed in."

"It was a stupid move."

As soon as he started filming, a Humvee came at him. "I was surrounded by five, six, seven American soldiers, guns pointed. All screaming, just to scare me." He was made to lie on the ground, then was handcuffed and detained in the Humvee for two hours until his bureau chief intervened.

In 2006, when the violence between Shiites and Sunnis escalated, Ali felt it was no longer safe for his family to stay in their Sunni neighborhood. So he rented a large apartment in Damascus, Syria, and asked Saif to take their family there. As the eldest brother, "he was the man of the house," Ali said.

"I was single; I didn't care about my safety, and I couldn't leave work."

He convinced his brother to take some time off. Ali moved into his grandmother's house in a Shia neighborhood.

But after a month, Saif, bored and missing his life in Bagdad, decided to come home for a visit. His half-sister, Fatima, and her two sons, 9 and 14, came along.

The western territory they would be crossing was Sunni, controlled by Al Qaeda. "We heard they were targeting cars coming and going from Syria," Ali said, "taking people's money, their jewelry. If someone proved they were Sunni, they left them alone."

But Saif was not worried: "He didn't believe in these stories," Ali said,

"that people from another sect would do that. He'd say, 'We're all Iraqis.'"
And Ali himself thought these incidents were rare.

Ali waited an hour for his brother at the Baghdad bus terminal. Another hour passed. Then it started getting dark. "During those days, the streets were almost empty," he said. It was dangerous to be out after dark.

"My grandmother kept calling my uncle, 'Get Ali to come home!'"

Ali was not alarmed that the bus was late. "I thought maybe there had been a delay or something. This happened all the time." He decided to go home until his brother called.

———

At 9 p.m., Fatima called, hysterical: The bus had been stopped by gunmen. Saif and her two boys had been dragged away.

Ali collapsed on a couch.

When he awoke, his aunt was standing over him, screaming, "What happened to you? Your lips are white. Your beard has turned white!"

For a few days, Ali was in shock. He did not say anything to his aunt, his mother, or his sisters. His mother kept calling: "Did Saif get there? Is he safe?"

"Yes, yes," Ali answered, numb. "He's here. But he's busy. I'm busy. He's working. He's staying at the TV station."

Finally, his mother decided to get on a bus and come to Baghdad.

She was not thinking about the danger, Ali said: "She didn't care."

Then he did not say anything more.

When asked if he has recovered, Ali shook his head and said, "Still," meaning that he is still in pain.

He said some refugees get counseling at the Community Health & Behavioral Services Center in Utica. He has worked there as an interpreter and found the experience disturbing.

That is not for him, he said.

30. DEPLOYED

IN MARCH 2018, things started happening very quickly for Ali.

He got government security clearance: The next day he got a job offer for a yearlong interpreting contract in the Middle East. Then he flew down to North Carolina for a physical and a battery of tests.

He had to wait two weeks to be cleared. Then he was told he was being deployed in three days.

He wanted this so badly; it was a chance to make some real money. He hoped to come home with about $80,000 saved to buy a house.

Ali and Heidi are stoical; they are used to waiting. She had waited 10 years, until her kids got older, before leaving her marriage. And Ali—from living under the thumb of Saddam Hussein, from being an immigrant, from dealing with the pain of his brother's death—has developed a deep patience.

They felt they could get through a year apart: They hoped to be together in Utica the following spring.

Yet they are realists—they know that relationships change, that political landscapes shift. Epidemics and wars break out.

Nothing is certain.

Ali and Julia were now buddies; they had all recently gone on a family vacation to Atlantic City, taking Kurrine along. When Ali returned from the Middle East, Heidi planned to introduce him to her two grown sons.

"That's our last little hurdle," she said.

Ali was told all his communication would be monitored. Heidi understood he would not be allowed to talk about his work or even tell her where he was stationed.

The couple rushed to put things in order: Ali wanted Heidi to get a used car before he left. They found a 2014 Hyundai Elantra, with 19,000 miles on it. "I certainly didn't have the $1,000 down payment," Heidi said. "But I used my car loan payment from that month, redid my budget, and Ali kicked in."

Even with Ali away, they would still be able to afford the $900 apartment on South Street. Their landlords, who lived in Philadelphia, had already given them a break on the rent, because Heidi kept an eye on things and shoveled the property in winter.

Then right before Ali was to leave, Julia got sick. "I thought she had mono," Heidi said, "and that threw Ali into a panic."

"I'm going to get sick," he said, standing in the middle of their living room. He saw his plan fading: Once before, he was about to get an interpreting contract for much more money: $200,000. But a mistake in paperwork—about his birth date—had caused the whole thing to fall through.

He suddenly saw himself stuck in Utica with little work. They would have to keep renting.

But whatever virus Julia had, it ended quickly. Then a familiar bout of depression set in. After a week in bed, Julia emerged, tired, her hair greasy—but feeling much better.

Ali was gone.

31. THE KEY

A LL THROUGH MARCH, Mersiha and Hajrudin were anxious, waiting to hear if the bank loan for their restaurant had been approved.

But on a rainy April afternoon, Hajrudin, sitting on his living room couch, leaned back and smiled. Often when facing uncertainty, he thinks back to 1992, when he was a 22-year-old engineering student taking a semester off to work in Belgrade, then the capital of Yugoslavia.

"War starts—and you don't know what's going to be," he said. "You lose everything, and then sometimes you gain again."

Ellen DeGeneres was on the wide-screen TV, the sound muted. There was a large pie from Jonny's Pizza on the coffee table. Hajrudin and Mersiha each took a slice, put it on a white plate—and he began talking about when the world darkened.

"We were all living together," he said, referring to Bosnia's villages and cities, which were a mix of ethnicities and religions. "Not side by side—I don't like side by side! But *together*, like relatives."

Yet he knew that in Croatia, just across the western border, ethnic war had begun: Croatia had recently declared independence from Yugoslavia, and forces loyal to the newly declared state were fighting against Serbian control.

"You're hearing the news," he said. "But you still think bad things aren't going to happen."

Hajrudin had already served a year in the Yugoslav People's Army, which was required of all young men after high school. His aunt, a doctor, was paying for his college education. His mother, Razija, could not afford the tuition; his father had died at 39, and she had struggled to raise him and his four siblings.

On a late Friday afternoon, Hajrudin boarded a bus for Donji Vakuf, the small town where his family lived; he went home every other weekend. The bus was packed with about 50 people—all men, except for one woman. They were workers and students: Bosnians, Croats, and Serbs. An outsider could not have identified anyone's ethnicity, Hajrudin said: "We were all Slavs—we looked the same."

After a half hour, the bus pulled over at a checkpoint. It was usually manned by the Yugoslav People's Army, or the police force. But this time, a Croat soldier boarded, asking to see national ID cards. Croat soldiers surrounded the bus.

The soldier—looking for Serbs—was identifying people through the names on their ID cards.

Then he ordered everybody off the bus.

As they stood clumped together, the soldier said, "Serbs have to stay. Bosnians can keep going." Everybody knew that the Serbs would be arrested.

But the riders refused to be separated; the Bosnians would not board the bus. For five hours, they argued with the soldiers.

Finally, "they let us all go off together," Hajrudin said.

The Serbs were grateful to their fellow riders. "Thank you! God bless you!" they kept saying. And the bus continued into the darkness, past the small town of Travnik, "Mersiha's town," Hajrudin said, smiling at his wife, who was uncharacteristically quiet.

Finishing his slice of pizza, Hajrudin carefully wiped the coffee table, then brought his plate into the kitchen. Mersiha took another slice.

The bus climbed a steep mountain, he said, returning to the living room. The Serbs—who controlled the mountain—had set up a checkpoint. As the bus neared it, the Serbian riders broke into a nationalistic song, "March on the Drina." It gave Hajrudin—and the other non-Serbs—chills.

> *Sing, sing Drina, tell the generations*
> *how we bravely fought.*
> *The front sang, the battle was fought*
> *near cold water.*
> *Blood was flowing,*
> *blood was streaming*
> *by the Drina for freedom!*

"It's supposed to make people feel scared," Hajrudin said. The song commemorates the World War I Battle of Cer, in which the Serbian Army pushed thousands of Austro-Hungarian soldiers from villages they had taken; panicking, many soldiers drowned in the Drina River.

"It means the Serbs are coming. And when they come to your town—it's going to be slaughter. No one will survive."

"It's sung with pride," he added, "but not good pride."

At the checkpoint, the soldiers heard the loud singing—*How we bravely fought . . . near cold water*—and simply waved the bus on.

But as it pulled away, the Serbian riders kept singing. More and more aggressively. Everyone else felt cowed.

"They were saying, 'Now you're in our territory—let us show you who's in charge,'" Hajrudin said.

But then the bus finally reached Donji Vakuf, the last stop. The town had a Bosnian mayor. More than half its residents were Bosnians.

Some of the Serbs fell silent. But a hard-core group raised their voices.

"We were naïve!" Mersiha broke in, jumping up to put away the pizza box. "People changed overnight. Overnight!"

———

In Donji Vakuf, Hajrudin noticed that some friends he had grown up with were no longer around. "Where is Jovan? Where is Sinisa?" he asked.

Young men had been disappearing one by one, he was told: Some Bosnians had slipped into the woods to join paramilitary groups. Some Serbs had run off to join the Serbian Army.

"But I was still 100 percent sure the Yugoslav People's Army would prevent war," Hajrudin said. And so he returned to Belgrade Sunday night. For the next two weeks, he concentrated on his job as an apprentice welder. But during his next visit home, his cousins took him aside.

"It's not going to be good," they told him. "Don't go back."

———

A few days later, a neighborhood leader spread the word: Women and children were going to be bussed to a stadium in Split—a large city on the eastern shore of Croatia—for their safety. Hajrudin's mother immediately gathered her two daughters—the eldest was pregnant—and her youngest son. They each packed a small bag. Her other son—a year younger than Hajrudin—would stay with him.

"My mother was mom and dad, and everything," Hajrudin said.

Every month, she got a small check from her husband's pension, and with great care she managed to feed their family. "She'd buy flour first, then oil, then sugar," Hajrudin said. She put everything in a huge wooden pantry—a *spaiz*—that she kept locked.

Her children had never glimpsed what was inside.

Before she left, she handed Hajrudin a key.

"Take whatever you need," she said.

He was stunned. He knew what she was saying: You're an adult now. Take care of things.

They embraced. "We thought it would be for two weeks," he said about the separation.

That night, Hajrudin and his brother fell into a deep sleep. But then Hajrudin found himself awake. "I was so curious to see," he said. And going into the kitchen, he opened the *spaiz*.

It was a wonderland: There were ten 75-pound bags of flour. Scores of glass jars of plum butter, rose hip jam, roasted peppers and eggplants, and stuffed pickled peppers. There was dried mint and chamomile tea. Long strands of garlic. Sacks of potatoes and onions. And dried beef sausage—*sudzuk*.

There was enough to live on for six months.

"It's still haunting me," Hajrudin said, shaking his head, "how my mom managed."

Like many struggling Bosnian mothers—including Mersiha's—she would go to Italy, Turkey, Austria, and Hungary to buy goods cheaply. She would purchase Lacoste T-shirts, Levi's jeans, and sneakers, which she would then resell in Bosnia. The bus trip to Istanbul took two days; she would spend one day shopping, then return.

Bribes often had to be given at the borders. To fund a trip, his mother would borrow 500 deutsche marks—about $400—from her sister, then pay her back. Levi's, bought for 60 deutsche marks, could be sold for 100 at home.

She would return, exhausted, carrying two huge bags. "Me and my brother couldn't carry even one," Hajrudin recalled. Putting down the bags, she would say, "I need to sleep."

But after only two hours, she would get up and shower. "We'd make coffee for her," Hajrudin said. "She'd tell her stories: 'This driver was so nice, so smart, he negotiated . . .'"

———

Three days after his mother and siblings left, Serbs blew up the bridge that connected the two parts of town. Two people were killed, and many wounded. The windows of shops blew out. Power was cut.

A Serbian checkpoint—cutting off access to the main road—was set up.

Many people thought about fleeing but did not want to abandon their homes. But Hajrudin, his brother, and a few other men decided to try to reach what they called the "free territory"—Bugojno, a large town about eight miles away—controlled by Bosnians and Croats.

It was still daylight when they slipped into the nearby forest. Hajrudin had put on a dark green sweater, thinking it would not be visible. In his pocket, he carried his mother's cupboard key.

———

In the Omeragics' living room it was getting dark, and Elhan, their youngest, came in. "When are you going to be done?" he asked his mother, frustrated. "When is she going to go?" He pointed to me.

"Shush, Elhan, go play," Mersiha said, sending him off.

Nobody put on a light; the TV was turned to the local news.

"I don't consider myself brave," Hajrudin said. "But I don't consider myself a sissy. My grandfather said, 'Always be in the middle.'"

In the free territory, guns were given to those who signed up to fight the nationalists. The atmosphere was tumultuous; everybody was on their own. His brother stayed on as a firefighter. Hajrudin was sent to defend a nearby town.

They could see snipers and tanks on the surrounding mountains; the townspeople had already made a trench. "We relieved those who were there," he said. "At first, you feel 'I have a gun, nobody can hurt me.' That excitement lasts just a half hour."

But the Serbs did not attack the new recruits. Instead, they fired on the city, targeting Bosnian mosques and Catholic churches.

"You could hear them cursing," Hajrudin said. They were drinking Slivovitz, plum brandy. "They're shooting day and night when they're drunk."

Warily, Elhan slipped back into the living room. "Momma!"

"Soon—I'll be with you soon!"

Elhan made an unhappy sound like a puppy growling, then left.

Hajrudin folded his hands behind his head. "They tried to make you hate them," he said about the Serbs. Looking at Mersiha, he said, "But even now, we don't hate."

"Every family has someone mixed," Mersiha said emphatically, getting up to go see Elhan. Hajrudin would continue his story the next day. "My uncle married a woman who's a mix of Serb and Croat. My other uncle married a Croat. These families have kids."

32. WHO WILL HELP YOU?

THE FOLLOWING afternoon, the sky outside the Omeragics' living room window was slate gray. Hajrudin picked up his story: He was 25—and had been fighting in central Bosnia for three years—when he accidentally stumbled into hell.

"I was still in survival mode," Hajrudin said, sitting across from Mersiha, who had been up all night baking. "Some of my friends had been killed or captured. You feel it's just a question of time before you're killed."

On August 30, 1995, there was a stunning turnaround: After years of sitting on the sidelines, the United States and its allies were finally galvanized by the massacre of over 8,000 mainly Muslim men and boys in the small town of Srebrenica, near the eastern border with Serbia. It was the worst mass killing in Europe since the end of World War II.

NATO launched Operation Deliberate Force, bombing hundreds of Serbian targets.

"I was told about Clinton," Hajrudin said, referring to the allied forces' intervention. But he had little information about what was going on.

He was sent back to free his hometown; he was now part of the military police, authorized to protect all residents and town property. It impressed him that his commander had given orders to protect the Serbian Orthodox church.

Walking around Donji Vakuf, he was heartbroken. All the stores and restaurants had changed their signs from the Latin alphabet, primarily used by Bosnians, to the Cyrillic, primarily used by Serbs.

Three Bosnian mosques had been leveled to the ground. He was told the Muslim cemetery had been destroyed.

By the time he got to his own house, it was dark. The grass had not been cut in years. "The place was a jungle," he said. His mother had never come back; she had stayed at his aunt's house in Croatia.

He saw his brother—who served in another unit—sitting on the ground, smoking.

"Look at it," his brother said, indicating the house. They had not seen each other in three years.

"I can't see it in the dark. Let's come back in the day," Hajrudin said. Their father had built that house; it meant everything.

"Look at it!" His brother started crying. Sitting down, Hajrudin cried, too.

Together, they went over to the Muslim cemetery.

Most of the headstones were toppled, broken, or defaced. But they walked to the far end, searching in a corner.

"Thank God, my father's stone was still there," Hajrudin said. It had his father's name on it: Mustafa Omeragic.

———

What happened next still haunts Hajrudin.

His brother returned to his military unit, and Hajrudin was sent to help take back Ključ, a small town still held by Serbs. He and five others—all Croats—were told to wait for a brigade; they were replacing soldiers who had gotten drunk. "You could hear shelling far away," he said.

Suddenly, soldiers appeared. "I saw the Bosnian flag," Hajrudin said, and his commander moved toward it. "I followed."

They were immediately surrounded by Serbian soldiers. "Throw me your guns!" somebody said. Then somebody hit Hajrudin on the head, and his gun flew out of his hand.

"Who's the commander?" they asked. "Not me," said all the men except the commander, who was standing next to Hajrudin. A soldier shot him point-blank. Another soldier, loading his gun, pointed it at Hajrudin.

"I started saying my prayers," Hajrudin recalled.

But then somebody said to the soldier, "What are you doing? Do you know how many people from our unit they've caught? We need to keep him alive."

This terrified Hajrudin. He had heard what the Serbs did to prisoners: "They're asking you questions as a tank is going back and forth over you." He had seen soldiers who had escaped; some died afterward from internal injuries.

They asked where his unit was. "I lied to them," Hajrudin said. But he quickly realized they already knew. "They always had better intelligence than us."

They bound the captives' hands and forced them to march toward Mrkonjic Grad, an interrogation center, about 20 miles away. On the way they passed through a Serbian village. "Old guys, 90 years old, they're taking sticks and hitting us," Hajrudin said. They screamed, "Turks!"

The Serbian soldiers just stood by and watched. "I remembered when we captured their people," Hajrudin said, slowly. "We didn't allow anyone to touch those guys."

———

For three days, he was interrogated in a basement covered with water. There were wooden pallets on the floor, where he could sometimes lie down.

Beatings were constant; they especially targeted his knees. As they kicked, they asked, "What is your mission?"

"I don't know," he kept saying. "I've just been sent here."

Now sitting on his couch, Hajrudin gingerly touched his right knee. "It still hurts him," Mersiha said.

But the actual pain was not as bad as his fear: What would happen next? Would they cut off parts of his body?

He knew two of his interrogators. One was a Serb from his hometown. They had gone to the same university and played basketball together. "He was an architectural technologist. I was an engineering technologist," Hajrudin said. He recognized another by his mustache—they used to hang out at the same bar in Travnik. He had worked for the Yugoslav People's Army in intelligence.

The third night of his captivity, this man said, "Listen, this is what I can do for you because I know you and your family. We're going to cover you with a blanket and get you out." He told him not to ask where he was going. "I wish you the best." ———

When Hajrudin pulled off the blanket, he was given a pair of old shoes and a jacket. It was October, extremely cold. Along with other prisoners, he began a brutal 60-mile march to the concentration camp known as Kotorsko.

"They are waiting for you," he said about the camp's commanders. "They know you are coming." He and other new arrivals were lined up: Some were shot. Some were simply beaten.

They put them to work, forcing him and other Muslim prisoners to demolish a mosque in a nearby town, and to cut down trees and plant potatoes and corn.

The International Committee of the Red Cross sent food, toiletries, and cigarettes. "But since we hadn't been registered, we got nothing," Hajrudin said. When delegations from the Red Cross came to check on the camp's conditions, the guards hid him and other prisoners in the woods.

One thing is seared in his memory: a game the guards played with a prisoner nicknamed Beret.

They thought it was funny to name the tall, half-starved, fragile-minded prisoner after the elite US Army special operations force.

Hajrudin knew this man—also a Muslim—from his town. "He had mental issues before the war," he said. "But he didn't do anybody any harm." He had been a strapping 200-pound bartender at a local restaurant.

The Serbs would throw an imaginary soccer ball at Beret. He had to catch it—guessing where it would go, jumping from side to side, like a goalie. On his right were sharp-edged rocks; grass was on his left. "Usually he jumped to the left," Hajrudin said. "Then they'd say, 'No, we did it toward the stones!'"

For each "mistake," they punched, kicked, and hit him with their guns.

Hajrudin was watching this out of the corner of his eye. Just yards away, he and other prisoners were being forced to cut down brush, then burn it. "Guards were waiting by the fire," he said. "They'd beat you with sticks as you got close."

Beret kept jumping onto the grass, his hands reaching for an imaginary ball.

After five beatings, the guards said, "You did it wrong!" and smashed him a couple of times. He stumbled, trying not to fall. He knew if he did, they would only kick him again.

Then the guards turned away. "What—you watching?" they called out to the prisoners cutting brush. "Go work—go work!"

Beret kept standing there.

"He didn't know where to go," Hajrudin said. "He didn't know where to go."

Some prisoners by the fire signaled him to join them.

———

"I'll be right back," Mersiha told her husband and me.

She returned with a video clip a Bosnian friend had sent. "She told me she saw Hajrudin on YouTube." The couple had already viewed it.

Hajrudin was calm as the grainy black-and-white footage started playing. "This was taken November 7, 1995, when they liberated the camps," Mersiha said.

A line of men were shuffling forward. Pale, gaunt, their dark eyes large, they looked barely alive. "That's me," Hajrudin said, pointing to a small man toward the back, with his sharp, even features and high cheekbones. "I was 108 pounds. My head was bigger than my body."

The day he was released, Hajrudin had been waiting to eat lunch. "I didn't know about the peace agreement," he said, referring to the Dayton Accords negotiated on the outskirts of Dayton, Ohio, by President Bill Clinton; the Bosnian, Serbian, and Croatian presidents; as well as representatives from Europe and Russia.

The agreement was signed on November 21, 1995, with all parties agreeing that Bosnia would be preserved as a state, made up of two parts: the Bosniak-Croat Federation and the Bosnian Serb Republic.

The guards pointed to different prisoners about to be exchanged for Serbian prisoners of war: "You, you, you—take your stuff. You have to leave!"

"You don't know what's going on," Hajrudin recalled. "Will you be exchanged? Or killed?"

"Even when they read our names"—about a dozen soldiers were released—"you're thinking something can go wrong."

During the actual prisoner exchange, one Bosnian prisoner was beaten so badly, he was carried out in a blanket to a Red Cross van, Hajrudin said. "After three days, he died."

Hajrudin was matter-of-fact about his own health when he got home. "I was so dehydrated two men had to carry me off the bus."

Much later he realized that in the tumult of war, he had lost his mother's cupboard key.

———

For months after he got home, his mother baked an extra loaf of bread and put it on his nightstand as he slept.

"Sometimes, I'd wake up and eat a little bit," Hajrudin said. "Just one piece of bread—and you have peace of mind."

Other nights, he would lie there holding the loaf against his chest.

"Like this," he said, crossing his strong baker's arms on his chest, and closing his eyes.

He had bad dreams—guards hitting him but he could not feel any pain.

His aunt, a doctor, quickly recognized he needed to be treated for trauma, and had him admitted to a hospital. There, he was seen by a psychologist, a friend of hers. "He said the best treatment was to talk," Hajrudin said. "That when anyone asks you about the war—talk, talk, talk!"

"Another prisoner released with me didn't talk," he added. "He drank a lot, got into fights, and ended up in jail."

During his hospital stay, he questioned himself: Was he mentally ill? He hoped that his ability to ask the question meant he was not.

And he tested himself: What did he believe in? It comforted him that he had said the Shahadah prayer as the Serbian soldier was about to kill him. He realized that throughout the war, he had not lost his faith. "Believers have a better chance," he said.

His love for his mother helped him get through: "In the concentration camp, I would say to God, 'Let me live, so I can have coffee with my mom one more time.'"

———

His healing accelerated when he met Mersiha in July 1996 in Utica, through a first cousin. They immediately became close. "We helped each other," she said. "We talked—always for hours. That's when I heard these stories."

"But he was still not good," she said about Hajrudin's state of mind. "He could explode quickly," especially if other Bosnians in Utica—who had not fought—gave their opinions about the war.

But after they got married in 1998, "all that went," Hajrudin said, referring to his trauma. His recurring dream of being beaten stopped.

He rediscovered the sense of balance he had before the war. "My grandfather always told me, 'Balance is everything.'"

"He's a puppy," Mersiha put in about Hajrudin, laughing. "Since we got married, he hasn't raised his voice."

———

When Hajrudin, on a family vacation, drives through western Bosnia—where he was captured—he is tense. There is no stopping for gas or snacks. No bathroom stops. He wants to avoid being pulled over by the police.

And crossing the border into Croatia, he worries about being detained. When he was in the military police, he had captured and guarded Croats. He is afraid he will run into one of his former prisoners.

"The border makes him numb," Mersiha said, drawing her chair closer.

"Not numb, but uncomfortable," he said.

It has already happened: In 2006, he was walking along a beach in Baska Voda—a beautiful seaside town—with his two older boys, when he saw a powerfully built Croat in a T-shirt and shorts coming toward him.

Growing up, they had been neighbors: The Croat was one of three brothers, all athletes. "They were huge, built up, handsome," Hajrudin said. When the war started, they had joined the Croatian Army.

Seeing him, Hajrudin's mind raced: He had guarded the Croat in a prisoner-of-war camp—and years later had overseen his release during a prisoner exchange.

"I thought, 'If he attacks me, I have to defend myself.'" He worried about his boys—that they could get hurt.

But the Croat came up and gave him an enormous hug. "How are you?" he asked. He had heard bits and pieces about him; news about those in the diaspora travels fast. "How is life in America? These are your kids!"

"Look—my house!" the Croat said, pointing to a beautiful villa on a cliff. It had a large banner flying outside: *We are all NORAC.*

Hajrudin knew what that meant: support for Mirko Norac, a former general in the Croatian Army, who had overseen the murders of scores of Serbian civilians in what was called the Gospić Massacre. He was serving a 12-year sentence. Looking at the villa, Hajrudin remembered the Croat had been in a special unit. The rumor was they had taken loot during the war.

"Would you come in for a beer?" the Croat asked.

Hajrudin's face burned. His words tumbled out—he had to get back to Mersiha, who was waiting at the hotel. In his mind, he replayed every contact he had had with the Croat in the camp.

He was trying to remember if he had ever mistreated him.

I know . . . I know I never touched him, he said to himself.

When they said goodbye, the Croat said, "Remember, if there's anything you need—money, food—let me know."

When Hajrudin got back to Mersiha, he could not speak. He quickly downed four beers.

When he finally caught his breath, he told her the story. Mersiha said, "Why didn't you go for a beer with him?"

"I saw the general. No thank you."

"You're an American citizen. You don't have to be afraid of anyone!"

"I don't want to gamble," he said, reminding her of veterans suffering from PTSD who have committed acts of violence. "It could happen— you never know."

———

Mersiha nodded, recalling that conversation. It was getting late; she could hear her two older boys in the kitchen.

"They tolerate the peace," she said about the Bosnians, Croats, and Serbs. "But it's the Balkans. Throw a match—it could blow up."

Hajrudin shook his head. Despite everything he has been through, he cannot accept that.

He leaned forward, close to Mersiha and me.

"My grandmother said, 'Your neighbors are more important than your brother and sister. If you need help, who will help you? Your neighbor.'"

PART III **NEW AMERICANS**

33. THEY DON'T TALK ABOUT IT

FOR LUPWAY DOH, 38, a leader in Utica's Karen community, it is easy to pick up on the signs of trauma around him—because he sees them in himself.

We were heading toward Rome, a small city 20 minutes from Utica, to see a young Karen woman who had left her husband.

The husband—whose leg was amputated when he served in the Karen National Liberation Army—is addicted to alcohol. "He just had his fourth DUI," LuPway said. "He may be deported to Burma."

LuPway's sympathy is with the young woman, who was abused. But he—and other community leaders—have not completely turned their backs on her husband.

"A friend of mine helped him with his legal problems," LuPway said. If the husband were deported, it would be tough for him to survive.

"But he doesn't want our help now," LuPway added, sounding relieved.

In Utica, each refugee group has leaders, who assist those who are struggling. Mohamed Ganiso, the Somali Bantu community leader who owns a small trucking company, may be hauling cargo cross-country when he gets a call. Sakib Duracak, a contractor and the president of the Utica Bosnian Mosque, may be installing a Home Depot kitchen when his cell phone rings.

These leaders help solve disputes; offer guidance to those overwhelmed; raise money during a crisis; and sometimes act as liaisons between members of their community and the city's institutions: its hospitals, schools, courts, and police force.

And they may sometimes act as chiefs—decision makers—as LuPway and other Karen leaders did in the fall of 2019 when the young woman was thinking of leaving her husband.

LuPway—a soft-spoken man with a long ponytail—was born in Thoo Mweh Hta, a village of about 20 huts on the border of Burma and Thailand. As a child, he was always listening: When the sounds of gunfire and bombing came close, LuPway and his family would run to a Thai village an hour away, crossing the powerful Salween River. When fighting subsided, they would return.

"The threat was everywhere; there was no safety," he said.

When he was six, fighting along the border became more intense; he and his family strapped bamboo baskets filled with clothes and food to their foreheads, and headed deeper into Thailand.

Going down the river with his father, he saw a dead soldier floating by. This was not the first time. Playing with friends by the river, he would sometimes see the bodies of Burmese soldiers who had been caught spying. "We'd say, 'I saw it first!'"

LuPway knows he has been lucky: At the Thai refugee camp, where his family arrived in 1995, his teachers quickly recognized he was a gifted student. He was selected to attend Assumption University, a Catholic university in Bangkok.

He enjoys his work as a college counselor at On Point for College. He owns a two-family house in East Utica with a big yard, where he lives with his extended family.

But he carries around the sounds of warfare. Other Karen do, too.

"It makes us scared to do anything," LuPway said. "Is it going to be the right thing? Is it going to cause harm?"

"We try to avoid conflict and that turns into a vulnerability," he added. "You give away what you have—and people take advantage of your generosity."

The Karen—a tight-knit community in Utica of about 6,000—have in many ways been successful. Hardworking and anxious for their children to do well academically, they are open to interacting with other cultures. Many of the men work at factories, including the Keymark Corporation, Chobani, and Conmed; many women are employed as housekeepers at Turning Stone.

Their children are high achievers. "About 80 to 90 percent of our kids go on to college," LuPway said. There are more Karen students at MVCC than any other refugee group.

But there is a hidden thread of depression—and addiction—among the Karen.

Some men drink heavily at home, LuPway said, trying to blunt memories of the war. If a husband loses control, the wife may call LuPway or another community leader.

"I've seen a lot of women crying and screaming," LuPway said. "They're trying to relieve the stress."

He tries to mediate, and he encourages women to speak to their family doctor. "But the majority—they don't talk about it, even in their family."

If the husband is violent, LuPway calls the police. But the wives do not press charges, he said.

"Men are getting very clever," he added. Knowing they can be arrested for being physically abusive, they have changed tactics: "They say terrible things to their wives, push, and break things."

———

Dr. Natalie Hua, 36, a family doctor at the Sister Rose Vincent Family Medicine Center in Utica, located in one of the poorest sections of Cornhill, does not claim to know what her refugee patients have been through. But she arrived at 16 from Vietnam—not understanding a word of English—so there is a level of awareness.

"I heard the stories growing up," said Dr. Hua, who lived with her grandparents in Brooklyn; her grandfather was a political refugee.

Dr. Hua is one of dozens of immigrant and refugee doctors working in the Mohawk Valley Health System. "I realized we didn't have the cultural competency for such a diverse community," said Dr. Mark Warfel, chief experience officer and former director of the St. Elizabeth Family Medicine Residency Program. "Most people coming from medical school have no understanding of refugees' problems. I felt we should recruit."

In 2000, Dr. Warfel began reaching out to young doctors—from Russia, Burma, and Bosnia—helping them through the steps to become viable applicants. In recent years, about half the medical residents have been immigrants.

They care for patients dealing with trauma and depression—and at high risk for diabetes, hypertension, high cholesterol, and obesity. Some cannot read or write; many have never been to a dentist.

The Burmese diet—heavy on rice and low on protein—contributes to an increase in diabetes, Dr. Warfel said. And refugee kids, just like American kids, gravitate to sugary snacks and drinks. During checkups, family doctors talk with parents and kids about healthy eating, and encourage kids to get outside.

"Green stuff?" Dr. Michael Nemirovsky, a family doctor, asked a lively 10-year-old Burmese boy during a recent checkup. Dr. Nemirovsky made a deal with the boy to try some greens.

It will not be easy: There are no grocery stores within walking distance in Utica's poor neighborhoods; fresh fruits and vegetables are a luxury. It is a pattern repeated in disadvantaged areas across the country.

Utica's children face a serious threat: The city has a higher rate of lead poisoning in children than Flint, Michigan, did at the height of the city's lead contamination crisis.

In Flint, 5 percent of children tested under the age of 6 had elevated blood lead levels, which is twice the national average. In East Utica and Cornhill, 36.65 percent of children under 6 who have been tested have elevated levels.

Most of the city's housing stock—as in other Rust Belt towns—was built before 1978, when the federal government banned consumer use of lead-based paint. Refugees are particularly at risk: Upon arrival in Utica, they have often been placed in poorly maintained houses, where kids may be exposed to lead through plaster dust on windowsills and old paint chips.

Some families live in homes rebuilt after fires. "When a house burns down, lead stays in the soil," said Dr. Stam, who has worked with refugee children treated for lead poisoning. Kids playing in the backyard may get soil on their hands. Later, if they have a snack—without washing their hands—they can ingest lead.

Refugees are also exposed to lead through certain spices, herbal medicines, incense, toys, and pots brought—or imported—from their home countries. The traditional yellow face paint used by Burmese women contains lead.

In recent years, there has been a push to test all 1-year-old and 18-month-old children. If a child has elevated blood lead levels, they are monitored by a doctor—and the county's Lead Poisoning Prevention Program does a home inspection to try to identify the sources and educate the family about things they can do, like using wet cloths to get rid of lead dust.

Zahara's two little boys—and Sofia's daughter, Amrah—are among the thousands of Utica kids affected.

All three were diagnosed with lead poisoning while living in their grandmother's old house on Rutger. "They could have eaten paint chips," Sofia said.

When Zahara moved into her new house, her sons' blood lead levels improved. Amrah's improved while living with her mom in the new apartment.

There is reason to be hopeful: In 2018, Utica was awarded a $3.5 million grant from the United States Department of Housing and Urban Development to help remove lead hazards from homes.

And testing is slowly paying off: In 2007, 39.6 percent of Oneida County children under 6 who were tested had high blood lead levels. In 2016, that dropped to 22.5 percent.

———

Dr. Hua sees a link between her grandparents and her patients: "The way they view pain is very different from Americans," she said. "They don't even mention it; it's a part of life."

When her grandmother fell down the stairs, her CAT scan showed a brain bleed. "She's like, 'I'm good, take me home, I'm fine!'" Dr. Hua recalled, laughing.

Recently, during an examination, Dr. Hua lifted a Somali patient's shirt—and saw hundreds of tiny scars on his back. At first, she thought it was a cultural or religious practice. But he explained the scars were from a traditional treatment he had 20 years ago for back pain. Medicine was inserted through the cuts in his skin.

When Dr. Hua asked, "Do you still have pain?" he said yes. An x-ray showed evidence of an old injury from a fall.

"But he didn't complain," she said. "He didn't ask for pain medication."

Many of Dr. Hua's patients have PTSD—but decline counseling.

"It takes a level of trust before patients will share these things with us," she said. "There are so many roadblocks."

"It's almost like the sun, the moon, and the stars have to line up," she added, before a patient will get therapy.

So, she tries to meet with her patients more often, hoping they will eventually see Dr. Katherine Warden, the only clinical psychologist at the center.

But patients often cancel follow-up appointments. As a first-year medical resident, Dr. Hua was crushed: "I took it very personally." But then she realized some of her patients have transportation issues. Family crises can crop up.

Now, she gives her patients tools they can use at home: breathing and relaxation exercises.

Recently, a young refugee who was sexually abused as a child had a panic attack in her office. "I turned off the light, did guided breathing meditation with her," Dr. Hua said. "She calmed down."

———

Dr. Warden, 34, director of behavioral medicine at the St. Elizabeth Family Medicine Residency Program, has an open approach when counseling her refugee patients: "I don't make people tell me their stories," she said. "It can be retraumatizing."

She lets her patients choose: "If they want to discuss the trauma, they can. But sometimes it's OK to let it sit and be healed."

There is a misconception, she said: "A lot of people think we should be emotionally pain free. That's completely unrealistic." She works with her patients to find a level of pain that is tolerable. "It's becoming used to the new normal."

When first meeting a patient, Dr. Warden tries to find out: What does your anxiety or depression prevent you from doing? What cultural barriers are standing in your way?

Then she comes up with a plan. "That's more effective than trying to talk about how we feel about things."

If patients are afraid to get in a car, she will practice guided imagery with them in her office. Eventually, she will take them out driving.

If a patient has social phobia, Dr. Warden will take them to a nearby coffee shop. As students work at their laptops and families stream in and out, Dr. Warden encourages her patient to order a cup of coffee.

"The point is to become desensitized in a crowded place," she said. And then take another step: Make small talk with a stranger.

"I point out things that work," she said, smiling. "'I like your jacket.' 'The weather is cold today.'"

Whether therapy is effective depends on a lot of factors, she said: the severity of the patient's psychological condition; the patient's general neurological-cognitive capacity; the effectiveness of the translator; the level of family support.

"And how willing they are to engage with the things I say to try," Dr. Warden added.

But it is really about establishing a relationship: "Patients respond if they feel the therapist is empathetic, and genuinely out for their best interests."

Any grasp of English helps, she explained. "But I have made wonderful connections with people who don't speak a lick of English."

Women in violent relationships rarely find their way to Dr. Warden's office. They are mostly locked into their situation and are only identified when the police are called. Social workers will then offer them counseling and shelter through the YWCA Mohawk Valley, which manages the city's emergency domestic services.

But sometimes a woman in an abusive situation comes in accompanied by her husband. If Dr. Warden senses the woman feels scared or uncomfortable around her partner, she asks him to leave the room. "Sometimes, the patient will open up about their troubles immediately. Sometimes not."

Dr. Warden will offer options. "I never tell a patient she has to leave. I let her make up the pros and cons."

Most refugee women—for cultural and economic reasons—choose to stay with their partners.

Dr. Warden helps them navigate their relationships: "For two sessions, I'll let a woman talk nonstop about her spouse."

Then she shifts the focus. "I'll talk about how we can change our own thoughts and behavior, and our priorities."

———

The young woman who left her abusive husband opened the door. Shyly—but confidently—she showed LuPway and me into a large living room.

She had recently moved in but will not be staying long, she explained. The subsidized duplex apartment is $700 a month—too expensive given her salary as a housekeeper at Turning Stone. She is looking for another place.

There was little furniture—just a few chairs and a folding table. But there was a Karen flag on the wall, along with photos of her five kids, and a large portrait of her parents on their wedding day: two solemn-looking young people in traditional clothing.

Her own marriage was arranged by her mother, she said, as LuPway translated from Karen. "These marriages are not always peaceful," she added, smiling.

Though she was coming out of a violent marriage, there was a sunniness about her. Her round face was framed by straight-cut bangs, and she wore a batiked top and pajama bottoms that had teddy bears on them. Her toenails were polished blue.

Her mother had hoped the young man would provide protection for their family; the young woman's father had recently been killed by the Burmese military. But her husband drank and was abusive from the start. "I was too young," she said. Her marriage took place when she was 13. "I didn't know right and wrong."

Her mother witnessed some of the abuse. "But she couldn't do anything about it."

Yet later, when they were all living in a refugee camp in Thailand, her mother suggested she take her kids to a town and find work. But she stayed.

The final straw came late at night, four months ago: Her husband's friends were over, drinking, and talking loudly. "I had to go to work soon," she said, and told them to be quiet. Her work is arduous; she cleans eight or nine large hotel rooms per shift.

After his friends left, her husband opened the front door and all the windows. It was a cold November night; the children were asleep. He started calling her foul names, screaming so the neighbors could hear.

Yet, she has worse memories from childhood, she explained: Burmese soldiers captured her father, used him as a porter to carry their military equipment, then killed him. Her cousin's husband was tortured. Six members of her family lost their legs to land mines.

"We had to suffer a lot when we were kids," she said.

A couple of years ago, her doctor diagnosed her as having PTSD and suggested therapy. "But I was too busy," she said. "It did not happen." Taking antidepressants helped. "But if you take them too long, then stop, you feel frustrated."

After the frightening incident in November, she spoke to LuPway and other community leaders. They said she was free to leave her husband. When she moved out, her husband said, "You find your own way!"

"Yes, I found it," she told LuPway and me. "I always listened to my parents. Now I'm an adult and can do my own thing."

But then her face clouded over. "If he calls, then I don't want to do anything. I start getting nervous, I can't breathe—all these combined feelings."

———

When LuPway got back in the car, he was quiet. Then he said that after dropping me off, he was going to the cemetery to meet the family of a close friend. His friend—who suffered from depression—had recently killed himself.

"We are self-treating," LuPway said, referring to how his community handles trauma. "A lot of us go hiking. We cook in the park in the summer." But it is an uphill battle: Not long ago, he took his close friend to the Finger Lakes.

"I think I handle my trauma pretty well," LuPway added. He often heads to Bald Mountain in the Adirondacks with friends. "By the time I reach the top, I feel better."

And he spends a lot of time in his backyard, growing the vegetables of his country: long beans, pumpkins, and tiny, hot red peppers.

But when nothing works, he drinks a shot of whiskey. "Some nights you cannot really sleep," he said. "Once these thoughts kick in, you can't really kick them out."

34. ON THE BRINK

L IFE IS CRAZY!" Sadia said, laughing, as she patted her belly. "I'm fat now."
Dressed in a sweatshirt and long skirt, Sadia looked rosy, and about 30 pounds heavier. She had been living in the apartment on Dudley Avenue for a year.

"I think I'm perfect," she added, standing in her living room, which had a new cream-colored couch and pillows, a coffee table, and chairs. "There's nothing wrong with a little extra. Ralya says I look 'yummy, yummy.'"

Ralya, who had stopped by after work, laughed.

Chol had moved in with Sadia.

"Before I had an eating problem," she said. "I'd take a bite and I'd feel full. Now I'm happy."

Sadia went to change into her Turning Stone uniform; she had been working as a server, doing the night shift, for almost a year.

Sadia returned in a crisp white shirt and black pants, her hair pulled into a tight bun. At Walmart, where Ralya and Mana worked, female employees are allowed to wear traditional clothing and hijab. At Turning Stone, a uniform is required—and hair must be left uncovered.

Sadia hated the policy; she felt exposed without a head wrap.

But she found the resort a decent place to work. "They help you," she said about her bosses. If you work hard, "you can become a manager, a supervisor, a lead."

"That's inspiring for some people, but not for me," she added. "I don't like the crowd." Guests sometimes complain that someone spat in their food or put hair in it. "You can see they're lying. But the guest is always right."

"Same thing at Walmart," Ralya said, laughing.

"It's all about the guest!" Sadia said. She imitated her manager: "'If you're sad, leave it at home. It's all about the guest!'"

The sisters laughed.

"I don't like my manager," Sadia added. "Not that she did anything wrong to me. She just has a bad vibe. I definitely have to go back and finish Math."

A young woman—a coworker, also in white shirt and black pants—walked in. She had come to give Sadia a lift.

"I thought you forgot about me!" Sadia said, and headed out the door.

———

A few months ago, Sofia and her baby moved back home.

She had loved being on her own—and she relished working full time and splitting Amrah's care with Sadia.

But from the start, her mother refused to accept her moving out. She called constantly, demanding she come home.

When that did not work, "she sent relatives to take my stuff," Sofia said.

Sofia would come home from work and find her bedroom in disarray. Drawers and closet doors were open, her favorite dresses and scarves gone.

"When Chol moved in, that was the end," Sofia said. "My mom started threatening me: 'If you don't come home, I'm dragging your body out.'"

Sofia understood her parents were not going to change—and she did not want to risk a complete break. She hoped to figure out a way to be happy—but still have her mother's approval.

"Your mother's blessing is the best thing ever," Sofia said. "And her curse is the worst. I'm not like Sadia. She doesn't care what people think."

———

At noon the following day, Sadia lay on the couch, wrapped in a blanket. She was thinking about her birthday.

She was turning 20 in three months: It was the end of her teen years.

And her thoughts turned to Chol: "I feel like I've argued with everyone my whole life," she said. "I just can't argue anymore. If Chol and I have a fight, we get over it as soon as we can. I can't hold a grudge with him."

"He makes me think about my actions: What's the consequence?"

From the start, Chol struck her as mature. "He had it all together," she said. He graduated a semester early from high school and worked at a car dealership, cleaning vehicles to be resold. "He was building his credit. He bought himself a car—a nice car."

She was impressed by how focused he was: The next fall, he began college.

Sadia longed to find her own niche: "I want to do something I love." Then she added, teasing, "Maybe I'll be like Cardi B," the rapper who as a teenager worked in a supermarket, then as a stripper, before making it big.

Chol's family had immediately embraced Sadia. "I love his whole family," she said. "His mom is a stay-at-home mom. His sister is a nurse." His dad works as a supervisor at a factory in Syracuse.

They encouraged the underweight girl to eat. "Chol says, 'You can't be so picky. You got to eat like my family.'"

"Everyone in his family is *thick*," Sadia said, explaining that they are from the Dinka tribe of South Sudan, but do not have the slender build of many Dinka. "They've got big old booties and big boobs. They look good."

"It's African," she said. "I like that."

But then, getting up for a glass of water, she fell back heavily, laughing. "I can't even get up no more!" she said. "In the morning, I'm like—uh, uh, trying to get out of bed."

Chol's mother called every day to chat. And brought her homemade cookies with images of different flowers on them.

"Chol knows that I love his mom way more than I love him," Sadia said, smiling. She and Chol considered themselves married. His family did, too.

But Zahara was extremely upset: There was no marriage contract. No dowry.

This did not bother Sadia. "They're putting the dowry together," she said about Chol's parents. "They're not in a rush."

Sadia was in no hurry to start a family, she said. For a while, she was taking birth control pills, but stopped because she was getting rashes.

She was not worried about getting pregnant: "We're too tired to have much sex," she said, laughing. "We're both working too hard."

If she does have kids, it will not be one after the other, she explained. "I don't respect the whole Somali Bantu kid thing. You can't just pop out a baby and have the other kids take care of it. Kids need attention. A whole lot of attention."

"That's what they don't understand," she said about the women in her family.

"You can't have a teenage life if you're always taking care of your siblings."

She wrapped the blanket more tightly around herself.

"I broke away," she said, "because I felt like the least important one. I've been through a lot."

"But I'm so glad I got to go outside and be with my friends." She glimpsed a bigger world.

Sadia had a Yemeni friend at Proctor whose family kept her inside. When they visited Yemen, she had to wear an abaya.

This girl had a Michael Kors bag and the latest iPhone: It killed Sadia to think of having such great stuff—but not being able to show it off.

"If I had a Michael Kors bag, I'd have worn it to the mall!" she said, laughing.

Sadia's life is less turbulent now: She is getting along a bit better with her mother; she has recently joined her older sisters in helping pay their mom's electricity and cell phone bills.

But on the brink of adulthood, old hurts remain: "If my mom had to give one of us up," Sadia said, "she'd give my ass up."

35. SOLO

HEIDI did not know what the year ahead would hold.

She had never lived alone: She had lived with her parents, with roommates. With her ex-husband and kids.

Julia had lots of suggestions: "Momma, you just got to take it one day at a time. We got to have fun." She wanted them to go to rock concerts; take trips to Syracuse and Saratoga; and buy camping equipment and head to the Adirondacks.

"Woman, slow down!" Heidi said.

In her eyes, everything Julia suggested cost a lot of money. "I just want to surprise Ali, and actually save a bunch of money this year," she said. "I've tried my whole life. I can't save a dime—and I'm almost 50!"

"Ali makes a dollar stretch very far," she added. "I burn it." But she planned to take Julia to visit a couple of upstate SUNY college campuses in the fall; Julia was interested in becoming a veterinary technician. That was as far ahead as Heidi could see.

The first Saturday night, after Ali left, Heidi called out from her bedroom: "Julia, I have nobody to sleep next to. Come sleep with me!"

Julia was in Ali's chair, watching TV; she had covered herself with Ali's blanket. She mumbled something.

"Julia, come sleep with me."

"I'm watching."

"Julia, please?"

Julia waited. Then, sighing heavily, she untangled herself from the blanket, got up, and went into her mother's bedroom.

———

Six weeks later, everything felt different.

Heidi had always smoked on the porch. Now, she started smoking inside the apartment.

She missed the smell of Ali's hookah. "It's a cherry molasses, welcoming kind of smell."

She started feeling less social: "I spend half the weekends sitting in that chair," she said, pointing to the recliner next to Ali's. "I'm just kind of a hermit now." She did not see Karen, Bob, or Dana that much.

Even Julia stopped by less often. She had a new puppy she was in love with. Also, Heidi started letting her use her car. But they texted every day.

"I think everybody's kind of leaving me alone," Heidi said, "and I'm grateful for it."

She had time to reflect: She thought about her marriage—and why she had been the one to move out. For so long she felt guilty about this.

Though she loved her children deeply, "Dan was the nurturer," she said. "He was definitely more hands on. I was very pragmatic with my kids—facing things, saying what's on my mind."

They lived in the neighborhood where her husband grew up. Her kids' grandmother and two aunts lived a block away. "They're wonderful," Heidi said. "They had a big hand in raising our kids."

She felt she could not uproot her children from their world.

Though it often felt as if her heart would break, she had returned every night to spend time with them and tuck Julia into bed.

———

His first six weeks away, Ali struggled.

He shared a room, small as a cell, with a young Iraqi-American who rarely looked up from his computer. He refused to speak Arabic with Ali. There was a metal locker between them to give a sense of privacy. There was no bathroom—they had to walk to an outside building five minutes away.

During the day, it was 120 degrees. "Even at night it's hot," Heidi said. "The cold water is hot. You can fry an egg on anything you touch."

The dining hall was a welcome respite. There was a sumptuous 24-hour buffet, with dishes from cuisines around the world.

Initially, Ali went at it with gusto. "Excuse me, my hands are full of crab legs," he told Heidi during a phone call.

But he quickly tired of the buffet. He felt depressed. He lost 10 pounds. He told Heidi, "Pray I make it through at least six months."

Then he made a close friend, also Iraqi.

His new buddy, Bill, was about a decade older; he lived in Texas with his wife. He was Christian, but the two men shared a similar cultural sensibility and sense of humor.

"Ali's extremely modest," Heidi said. He was taken aback that in the public shower, the Americans walk around naked, that "they just don't care."

"Ali and Bill call them Tarzans," she added, smiling.

Ali created an outdoor resting area for the two of them, behind the living quarters. He cleared out debris, put up a tarp, had the engineers build chairs and a table, and brought over an outdoor water cooler and hookahs. He called it Ali Baba Cave.

But he needed a spot to pray. It was hard to find somewhere clean and private. Then, walking around the base, he stumbled on a small chapel.

He spoke with the priest, who gave him his own special area in the back; he started praying there five times a day.

36. RAMADAN, 2019

THAT RAMADAN was a time of transition for Ali, Sadia, and Mersiha. Ali was adjusting to the extreme heat as he fasted. "He's just trying to get through it," Heidi said. Sadia felt exhausted and nauseous, falling asleep the second she got home from work.

And during that month of fasting and prayer, Mersiha and Hajrudin were stepping away from their old world.

They finally closed on their restaurant. And then Hajrudin did what he had dreaded—he quit his job at the senior adult facility, giving six weeks' notice. Afterward, walking toward his car, he felt as if he were flying out an open window, with no mattress below.

Mersiha, too, was full of doubts. "I keep thinking, 'How is this going to work out?'" she said. But then she would think about their years catering: "We are hardworking people. We are ready."

In any case, "there is no going back now," she said, laughing. "We are so done, done, done!"

Mersiha had wanted to wait until after the closing to show her kids the restaurant, and the apartment above it. The three older ones were anxious to see it.

But Elhan refused. "He hates the place," she said.

Elhan was disturbed by all the changes swirling around him. He did not want to move.

Recently, driving down Rutger Street, Mersiha pulled over and pointed to the sprawling old restaurant.

"See, Elhan?"

"No!" he said, refusing to look. "I'm not leaving my house. You can go."

She tried to reassure him: When they moved, he would have a nice new room. They would bring all his favorite things.

"How can you leave *grandma's* house?" he asked.

Mersiha was surprised: He never knew her mother, who had died before he was born. But he had grown up hearing stories. They called their living room couch "grandma's couch."

Mersiha was quiet for a second. "We'll bring grandma's couch," she promised.

"We are the family who never moved," she told me, sighing. "The kids were born in that house, grew up there. This will be a new adventure for us."

———

The fabric of their family life was changing.

Faris graduated in the top 10 percent of his class at Proctor High School and got a full-tuition scholarship at SUNY Poly to study computer engineering technology. "Now two kids are out," Mersiha said, proudly. Ismar was now a junior.

But what made her happiest was how the older boys had turned out.

"They're very humble kids," Mersiha said. "Not the ones to brag."

They understood their parents' lives were about to get more difficult: They pitched in, driving long distances to deliver cakes and babysitting the younger kids while Mersiha shopped for new restaurant appliances: a cake mixer, a convection oven, a display refrigerator, and a refrigerator/freezer combo.

Ajla—a quiet figure in their harried household—was fasting for the first time. "It was her decision," Mersiha said. "I told her, 'Do it when you're ready.'"

Mersiha suggested she start by fasting on the weekends. But Ajla, 12, said, "No, Mom, I want to do it every day."

"She did it easily," Mersiha said. "Much better than we did." Elhan—not wanting to be left out—pretended to be fasting. But he also took a first step: He skipped drinking water from 3 p.m., when he got home from school, until dinner.

It is not easy being a professional cook during Ramadan: Hajrudin usually taste tests everything—soups, stews. Fasting, he simply looks and sniffs.

But Mersiha will put a crumb in her mouth. "I taste—for salty or sweet—then spit it out," she explained. "If I accidentally swallow, it's OK. We're not perfect."

Ramadan is not just about fasting, she said. "It's doing your everyday work and thinking of others who have to go through that suffering every day." It bothered her that her students, exhausted from fasting, fall asleep at their desks.

"I'm like, 'Hello! I'm fasting. It doesn't mean you get to do nothing.'"

———

Mersiha longed for her mother: When she was alive, they spent the holiday together. A few mornings she woke up crying, especially at the approach of Eid al-Fitr, the celebration that marks the end of Ramadan.

Mersiha awakened at 4:30 a.m., anxious.

It was Eid: She quickly got her sons ready for prayers in new, freshly ironed clothes. At 5:40 a.m., Hajrudin and the boys left for the mosque. "Only men go to Bajram namaz prayers," she explained.

Afterward, her husband and sons went directly to her mother's grave at Forest Hill Cemetery in Utica—a burial ground for all denominations—"to say a prayer for her, and for everyone in the cemetery," Mersiha said.

When they returned, she brought out desserts: Her mother's baklava. Her grandmother's hurmasica, a buttery, oblong pastry. And her aunt's jabukovaca, a delicate apple strudel. It was her way of honoring the three women most important to her.

Then she gave out presents: a bottle of Dior cologne for the two older boys to share, and prepaid Apple music cards. She gave Ajla, who loved to draw, a sketch pad and colored pencils. Elhan got Lego blocks.

"Then I went by myself to see my mother," Mersiha said.

It was 11:30 a.m., a beautiful, chilly June day. Mersiha drove to the third section of the cemetery, up on a hill. Then she crouched by her mother's headstone: *Muratovic Ismeta Rod Tekac, 1950–2003, Bosna-USA.*

"As soon as I got there, I started crying," she said. "I couldn't stop."

She got things ready: She cleaned out the vase of forlorn flowers, still there from her last visit—and replaced it with a pot of red roses and white carnations. "In Islam you're not allowed to plant at a gravesite," she explained. "My mom loves roses."

She said a prayer.

And then she began talking to her mother—about Elhan, the funny things he says. "Oh, my God, Mom!" she said, starting to laugh.

She talked about Ajla—how reserved she is. And kind. "Mom, you would like having her help you—she's very patient."

She told her mother how a classmate of Ajla's had refused to return an Islamic book she had lent her. When Mersiha asked the imam for help getting it back, Ajla was distraught; she did not want the girl to get into trouble. "She said, 'Look mom, I found another book I can use!'"

Then Mersiha sighed.

"Mom, you would be so proud that your daughter and son-in-law are getting a restaurant. And you would be so much help if you were here today."

"I will need your help now more than ever."

She added, quietly, "You were such an awesome cook."

On Eid, Mersiha often saw deer in the cemetery. And she always saw butterflies.

It might just be superstition, she said, but she felt the deer and butterflies were signs of her mother. Yet that day—beginning to get cloudy—there were none.

She sat there for about half an hour. Then it started to lightly rain. "Is this you, mom?" she asked, smiling.

"Are this happiness or sadness?" she added, her English slipping for a second. "I know it's a little bit of both."

37. THE MAYOR'S SWEEP

THE NEXT DAY, it was still raining. Mayor Palmieri—5' 11", with salt-and-pepper hair—strode down Bleecker Street, holding a big pair of red pruning clippers. He cut off a low-hanging branch of a tree. Then another. Wearing a dark suit and tie, he signaled a guy in the truck following him to pick up the branches.

His team fanned out behind him: a mix of police officers, firefighters, city engineers, and the heads of various community organizations. Every Wednesday for the past eight years—except during the harsh winter months—he and his team have swept through a different part of the city: run-down blocks of Mohawk Street or a coming-to-life stretch of Genesee.

It is a chance for the mayor to connect, kibitz, troubleshoot—and also campaign for a third term. In 2017, the Utica Common Council passed a local law to extend term limits to 12 consecutive years. A Democrat, the mayor was facing a primary challenge in three weeks from Joe Marino, a city councilman representing East Utica.

"It's the mayor's favorite part of the job," said Marques Phillips, formerly Mayor Palmieri's chief of staff, about the weekly sweep; he is currently Utica codes commissioner and director of city initiatives.

The mayor wanted to give people without access a chance to meet and build a relationship with somebody in city government, he added. "Then if you have a problem, you can figure out who to call."

Not breaking stride, the mayor, 68, cast a homeowner's critical eye on the condition of sidewalks and storefronts. Raising five kids in East Utica, where he still lives with his wife, there was a routine, he said: "Saturday mornings, the kids didn't sleep in. It was breakfast then yard chores."

For 30 years, before becoming mayor, he was a salesman in the carpet and roofing industries, traveling throughout the Northeast. He also represented East Utica on the Common Council and served as deputy public safety commissioner and codes commissioner.

Despite the rain, the mayor's team was cheerful; many have known each other for decades. A firefighter ran out of the Bleecker Street firehouse and quickly hugged Lonnie Jenkins, a tall man who is the recreation director for the City of Utica Youth Bureau. As he walked, Mr. Jenkins, a seven-year veteran of these walks, stoically picked up pieces of litter with a grabber and put them in his bucket.

A thin Black man, all in red—baseball cap, sweatshirt, and sneakers—approached.

"Mayor, I got an eviction notice," he said, explaining he had recently been laid off. "I have a new job starting Monday. But I'm short $440 for rent."

"Do you get Social Security?" the mayor asked.

"I'm only getting $650 a month. What can a man my age do?"

"Who is your landlord?"

"His name is Will. But my real landlord is in Washington, DC."

Jimmy Dongsavanh, a young police officer who is a member of the department's community outreach team, interrupted: "Call 211, they'll give you a list of different social service agencies."

"Will they give me money?"

"Nobody will give you money," the mayor said, firmly. "But the eviction process doesn't happen so fast. Go to the judge and show them proof you got a job."

"Walk with me," the mayor added, "because I got to walk." He picked up twigs and fallen branches as the man fell into step with him.

"Now, what are you going to do?" he reminded him.

"I'm going to tell the judge I have a job."

After the man left, Mr. Dongsavanh turned to the mayor, and teased him. "If you'd given him the $440, that would have been cut short."

Crossing the street, the mayor and young police officer entered a large Vietnamese grocery store and greeted the store's owner, a thin middle-aged woman with a dark bun. Mr. Dongsavanh, who is Vietnamese-Laotian—the first Asian on the police force—chatted with her as the mayor wandered around, looking at the open barrels of fresh melons and dried shrimp.

"Jimmy's known the owner a long time," the mayor said. "She's the mother of his friend." The mayor, who relishes Utica's diversity, added, "Jimmy's fiancée is Italian-Lebanese."

The mayor passed Florentine Pastry Shop, an almost 100-year-old Italian bakery, then a few empty, desolate-looking storefronts. For decades, Bleecker Street has been struggling to make a comeback.

A well-dressed man in his thirties stopped him.

"Mayor, if you would do this one thing for the Muslim community, we would be so grateful."

"What is it?"

"No school on Eid," the man said, referring to the holiday, which had just ended. "If you could push it as a school holiday. New York City has it. Buffalo too. Syracuse—they're voting for it."

"I visited the Kemble Street mosque during Ramadan," the mayor put in.

"But what about making Eid a holiday?"

"I'll look into it at the Conference of Mayors."

Continuing down the street, the mayor said, "The guy owns real estate—convenience stores and housing. Very successful."

The mayor passed Caruso's Pastry Shoppe: Behind the counter, the owner, Carmela Caruso—who has spent a big chunk of the last 50 years in that spot—chatted with a customer.

An overwhelming smell of fried food wafted from a new storefront.

Mimi Anderson, 28—along with her husband—had recently opened a fried chicken joint. It was just a counter, with orange Formica tables and chairs. Though it was 1 p.m., the place was empty.

But generally, they have been busy, Ms. Anderson said: "We already need a second fryer, but it costs $5,000. We'll have to wait." The mayor asked what she thought about Utica.

"The rent is great," she said, "especially compared to where I'm from, Cypress Hills, Brooklyn. There's no traffic. Nobody's in a rush."

Her family's here to stay, she added: She and her husband have a three-month-old daughter. Her husband owned a construction company in Brooklyn and is trying to get a contracting license in Utica.

"New apartment, new baby, new business," the mayor said.

And yet, a year later—like many small businesses trying to get a foothold—the fried chicken joint was gone.

The bearded owner of a bodega across the street signaled him: "Come see!" Entering, the mayor looked around the narrow, fluorescent-lit store. The last time he visited he had admonished the owner about how dirty it was.

"Very nice. Much better!" the mayor said.

It started raining harder. The mayor, who refuses to use an umbrella, stood on the corner. One of the men in his entourage—tall and broad shouldered—pointed to two houses across the street, next to a church. They were in good shape and freshly painted.

"A guy I know bought that house," he said, pointing to the one on the left, "fixed it up himself, and made it into apartments. But he wanted something for himself, so he bought the other one."

The two men stood in the rain, surveying the houses.

"Smart," the mayor said.

———

An hour later, the mayor was back in his office, his white shirt dry. Around him were large renderings of the next stage of Utica's development: the downtown hospital, now projected to cost $548 million, and Harbor Point Project, a plan to develop more than 100 acres of property around the city's historic harbor between the Mohawk River and the Erie Canal.

"I'm the salesman," Mayor Palmieri said, smiling.

In recent years, the mayor has matched almost a dozen abandoned buildings with developers. They have been converted into loft apartments, offices, a grocery store, and a restaurant.

Two new hotels have opened on North Genesee, and two old ones have been given new life: The downtown Radisson Hotel was bought by Marriott and underwent an expensive renovation. And the Hotel Utica was gracefully restored under the Hilton flagship.

New retail stores have appeared, including the outdoor gear store Bass Pro Shops, part of a national chain, and Stewart's convenience stores.

Many people feel downtown is the favored child.

"Do I want to complain about progress—no!" said Samantha Colosimo-Testa, a teacher and former city councilwoman from North Utica. "But there are other areas in the city needing attention."

Some residents would like to see more money spent on quality-of-life issues: fixing deteriorated building facades, cracked sidewalks and roads, and run-down local parks, and funding policing programs to help underserved neighborhoods deal with gun violence.

Ms. Colosimo-Testa would like City Hall to appoint a coordinator to help the refugees adapt. "And to show them what the city has to offer—bike trails in Proctor Park, the Utica Zoo, and the museum," she said, referring to the Munson-Williams-Proctor Arts Institute, the city's fine arts museum.

"They need to know there's things to do besides staying in the house. It's their community, too."

Utica's population is again dwindling, according to recent reports. Between 2014 and 2018, the city lost approximately 1,300 residents.

The pipeline of refugees has been cut to a trickle: In 2020 the city was expecting only about 100 new refugees, according to Shelly Callahan, though there was an expected secondary migration of at least 100 refugees from other cities.

"We're right on the cusp, just holding steady," Ms. Callahan said about Utica's population. It has led to a workforce shortage at companies like Keymark, International Wire, and Turning Stone, which have relied on refugees' labor.

Other Rust Belt cities—in upstate New York and across the country—are also again experiencing population decline. The United States planned to admit no more than 18,000 refugees in the fiscal year 2020, down from a maximum of 30,000 in the one that ended September 30, 2019, according to the Pew Research Center. This will be the lowest number of refugees resettled since 1980, when Congress started the program.

"You have all these communities competing for refugees," Ms. Callahan said. "States are thinking, 'How can we attract population?'"

Refugees helped boost southeastern Michigan—which includes Detroit—contributing up to $295 million to the local economy in 2016 and creating between 1,800 and 2,300 jobs, according to a 2017 study by the nonprofit Global Detroit and the University of Michigan's School of Public Policy.

But the region's recovery is fragile: Roughly 70 refugees arrived in 2018, in contrast to the 21,000 refugees—mostly from Iraq—resettled over the previous decade. The automotive industry and construction companies are struggling to find workers.

Yet Mayor Palmieri says he is not worried about population decline. Small drops in the census do not mean much, he explained: "Many people are afraid to be counted." Kids, opening the door, "often say their elders aren't there."

Another reason he is not concerned: "Once President Trump is out of office, the numbers of refugees will go up."

Utica is not utopia, but it has welcomed refugees, he said, "because we're based on immigration. The immigrants, who came 100 years ago, worked extremely hard to be accepted."

He knows this firsthand: One of his grandfathers arrived from Sicily; the other from Calabria. As a kid, he saw that Italian immigrants were looked down on: "They were viewed as uneducated," he said. In elementary school, he was called names: guinea, greaseball.

"Even in my work as a salesman, innuendos were made. 'You meatball guys.' Occasionally, I'll still hear the rumblings of it."

The mayor has a new reason to feel upbeat: "Cree is coming," he said.

Almost three years before, the $2 billion Marcy Nanocenter plan had fallen apart. But recently Cree, a semiconductor company based in North Carolina, announced it was going to build a $1 billion factory to make silicon carbide wafers in Marcy. Governor Cuomo's office pledged that New York State would provide a $500 million grant.

This would mean a big boost for Utica, though the number of new jobs has not yet been announced. The facility is supposed to be completed in 2022.

———

Mayor Palmieri feels there is no going back: "Utica will be the best little city in America."

He envisions it as a vibrant mix of native Uticans, refugees, retirees, entrepreneurs, and artists moving from downstate, young professionals, families, the staff of the new Downtown Hospital, techies who work at Cree, and visitors.

Many in Utica's Black community do not feel included in this vision.

African Americans have had a longtime presence in the city: Many arrived as itinerant farmworkers—picking green beans—during the Great Migration, then decided to settle in Utica. They were marginalized from the start.

They rarely got jobs in the mills and factories. They knew to avoid certain parts of the city—like Genesee Street, near the elegant Kanatenah Apartments.

Even now, there are few African Americans in leadership roles within the city's institutions.

"What hardworking Black people have noticed in Utica is that historically they didn't get the niceties and access," said Patrick Johnson, who serves as a liaison between law enforcement and the community. His family was one of the first Black families to move into Cornhill, a middle-class immigrant neighborhood, before the city's decline.

It is now predominately working class and poor. Black people and refugees are neighbors.

Many African Americans feel the refugees have been given opportunities—and support—not available to them.

"The hand of welcome is not offered to the Black community," said Freddie Hamilton, an activist and former councilwoman, who moved to Cornhill from Brooklyn about 10 years ago.

This is due to the country's troubled past, she added: "Black–white relations are tough because of our history of slavery, Jim Crow, and institutionalized racism. These are much harder issues to deal with than welcoming new people to America."

The refugees arrive with a different worldview: "They start fresh. They view America as opportunity. They have more hope."

———

For the mayor, the new hospital is at the heart of the city's reblooming. But he is also excited about the Nexus Center, a $44 million sports center, which will be adjacent to the Adirondack Bank Center, home of the Comets. The project—to be paid for by New York State and Oneida County—is designed to have ice hockey rinks that can be changed into turf fields for lacrosse and soccer.

For decades, politicians have talked about developing Utica's neglected harbor, which includes two decayed historic buildings by the waterfront. The mayor wants to turn it into a hub where people can live and work—and also stroll, eat, listen to music, and shop.

City Hall has created renderings of residential and retail spaces; an amphitheater; and public plazas with fountains, period lighting, and native plants.

The city and state have taken initial steps: The state provided $6 million to improve the entrance to the harbor and to reconstruct the concrete bulkhead. The city has improved the roads leading to two areas of the harbor, hoping to attract private investors.

Always optimistic, the mayor said he expects "shovels in the ground in 2021."

———

The next day, I walked down Hotel Street—past a couple of abandoned 19th-century brick houses—heading toward the harbor. Water Street was ahead, and beyond that a long field before the narrow brown ribbon of the Mohawk River.

A bit farther, across the railroad tracks, is the land designated for Harbor Point.

A man was standing in the field, holding a huge, handmade kite, like those I had seen downtown.

Wearing a baseball cap with black pom-poms over his ears, he signaled to me: "Come!"

I made my way toward him, crossing traffic: His kite had a purple and blue butterfly painted on it. And there was another kite—with pastel-colored fish—attached to a makeshift stage.

"Everybody calls me Kevin the Kite Man," he said. A small Black man with a weathered face, he has been making kites for 15 years.

His real name is Kevin Hines. Born in Philadelphia, raised in Brooklyn and Harlem, he arrived in Utica a couple of years ago and is staying with a relative at a housing project downtown.

He is an ambassador of kites: "I've put them on the roof of Madison Square Garden. I've brought them to the UN. I put them around Utica. I'm trying to show people to aim high."

"It gives you a feeling of freedom," he said about flying kites. "Independence. You've got to do it by yourself." He has taught kids, pregnant women, and people in wheelchairs.

He is comfortable in Utica; residents chat with him as he places his kites in odd spots. He got a young couple to fly kites in the snow.

The city has given him ideas: At night, he attaches lights to his kites. He wants to paint a mural on multiple kites—and fly them together.

"We got to have a city-wide competition."

He has his own technique: "Let me show you."

He placed the string of his butterfly kite in my right hand. "That's your anchor." He put the ball of string in my other hand.

It was a sunny day, with some wind coming off the water. "You don't let out a lot of string, just keep tapping up," he said, showing me how to let go of a little string at a time. He made a soft sound—"puh, puh, puh."

I was surprised: The kite rose easily—like a butterfly above the field.

"If it sinks, just lift your hand," he cautioned me. "Just let the wind do the work."

38. SADIA'S LIST

SADIA moved slowly around the new apartment she and Chol had moved into; she was wearing a patterned baati—a long, loose dress—and a knit cap.

"I'm five months pregnant," she said, smiling. "I was shocked—but happy. At first, I wanted a girl, somebody to dress up with. But I'm happy it's a boy."

Did she remember saying, at 15, she would have one child, a boy?

"No!" she said, laughing.

Since the start of her pregnancy, she has had stomach pain; she can hardly eat. "I don't like feeling sick," she said. "But outside of that, it's the biggest blessing I ever had. In life, I feel like I had to deal with a lot. I finally have peace."

Sadia has circled back to Rutger Street, several blocks from her grandmother's house, though she has no contact with her. Her apartment —near Proctor Park—is on the first floor of a Victorian house painted white with blue trim.

Sadia seemed more focused: She was working at a local greenhouse, spraying and cutting tomatoes. She had no complaints. Her hours are 7:30 a.m. to 4 p.m. But she always stays till 5 p.m., she said.

"You work fast. It's safe and close by, and it's exercise."

She was also taking classes at BOCES, trying to get ready for the math Regents. She was frustrated that she kept failing the practice tests.

But her old dreams have come back: "I feel everything's ahead," she said, sitting on a couch with big pillows. "Not the modeling part," she added, smiling, "because I'm chubby and the shortest person ever. But I still want to write—I write in my notebook all the time."

And yet, something tugs at her: "I know you're supposed to work hard all the time for *yourself*," she said.

"But some people find their purpose in their kid."

"I'll have to work 10 times harder now," she added, heading into the kitchen past a hamburger and some onions, sitting in a skillet. "I don't want to talk about the stuff I'm going to do—just do it."

The apartment was spare, but you could feel Sadia's flair: There were white candles and anemones in a vase on the glass-covered coffee table. In the master bedroom, a zebra-striped quilt covered a mattress on the floor; a clothing rack was draped with yellow, red, and purple scarves.

"Chol's excited about the baby, especially since it's a boy," Sadia said, peering into the second bedroom, which she will turn into a nursery. Chol was taking time off from school, working as a card dealer at Turning Stone to earn money.

His family was extremely supportive. "His mother loves me to death," Sadia said, smiling. "She always checks up on me." Every few days, she brings big containers of food—homemade bread and meat stew soup.

How does Zahara feel about her pregnancy?

"She doesn't say nothing bad about it," Sadia said, shortly.

She was hurt by her sisters' response: "I always feel locked out by them. But I would give them the world."

It was Sadia's day off; she was exhausted and wanted to rest. But she felt pressured: She wanted to get the baby's room ready. She wanted to pass the Regents and start taking classes at MVCC. "I'm so stressed," she said. "I would just love to go somewhere and cry, but I've got to be strong."

"It's so hard to succeed in this world," she added, "though it's easy for some people."

Recently, it hit Sadia that she suffered from depression. It started in middle school but got worse after the big fight with her mom. "I still have to deal with it," she said.

Has she talked to a therapist?

"No, I can't afford it."

But she sought help senior year, she added. She went to see her guidance counselor after returning from Lewiston, Maine.

"I said, 'Hey, can I talk to you?'"

"I told her everything: 'My life is falling apart. I'm homeless. I don't feel safe at home—I feel it's like mental abuse.'"

"She didn't try to comfort me. She didn't say, 'Let me find you a place to stay tonight.' She just goes, 'I'm going to call your mom.'"

Zahara came to the counselor's office; the two women spoke as Sadia sat there.

"I know how kids are," Sadia recalled the counselor saying. Sadia felt her mom and the counselor were discussing all the things she did wrong.

"Honestly, I just blacked out, and went back to class."

A week later, Sadia finally went home. "The counselor never even called to see how I was."

Sadia, now 21, glanced toward her baby's room. And her spirits lifted.

Smiling, she showed me a list she had made: 30 things to do before the baby's birth.

It included: *Glow in the dark stickers, Lavender, Eat healthy, Save money for my first baby trip, Go back to school, Get my baby pictures, Food stamps, Make a dentist appointment, A video camera and lights, Start a small line of lipsticks and gloss, Prayer I need to start ASAP.*

"I'm going to do audio books with my baby," Sadia said, firmly. "I'm going to read a poem to him every day."

"I want him to know me. I write to him every single night before I go to sleep."

39. THE VISIT

ALI looked tan and extremely fit on his visit home, after being away for eight months—and somehow bigger than before, sitting in his living room in Utica, near the large portrait of himself.

But he looked shell-shocked.

Heidi knows that switching worlds is not easy.

There was a previous visit home, months ago—for just a few days: At the airport, they kept checking each other's faces, delighted, then they would look away.

But the visit was taken up by mundane things: Ali gave his old car to Bob. Had a doctor check his knee. He bought a virtual reality headset, and a pair of military pants at the army/navy store. Afterward, they said to each other, "Did that even happen?"

This visit would last two weeks.

Heidi looked radiant and a bit nervous. She was wearing makeup—rare for her—and a pretty, low-cut blouse. Recently she had decided to quit her job; she was now working in the office of a social services agency that worked with foster kids, and she loved it.

She shot a look at Julia, sitting in Ali's recliner. "Julia—that's Ali's!" she said.

But Julia—laughing and chatting with Kurrine, who was in Heidi's chair—ignored her. They were in a giddy state: They had just gotten acceptance letters from colleges. Julia would be going to SUNY Delhi, Kurrine to SUNY Buffalo.

Ali, sitting on the couch, did not seem to mind. He smoked his hookah, waiting for Bob and Dana to arrive.

Heidi sat next to him, quietly, then went to check on dinner.

Ali came over to me and started talking about his work, interpreting for high-ranking coalition officers advising the Iraqi forces.

"It's 12 hours a day, and we're on call 24/7," he said. "It's exciting, addictive."

He is finally allowed to say where he is based: "I'm in the middle of Baghdad," he said, grinning.

His team is within a small area of the Green Zone, which was the governmental seat of Saddam Hussein's Baath Party before the invasion.

"We're not free to come and go," he explained. "But everything is close to us: the chow hall, gym, movie theater. There's an Iraqi rock band and a fire pit."

"But I'm 10 minutes from my house," he said, quietly. "And I can't go home."

Initially, Ali did not tell his family he was in Baghdad; he worried about their safety. But his team manager said he needed to inform them: "We don't want them going to the embassy asking for you."

The manager said he would arrange for Ali's family to visit. It would be highly secret. Nobody would see them leaving their house.

"I told him no," Ali said. "I can't see my mom and sisters for a day, and then say goodbye. And I can't guarantee their security. I can't risk it."

"So, I'm home—and I'm not home."

Yet his mother is happy he is nearby, he added, smiling. "She told me, 'We feel like you never left.'"

Karen arrived and gave Ali a big hug. "KK!" he said, affectionately. She had driven Heidi to the Syracuse airport to pick him up.

"Dana just called," Heidi said, coming out of the bedroom. "She, Bob, and the kids all have the flu—they can't come."

Ali looked devastated.

"Do they need help?" he asked. "I can drive them to the hospital."

"They're just in bed," Heidi said. "We'll see them next week when they're better."

"Ask them if they need anything."

For a few minutes, he was quiet.

What has eased his time away is his friendship with a new roommate. "He's a character, very funny," Ali said.

The room they share is tiny, and when Ali first entered, he brought along a curtain, thinking they would divide the room for privacy.

"My roommate said, 'You don't need that. I won't look at your bra and underwear!'" Ali laughed.

Two big men, they manage to coexist: Both use the middle of the room for prayer. They like Arabic TV on, even when they sleep. They like drones, soccer, hookah.

"After work, I put on my headphones," Ali said, "go on YouTube, and play stand-up comedy in Arabic. I fall asleep in five seconds."

Looking around his living room, he drew a circle in the air: "I miss all this," he said. "Heidi and home. Julia. Bob and Dana, their kids. KK. And the lakes."

"Shopping," he added, smiling. "Ollie's, Best Buy, Walmart. I miss looking—and the possibility of buying."

And yet, he was signing up for a second year in Iraq.

"I just did the medical exam yesterday," he said. He is waiting to be cleared.

After completing a second year, he would have enough money to buy a house without taking out a mortgage. "I don't like payments," he said. "Even if I buy a car, I pay outright."

For $70,000–80,000 cash he and Heidi could get a three-bedroom house. "I like this section of East Utica, close to Proctor Park." He would also consider New Hartford. "It's cleaner, greener."

But there is another reason he is signing up again: The work is riveting to him.

"When we're making plans to do something, and it happens, it makes me very happy," he said. "Every word I say or translate—if it helps capture or kill a terrorist, I'm glad."

"We are brothers," he added about his team. "Even before I left Iraq, they called to say they missed me."

Ali's team is based near the courthouse—set in the old Baath Party headquarters—where Saddam was tried and convicted.

For years, Ali has been fascinated by the courthouse. "They turned it into a museum," he said. But he never got to see it. "They had tours, but then stopped giving them. I wanted to see the court so bad."

Saddam's trial was a turning point in Ali's life.

Saddam was being tried, along with seven others, for the torture and killing of 148 Shiite men and teenage boys from the town of Dujail, 35 miles north of Baghdad, after an assassination attempt against him there in 1982.

The trial itself seemed like a miracle to Ali. "If anybody had told us we'd be in charge . . ." he said, shaking his head. "We suffered so much under Saddam."

Ali was a public affairs officer, organizing Arab media during the trial. He and his team spent six months preparing for it, making sure every Arab household had free access.

"I'd worked so hard, I thought I'd be the first person in court," he said. And on the morning of October 19, 2005, the first day of the trial, he dressed carefully, in his best suit.

When his supervisor told him to stay in the office to monitor the coverage, he was crushed. "I took off my suit and tie," he said, "and lay down."

During that first session—which lasted only three hours—Saddam remained defiant. He made fun of the American military occupation. He refused to recognize the court's authority.

The trial was adjourned until November 28 to allow Saddam's lawyers to prepare.

The night of the 27th, a friend from the American Embassy called Ali: "Are you ready for tomorrow? You're going."

This time, Ali dressed differently: "I put on Italian black boots, black pants, a black shirt, and a long, black leather coat," he said. "I had a little hair then," he added, touching his bald head, "and I put it back with gel."

"My friends called me the Angel of Death."

In the courtroom, journalists and high-ranking officials of the new Iraqi government sat behind bulletproof glass.

Ali was behind glass, too. Right by the exit door.

"I was standing and waiting. I was like, 'Please God.' Then the door opened."

"He's a tall man; his skin was yellow-white," Ali said, describing Saddam.

In his manacled hands, he held a green-backed Koran.

"Saddam walked like he was tired, until he was in front of me," Ali said.

"Then he stopped and looked at me from my black boots to my black shirt."

Ali jumped up from the living room couch—and crossing his arms across his broad chest, showed me how he had stood, glaring at the former dictator of Iraq.

For Ali, this encounter was real—and personal. As a child, he was terrified his Iranian mother would be taken away by the police. As a young man, he lost his brother and nephews to Sunni insurgents.

He blamed Saddam for Iraq's fall.

"Iraq was the number one country in the Mideast," Ali said. "A rich country. With one job, you could support a family. People were happy. Through Saddam's stupid strategy—surrounding himself with people of his tribe, who were loyal killers—he got us into the eight-year war with Iran."

"Half of Iraqi young men were killed," he added. "It was hard to find a piece of bread or cooking oil. People forget that."

There was laughter coming from the dining room table: Two old friends of Heidi's had arrived. Heidi was telling a story about a surprise 22nd-birthday party she threw for Karen.

"I brought in this beautiful chocolate cake," Heidi recalled. "Karen kept saying, 'Oh, I'm so surprised!'"

"I said, 'No, you're not! You've known about it for weeks. You told me everything you wanted!'"

A massive cake fight started: Heidi pushed the cake into Karen's face. And Karen—small but strong—lunged at Heidi, toppling her.

"Everybody jumped in," Karen said, laughing.

Later, "we all went up to the bathroom, took off our clothes, and washed ourselves," Heidi said.

Just as the story was ending, Ali came over. Sitting down next to Heidi, he smiled. He helped himself to some salad and orzo with olives and almonds, and began eating.

40. RENOVATING

AS SOON AS Hajrudin started renovating the old restaurant, he found extensive water damage behind the decrepit wood paneling in the party room. Behind the large refrigerator. Behind the acoustic tile in the ceiling. Under the long bar, and under the floorboards.

This infuriated—and energized—Mersiha.

"He hid it!" she said about the former owner, recalling how he had refused a second round of inspections. The inspector had been unable to move the refrigerator to see what was behind it. She wished she had stuck to her offer of $165,000. "If I see him now, I will not be quiet!"

Hajrudin took this setback—which would cost them thousands of dollars—as if he had been slugged. Mersiha had never seen him so disappointed.

"I just don't have the strength," he told her.

He worried—maybe he should take a part-time job to help pay for the extra costs. But Mersiha reminded him that he would make so little—it was best to keep renovating the restaurant full time.

She opened four new credit cards.

Hajrudin dug in: He changed the basement beams, cleaning and bleaching everything. Then he put in new walls and flooring. He rewired the electricity and put in new outlets.

"He started to see there's light at the end of the tunnel," Mersiha said.

Mersiha was in contact with the owners of cafés she admired in England, Italy, and Croatia. Talking with them helped crystallize what she wanted: a cool, colorful environment that would draw in young people, as well as others. She wanted her café to have a European feel.

Her model was EL&N, a chain in London. "It's the most Instagrammable café," she said. "In every corner, you can take awesome pictures." The cafés have pink banquettes, smooth surfaces, and walls of tiny fabric flowers.

Mersiha expressed disdain for a popular brick-walled café in downtown Utica. Old-fashioned is out, she said. "A modern look is in."

She planned to have a curtain of flowers, like EL&N's, at the entrance, where people could take photos; she hoped it would distract customers from the restaurant's run-down facade. Next year, after they make some money, the couple plan to renovate the facade.

Mersiha carefully chose every element of the new restaurant: pink and blue jelly glasses, white plates, comfortable velvet-upholstered chairs and love seats. Seating will be roomy—so people can relax.

But it is all about getting on Instagram, Mersiha said: She is proud she has 16,000 followers. All day long, she connects with them. People keep asking: "When will the new restaurant open?"

———

To walk through the restaurant—an enormous construction site—is to be daunted by what the couple have taken on.

The former owner left a lifetime of debris—sports trophies, broken machinery, old lamps—which will have to be dumped. Plates, mugs, and cups are stacked everywhere. Old wires are strewn about. The big kitchen, with its old, stainless steel counters, looks Dickensian.

The couple have been renovating the party room so they can start catering. One wall was just painted—a cool, pearly gray. But the room is jammed with a dozen tables covered with junk; a frayed red carpet is underfoot.

A long, dark corridor opens onto the cream-colored ballroom. There is room for dozens of tables. But it looks abandoned, eerily empty, except for an army of black and burgundy chairs.

The café—the heart of the complex—is quickly coming together.

On a recent Sunday at 6 p.m., Mersiha brought a pizza for Hajrudin, who was working alone. He had just put in new wood floors. The ocean-gray wall facing the mahogany bar seemed to glow.

As they stood by the bar, admiring how wide and elegant it is, Hajrudin said, "We can put stools here, and customers can sit."

"No," Mersiha cut him off. "I like that space open."

"But it would be so pleasant—"

"No!"

But there was no hostility. They wandered around the empty space, talking about things to be done. Mersiha said she would start painting the party room on Monday.

There was an underlying sense of urgency. It was October 2019; they were hoping to open in December.

She and Hajrudin felt the gravity of their situation.

Their upstairs tenant had recently left; the apartment's toilet had leaked through the restaurant's ceiling. The whole apartment now needed to be redone.

They had taken money out of their 401K to buy the building. Everything since then has cost far more than they expected. They were out of cash.

"My husband thinks I'm too far out," Mersiha said, gathering some bags as she and Hajrudin got ready to leave.

She knew they were on a cliff: "We don't know what's going to happen." They could fail.

She shrugged at the thought. "We will handle that. We have been through worse."

She shut off the café's lights; their kids were waiting for them at home.

"There's no success without risk," she said.

41. THE BABY SHOWER

THERE WAS some confusion about when the baby shower would start: Sadia had told people 2 p.m., then pushed it back to 5 p.m. The address she gave turned out to be a locked church on a quiet street in Syracuse.

"Just come over to my in-laws' house," Sadia said when people called, confused. Then everybody could head to the party together.

But at 5:30 p.m., Chol's family was still getting ready.

"Africans are always late," Sadia said matter-of-factly.

It was a hot July day: In an upstairs bedroom, Sadia leaned close to a fan and closed her eyes. She was wearing a long-sleeved shift to protect her party dress—it was making her even hotter. Only two weeks from her due date, even walking was difficult.

She wore mermaid-colored eye shadow, and her hair—generally hidden under a head wrap—was in long strands of dense curls. Chol—a thin, sweet-looking young man—popped in for a second to check on her, then headed back downstairs to run party errands for his mother, Amal, who had been cooking for two weeks.

Some of his siblings fanned out around Sadia. Chol's 9-year-old brother was ironing his pants on the bed. Another brother was lying down, watching a video. A teenage sister was helping an aunt with the delicate job of pasting on false eyelashes. His youngest brother—a stocky 5-year-old in shorts—was vigorously applying lotion to his arms.

"Bro, can you put some on me?" Sadia asked. She indicated her feet, covered in a lacey henna pattern. Slipping off the bed, the little boy began rubbing cocoa butter into them.

"Thank you."

Sadia's family was new to the idea of a baby shower. "We're not really sure what it is," said Sofia, who had just arrived with her daughter. "But it seems like a good idea," she added, referring to the gifts. "I wish I'd had one."

The baby shower was Amal's idea. Tall and elegant in a long traditional dress, she moved around her small kitchen, ladling beef and lamb stew into large aluminum trays and packing up salads, macaroni and cheese, and cakes.

Sixteen trays had already been taken over to the local school, where she had rented an event space in the basement. The DJ was already there, setting up. Blue and white balloons were hung, as well as a sign: *Welcome Little Prince.*

Sofia was one of the few people attending from Sadia's family.

Ralya was also there: She had recently married Siddi, a good-natured young Somali Bantu man she has known since middle school. It was not an arranged marriage; they dated for two years.

He appreciates Ralya: "He knows I have a wild side," she said, laughing, "that I've always been spoiled."

The couple did everything *right*: Siddi asked her grandmother's permission to marry Ralya.

"I prayed money for him!" Halima told Ralya, meaning that she had prayed for a good man—and given money to charity to help her prayer along.

Siddi's family provided a dowry of cash, dresses, scarves, jewelry, furniture, rugs, drapes, and a large-screen TV.

The couple had a big Somali Bantu wedding at an Italian banquet hall in New Hartford. Ralya honored the traditions: She made five entrances in five splendid outfits. As she sat in a gold-painted chair, her aunts lovingly draped colorful scarves over her head and showered her with dollar bills.

The couple waited to have sex until after their wedding.

In contrast, Sadia and Chol broke every rule: Sadia got pregnant without any of the protections Zahara wanted for her.

"If your daughter is married the right way, everybody cares for you," Ralya explained. "My mom wants the same thing for Sadia and Mana."

Ralya did not even bother making an excuse for her mother's absence from the baby shower. Zahara had not wanted her younger girls to attend.

"Sadia and my mom," Ralya said, shaking her head. "I leave them to God!"

At 6 p.m., Sadia's father-in-law, Moyluk, a kind-looking man in a Panama hat, was still greeting his relatives arriving from Rochester. Their cars, parked on the street, were stuffed with gifts: baby clothing, jumbo packages of diapers, blankets, and toys.

Moyluk signaled for his youngest daughter to give those arriving a bottle of cold water.

The small house—though darkened by window drapes—was sweltering.

Sadia sat on the living room couch, trying to stay cool. Chol's aunt offered her Sudanese flatbread; she shook her head. "The things I used to like, I don't like," she told me. "But I never drank tea before—you fill it with powdered milk. It's delicious."

Sadia checked her makeup, using her iPhone. She nodded at her reflection, pleased: "I still got it."

Suddenly, Moyluk announced they were leaving for the party.

Sadia struggled to take off her long shift. But her belly was too big. She collapsed against the couch, laughing.

Chol's teenage sister—a bandana over her long braids—helped her peel it off.

And then Sadia's party dress was revealed: She was wearing a low-cut white minidress, skintight over her baby bump. A gold necklace and bracelets glowed against her skin.

"My mother-in-law gave them to me," she said.

For years, I had only seen Sadia covered up, head to toe. Even she looked shocked. "I've never worn anything that showed so much," she said, looking down at her cleavage.

But she was happy. And her young sister-in-law gently put her hand on Sadia's belly, stroking it to help her cool off, before getting into the car.

42. THEIR GENERATION

SADIA found a way to see her younger sisters: Ralya brought them to her house on Jay Street, which she rented from her mother, and Sadia visited them there.

"My mother doesn't want them to see me," Sadia explained.

She felt particularly close to Zamzam, now a tall, thin 13-year-old. "She's the sweetest one in the family," Sadia said. But she knew how to stick up for herself. Recently another sister, who had just bought expensive makeup, teased Zamzam about having the darkest skin in the family.

"I don't need makeup for my beautiful Black skin," Zamzam said, and walked away.

Sadia no longer saw her younger sisters as so different from her: "They think for themselves," she said. "They uncover their hair, wear what they want, listen to what they want."

"But it's not just them," she added. "It's their generation. Their American generation."

At home, Mana was still in charge—yet things were shifting.

Their mother was working full time at Walmart, after giving birth to her 13th child. On a Friday afternoon, Mana assigned her siblings the formidable task of cleaning the whole house.

She promised: If they did a good job, she would take them to a fair in Utica.

This was a big treat. They had all gone last year and loved it—no ride was too scary for the older kids. Mana had already bought the tickets, which were expensive.

But they would have to hurry. It was already late afternoon, and the fair closed at 8 p.m.

"They suck at cleaning," Mana said matter-of-factly.

The kids were making a racket on the second floor. She yelled up at them, "No clothes or garbage on the floor!"

Picking up Luqman, her new baby brother, she kissed his cheeks, then tickled him under his arms; he giggled wildly. Mana mentioned Sadia's pregnancy: "I'm happy for her."

Mana had always thought she would be the one with kids and that Sadia would not. "It turned out the opposite," she said quietly.

As always, Mana was wearing a headscarf and long skirt; the word *Love* ran down the sleeves of her blue jacket.

Like a queen, Mana has her methods of control.

She rewards those who are good, with candy from Walmart. Those who misbehave get ignored. This works, she said, "because they all want my attention."

In high school, "I worked all the time," she said, referring to running the household with Ralya. When their two little brothers were diagnosed with lead poisoning, she and Ralya dealt with the doctors and got the boys into Head Start and a special tutoring program.

There was no fun, no outlet: "I didn't have a cell phone or tablet, like my younger sisters do."

Now it is her turn: She expects to be waited on.

"The children wake me exactly at 9:30, when I need to get up for work," she said. "They lay out my clothes, bring me food and water. And they clean my room."

Halima, 14, approached Mana.

I had never seen Halima without a hijab: Her waist-length hair was in a hundred tiny braids, some twisted into an elaborate knot on top of her head, some raining down. Instead of her usual long skirt, she wore tight jeans, torn at the knees.

"Ma'am," she said, smiling but cautious, "The fair will be over soon. Can we finish when we get back?"

"Ma'am!" Mana mimicked her, annoyed. "No, you have to finish now. Let's see what you've done."

Halima followed her upstairs. Mana swept past her 5-year-old brother in the hallway, gathering trash—old candy wrappers and a penny—into a garbage bag. Her 2-year-old sister stood watching him, transfixed.

Mana headed into her bedroom. It was large and sunlit, one of the nicest rooms in the house.

She stared at her double bed with its pretty floral quilt. And at the large pile of clothing in a corner.

"You didn't change the sheets?" she asked, furious. "You didn't put away my clothes?"

"It's too much work," Halima said. "Can't we do it later?"

"It's too much work?" Mana said, her voice rising. "Should I add more?"

"We're always working!" Zamzam said, appearing with a broom. She also was without a hijab, her hair in braids. She looked like an American teenager in a long-sleeved black racing shirt and jeans.

"I pay for the Wi-Fi!" Mana said. "You want me to cut the Wi-Fi?"

"Not the Wi-Fi," Halima said quickly, looking devastated. "We'll do it."

———

Twenty minutes later, on her way downstairs, Halima smiled and flashed a peace sign at Mana.

The gesture puzzled and aggravated Mana. "Oh, is that what people do now?" she said.

But then they were all downstairs, excitedly putting on sneakers. And they were one organism again.

It was lightly raining outside. The older children helped the younger ones pull on jackets. One of the boys wrapped a plastic bag around himself. Abdiwle—now a 6-year-old with a shy smile—left his pink stuffed bunny by the door.

Mana was as excited as the kids. She shepherded the youngest into the car, strapped the baby into his car seat, and waved to the others standing on the steps. They would walk the half mile to the fair, which was next to the Utica Zoo.

"They're precious to me," Mana said, glancing at the young ones in the back seat.

It was a gray day, and the fair was in its last hours. But there were still dozens of kids lining up to go on rides, many from large refugee families. A Dominican mother carried a big red panda she had won. A Vietnamese woman ran after her two grandchildren.

Ralya showed up, delighting her siblings. She was majestic in a long, purple patterned dress. Like her younger sisters, her hair was uncovered and twisted into long braids. She entered fully into the spirit of the fair: She paid $5 and tossed three balls into a bucket, trying to win a big, plush bear. Each one hit its mark—but then popped out. She was disappointed; they were superballs, with too much oomph to stay put.

Then she and Halima went on Avengers, a neon-blue roller coaster that rocketed to the side, then circled like a moon.

When the ride finally stopped, Halima hit the ground exhilarated, but unsteady. Ralya looked refreshed.

Mana did not go on any rides; the baby was strapped to her back. But her face—framed by her brown head wrap—was joyous and unburdened.

Laughing, she watched her siblings go on ride after ride. She threw her arms up; she called out to them. She took pictures with her cell phone. Disembarking, the younger ones ran to her, clutching her long skirt.

At that moment, it felt like Mana—adored and feared—would rule the house forever. The older girls were changing; they would grow up and be replaced by the younger ones. But Mana would somehow stay put.

Nobody could have guessed that in just months, Mana, 26, would remarry. Zahara arranged it; she knew the young man's mother from the refugee camp. He was 22 years old—and Mana liked him very much.

The teenagers buzzed around Mana before wandering off.

Zamzam ran into a classmate, a short Vietnamese boy with glasses, and gave him a hug. He came up to her chest. "That's my best friend," she said.

The light was fading. Soon their mother would be home from work. And Mana would leave for the night shift.

Mana gave a signal: Like a flock of birds, the 11 siblings started heading out.

43. SIX MONTHS

I'M LOSING IT," Heidi said, cheerfully, about her state of mind in the final stretch. In six months, Ali would be home. She pointed to the heaps of light blue, purple, and gray yarn on a bench in her living room, and to a blanket she was making for Ali.

"At night, I chain-smoke and knit."

To protect herself, Heidi tried not to pay much attention to news about Iraq. But at the beginning of October 2019, the news was alarming: Iraq seemed to be descending into chaos.

Violent demonstrations had broken out across the country, driven by people's anger about poor services, corruption, and unemployment. Counterterrorism police were sent to stop protesters from storming the Baghdad airport. And police had used tear gas, rubber bullets—and later live fire—to stop crowds from marching close to the Green Zone, where Ali was stationed.

A curfew had been imposed; the internet was temporarily shut down. During the first few days of protests, at least 91 people were killed and more than 2,000 wounded.

Heidi was distraught, wondering if Ali was OK. And she was frustrated, knowing that every text and email was monitored. Every day she asked him: "How are things going?" He always answered: "Everything's good. Don't worry."

Heidi forced herself to stop thinking about Ali.

She focused her anxiety on Julia, adjusting to her first year at college.

"I didn't realize the added stress of not having Julia here," she said. "I'm always worrying, worrying about her."

At night she could not sleep, picturing Julia drinking, then driving. Or flunking out of school. But Julia's behavior was relatively tame: At a party, she drank heavily from a punch bowl and called Heidi as she was throwing up. She got a dinosaur tattoo. Her midterm grades were mediocre.

Yet Julia was feeling happy, changed: For the first time ever, she had a male buddy to hang out with. She relished barn duty: feeding and cleaning the agricultural program's numerous cows and goats. She had always had wanderlust. Now on weekends, she drove long distances to see rock bands and visit Kurrine and other friends.

Julia was not sure how she felt about Ali being gone. "We didn't spend a huge amount of time together," she said.

And yet, she felt a connection.

When Julia first started working at her family's meat market and grocery, she was terrified. "I have such bad anxiety," she said. "I just wanted to cry the entire time." She found it hard to work the cash register and check people out, even though price tags were on everything.

So she went home, drew a picture of the register, and practiced doing totals. She got faster. Then she started getting lost among the freezers out back. "Get me the soup!" a coworker yelled.

"I'd ask like five people for help," Julia said. "Now I boss the guys. 'Get me the cheese!'"

Ali is persevering, too, she added: "He really wanted that job in the Middle East. He worked hard to get it. I'm proud of him."

Julia understood it was not just about the money: Ali wanted to go home.

She could relate to this: Julia's roots in Utica go deep. She is a fourth-generation Utican on her father's side. The family's Polish market—which her great-grandparents opened as a grocery in East Utica over a hundred years ago—is a local institution.

"If America got war-torn, maybe I'd move away," Julia said. "But then later, if things got better, I'd feel *I know Utica*—and I'd come back."

———

Ali changed physically.

He was homesick, and his disciplined schedule helped him get through the tension-filled days: work, gym, a little hookah, bed.

In a recent photo, he is standing in the allied forces gym, looking like a middleweight boxer. His face is narrower. Gone are the full-cheeked face and paunch he had living with Heidi in Utica.

He has a new set of teeth. They are blazingly white—and he looks delighted.

"I told him he'd better start drinking a lot of coffee," Heidi said, laughing.

Ali always had bad teeth, she explained, caused by tetracycline his mother took during pregnancy. For a long time, he needed major dental work but could not afford it. Then he went to Turkey—where dental care is inexpensive—and got implants.

It was torture: "He sat in the dental chair for seven days straight," Heidi said.

Ali was starting to dream about what he would do when he got home. He knew that first, he would need to recover: He pictured sitting for hours in his favorite chair next to Heidi, smoking his hookah filled with tobacco.

Then after a couple of weeks, he would start looking for a house in Utica. "He's adamant about it," Heidi said. "I'm not."

Housing prices have shot up since he left. Heidi showed me a photo of a small three-bedroom house in East Utica on the market for $130,000. "A couple of years ago, when we were looking, it would have gone for $70,000."

She worried about risking such a big chunk of money at their age. "It's a lot to think about. I mean, we're not 30 anymore." Ali is not fazed, she added: "He says a house is always a good investment."

"I think we should wait a little while, definitely till winter when housing prices drop."

There is a bright spot ahead. Ali might have a job to come home to: A friend is now managing an interpreting service in Utica that is expanding into the Cooperstown and Saratoga areas.

During their time apart, Heidi has never doubted that she and Ali love each other. Yet, as his arrival date neared, she was excited but also cautious.

"I really have no idea what will happen when he comes home."

Heidi herself has not changed much. She has been alone for 18 months, yet her personality is still ebullient. She wanted to lose weight; she lost 12 pounds. She wanted to save money; she managed to put aside $1,000, but then had to spend $400 on car repairs.

Did she become more independent?

"I was always independent."

44. HIS TEXT

AT THE END of October 2019, Ali told Heidi that his internet connection might go out. But he did not mention that the situation in Baghdad was much worse.

She already knew that. She still avoided TV news, but would google "Baghdad" and get bits and pieces of what was going on.

Protesters were pushing for massive change: They wanted Prime Minister Mahdi to resign. They also wanted a new constitution and a new electoral system to be put in place, so people could directly vote for the Iraqi president.

On the 28th, Tahrir Square, Baghdad's main gathering place and the entryway to a bridge leading to the Green Zone, was jammed with young people—some of them dancing and making music. But closer to the Green Zone, where Ali was based, demonstrators battled with security forces. A few days later, Mahdi offered to resign.

Ali never mentioned any of this. And Heidi tried not to think about it.

At the beginning of November, more than 200,000 protesters marching in Baghdad had a new demand: an end to Iranian influence in their country's affairs. Iran had been supporting powerful political factions and their militias since 2009, after American troops withdrew.

Then events escalated: Rockets, believed to be Iranian, hit an Iraqi military base near Kirkuk, killing someone identified only as an American contractor. He was an Iraqi immigrant, working—just like Ali—as a translator for the American military.

In retaliation, the United States struck five targets in Iraq and Syria linked to an Iranian-backed militia.

Iraqis were infuriated by this response; they saw it as a violation of their sovereignty. There were calls for the American military to leave Iraq.

Protesters broke into the heavily guarded Green Zone. They shattered security cameras at the American Embassy, scrawled anti-American graffiti on walls, and set fires.

Ali said nothing about this. But he texted Heidi: "Don't worry. I'm OK."

She tried to focus on that—but she was numb.

Three days later, the world was on edge: On January 3, a US drone strike killed Major General Qassim Suleimani, Iran's powerful top security and intelligence officer, as he left Baghdad International Airport in a convoy. Iran's supreme leader Ayatollah Ali Khamenei called for three days of mourning—and then retaliation. Across the region—and in America—people braced for Iran's response.

The next day, tens of thousands of pro-Iranian fighters marched through Baghdad, vowing revenge.

Additional troops were sent to the region. Iraqi lawmakers voted to expel American forces. And the American-led coalition suspended its campaign against ISIS, which Ali was working on.

Ali was out of touch for three days.

Heidi tries to take her cues from Ali. "He's always totally positive," she said. He never gets rattled. So, she kept pushing her bleak thoughts away.

But then she received a text: *You know what to do if something happens to me.*

Her heart dropped. The message seemed surreal; it was so unlike him.

She knew what Ali was referring to: Before leaving for the Middle East, he said that if, God forbid, he should die, she should split the money in his bank account with his mother and sisters.

"Make sure it gets to them," he said.

Iran responded to Suleimani's killing: It bombed two military bases in Iraq. No Americans or Iraqis were killed, though many were treated for traumatic brain injuries. In some parts of the world, there was a sigh of relief.

Ali finally contacted Heidi—and reassured her. All he could say was that his work was on hold—and his team had twice been moved to different locations.

She asked him to send a thumbs-up emoji every day, so she would know he was safe. And he promised that if he felt he was in great danger, he would request to come home.

His team was now living out of their bags, in case they had to move again. It was uncomfortable, especially since he loved clothes and had recently bought lots of things online. But instead of complaining, he joked about his 30 pairs of pants and sent Heidi a snapshot of a rack of them.

"I can't tell you how much I love and admire that man!" Heidi said.

He had been gone almost two years.

He had lived in a male environment with some of the elements of prison: narrow living quarters, limited access to the outside world. He loved the clear gray rivers outside Utica, but now he wanted to see blue, blue water when he got home. He wanted to travel with Heidi to Cancun or Hawaii.

"Can you please slow down?" she said, exasperated.

All she wanted was for him to come home. "He's always three months ahead of the game," she told me. "I just live in the moment."

But now he was not exactly sure when he would be back. His team had lost time, moving around during the political turmoil. Their contracts had been extended.

Once, in the middle of the night, unable to sleep, Heidi sent Ali an 85-line text. It began: *I know you can't respond, but here's what I'm thinking: I don't know if I can do this.*

He immediately wrote back a few lines—and an emoji of a face blowing kisses—that consoled her. "He never goes to any of the dark places I go," she said. "He has a good way of pulling me out of it."

Ali was excited about a recent purchase: He told Heidi he had bought an underwater drone online during a Black Friday sale. It was being delivered to their apartment.

He hoped to film steelhead in the Salmon River—or maybe bluefin tuna in Maui.

Heidi shook her head and smiled.

"I'm here—scared to death. And he's like, 'There's a drone coming in the mail,' as if he's just down the street."

45. ON THE RUN

IN UTICA, there are thousands of people who were once on the run from persecution and war: The Sudanese mother picking out eye makeup with her daughter at the Rite-Aid on Genesee. The Vietnamese woman working on her laptop at the back of the restaurant she owns on Bleecker.

The tall Serbian mother standing by the Salmon River as she watches her teenage son, a fly fisherman, tie intricate knots.

Sometimes, threats came out of the blue. Sometimes, they were building for decades. Within seconds, people had to make agonizing decisions.

When Ali picked up the envelope left on his mother's doorstep, he was puzzled. But then he saw two AK-47 slim-tipped bullets inside, and the handwritten note: "You betrayed your people. We will kill you when we see you." It was signed by al Mujahideen, a Sunni militant group.

It was 2004, and he was working as an interpreter for the allied forces. It was as if an alarm went off in his body: "I was shocked and angry," he said, and grabbing the letter, he drove to the neighborhood mosque. Earlier he had noticed a bunch of men with long beards, passing by his mother's house.

He parked on the curb, by the mosque's front gate, and stormed inside. It was after prayers, but there was still a group of men there. Standing in the middle of the prayer hall, Ali shouted, "Who is the imam of the mosque?"

The men looked at him angrily. "What do you want?" somebody asked.

Ali pulled out the letter. "Who put this stupid letter in front of my door? I want to talk to the imam."

"He just left for his house," somebody said.

Ali got the imam's address and drove there.

When he knocked on the door, the imam's son answered and took Ali into a guest room.

When the imam came in, he was very polite and welcoming.

Ali showed him the letter and said, "Sheikh, we have been living in this neighborhood for 25 years with no issues with anyone. We are a well-known family," he added, his face burning, "so who is accusing me of betrayal?"

"My son, I swear to God I don't know who did this," the imam said. "But since the sectarian violence started, strangers from Sunni areas have been coming into the neighborhood."

Ali left the imam's house—and decided to forget about the letter. But a few days later, he received another.

He knew what a second warning meant: death.

He ran to his room and packed a few clothes. Nobody was home; he had already sent his mother and sisters to live in Damascus. Then he jumped into his car and pushed the gas pedal to the floor. He did not stop until he got to his grandmother's house, in a Shia neighborhood, just minutes away. It was guarded by the Al Mahdi Army, a Shia militia, as well as by Iraqi police.

"No one was allowed in unless they lived there," Ali said. "It would have been hard for Sunni militia to get in."

Ali told his grandmother and his uncle, who lived with her, what had happened.

"My grandmother asked me to share my uncle's room," Ali said. His boss gave him an army cot, which he put into the small room. A reserved, considerate man in his fifties, his uncle would go to the gym or meet friends when Ali came back after work.

Ali missed his fancy, king-size bed and his guitars. Also, "I did not see my mom and sisters for a long time." But he was grateful to be alive.

His supervisor advised him to apply to a special immigration visa program, created for those who had worked for the US Army. It took over a year before he was approved—and then he flew to Damascus to see his mother and sisters and to pick up his visa at the American consulate. But then instead of flying to the United States, he flew to Baghdad.

"My boss freaked out to see me back at the office," he said. "But I told her I cannot leave now. I loved my job to no end."

A few months later, he was informed his visa was about to expire. His boss told him to leave. His mother pushed him: "Go, go!"

Ali said, "I left Iraq."

———

In her senior year of high school, Mersiha noticed what she called "little incidents." Soldiers—she did not know if they were Croats or Serbs—suddenly appeared in the road, asking for ID, when she was on her way to visit her aunt in Zenica, an hour away.

A few classmates were missing: They were Croats and Serbs, who lived in the surrounding villages. "They just stopped coming," Mersiha said.

But she did not dwell on this. She—along with the rest of the class of 1992—was obsessed with the upcoming prom.

It was a high point of the year for the town: Every May, people lined up on the main street, some kids perched on their fathers' shoulders. The graduates strolled past, sometimes as a threesome, arm in arm. The young men wore dark suits. The young women wore glamorous gowns—canary yellow, cobalt blue, and scarlet.

"We did not go as couples," Mersiha insisted. "But as a class. No one was left out—no one!"

The procession ended at the popular downtown restaurant Plava Voda —Blue Water—for a dinner of traditional Bosnian food and dancing. A few days later, every shop had prom photos taped to their front windows.

Mersiha knew exactly what she wanted to wear: a simple black dress like Audrey Hepburn's in *Breakfast at Tiffany's*. But she wanted a minidress, like the girls wore on *Beverly Hills 90210*. She argued with her mother, who insisted it cover her knees.

They hunted for this dress—but there was nothing like it in Travnik.

Then in April, a large box arrived from her mother's brother, who lived in Austria. When Mersiha opened it—pulling back the tissue paper—there was the elegant dress.

There was also a pair of long black gloves, just like Hepburn's in the movie. And a few hazelnut Milka bars, her favorite.

Mersiha did not have Hepburn's swanlike neck or fragile-looking body. She was shorter and shapely—and the dress looked great.

But just two weeks before the prom, Mersiha's teachers announced: "School is closed. There is war."

A few days later, Mersiha's mother heard that girls had been raped by Serbs in a village only 20 minutes away. This terrified her: She pictured her own girls being assaulted. "I can't live like this," she told Mersiha.

Her mother decided to send her daughters to Croatia, with her sister, for just a few weeks. She herself would stay in Travnik; she was afraid of losing her job as a salesclerk in a home-goods store. They needed the money.

This was not an easy decision: She had never been separated from her daughters—except for one time.

When Mersiha was seven, her father, who owned factories in Bosnia and Croatia, kidnapped her.

He had cheated on his wife when Mersiha was five. When Mersiha's mother found out, she wrapped Melissa in a blanket, scooped up Mersiha, and took them to live in her mother's house.

She refused any financial support from her husband. But she allowed an occasional visit. One afternoon, he asked if he could take Mersiha across the street to an ice cream shop.

When he did not return after 15 minutes, her mother ran into the shop. "She started screaming and pulling out her hair," Mersiha said. Her father had put her in a car and driven to the Adriatic coast, where he had a house.

A few weeks later, the courts forced him to bring Mersiha back.

This event immediately vanished from Mersiha's memory; years later, she heard about it from her grandmother. Her mother never spoke about it.

When Mersiha heard her mother's plan to send her away, she was angry: "How could you leave me?"

On a beautiful May morning, Mersiha—wearing her favorite jean jacket—and her sister climbed into their aunt's Volkswagen. It seemed everyone on the street was saying goodbye.

"I kept turning around to see my mother and grandmother crying at the window," Mersiha said.

They joined a convoy of thousands of cars, trucks, and buses filled with women and children. Everybody was heading to Split, on the Croatian coast. The highway was closed; they took an old, narrow route. The trip, which generally took 3 hours, took 24.

Men were not allowed to leave the country. But her uncle, the director of a large hotel complex, was politically connected: He drove them, as well as his wife and two young kids.

But like everyone else, they registered at the border as refugees and were given a yellow card, enabling them to get food from Caritas, a humanitarian organization. Then they were sent to a soccer stadium in Split, the same place Hajrudin's mom and siblings had gone.

Women and children were huddled together, lying in hallways and on the grounds, before being sent to a variety of temporary housing: tents, mobile homes, hotels, and camps.

After only a day, a friend of their uncle's arrived—and took them to a house on Brač, an island that was a ferry ride away. They were going to stay on the second floor; Mersiha's uncle had paid their rent. But the woman of the house resented the refugees.

The first day, she told Mersiha: "You are here. You safe. I won't tell the police."

This infuriated Mersiha: "To this day, I curse her for saying that. Why would she call the police? We were legal—we had refugee status." It was Bosnian men who were at risk.

Behind her back, the girls called the woman—who had long, dark curly hair—a witch. "She wouldn't let us use the shower," Mersiha said. "We had to wash in the sea—it was so cold. We got itchy from the salt."

And though her uncle had bought them all kinds of provisions—Nutella, juice, detergent—the woman kept them in a locked storage room.

The island, known for its beautiful beaches, was always insular. But once refugees started arriving, the residents became hostile. When Mersiha and her sister left the house to get milk or bread, the islanders leaned out their windows, staring at them and cursing.

Then in late June, as Mersiha, her sister, and cousin were sleeping, three policemen entered their bedroom.

"Get up—get up!" the police yelled. Terrified, the girls jumped up, wrapping themselves in sheets. It was a hot night; they were in their underwear. As one police officer came closer, Mersiha stepped in front of her sister and cousin to protect them. Using his rifle, the man lifted a corner of the sheet covering Mersiha.

"Are you hiding something?"

"No, sir, we don't have anything," Mersiha said, crying and shaking.

Then another police officer came into the room. "What the fuck are you doing?" he asked his friend. "There's only girls here." Somebody had reported that there were Bosnian men.

They left, laughing.

The girls hugged each other. "God sent that man!" Mersiha said.

Her uncle then moved them to a house in Split. It was on a hilltop, above a hotel filled with refugees from Bosnia and the border towns of Croatia, which were under siege by Serbs. Nearby, on the beach, was a refugee camp.

Mersiha felt safer: They were living with a family, and since there was a man in the house, "neighbors didn't treat us so bad," she said. The couple had a son, Robert, also 17. "He was a little gangster, a troublemaker. But he was really nice to refugees. Like a brother I never had."

One afternoon, Mersiha was sitting with her sister in the back of a bus, heading into town; Robert was in the front. A tiny, elderly woman started yelling at the two Bosnian girls, "You look like animals. You belong on a farm!"

Hearing the racket, Robert came running, his eyes bulging, "You ignorant old woman! If you ever, ever do anything to these girls, I will personally come knocking on your door."

Soon, all the borders closed.

Her uncle had been running humanitarian trucks from Bosnia into Croatia to help feed and clothe the refugees. He used to bring the girls news from home.

For a year, they heard nothing.

"We didn't know if my mother was alive or not," Mersiha said.

But she kept her anxiety to herself: Melissa was 16; willful. "I had to take care of my sister. We didn't have anyone but each other."

Other refugees were now living in the house. At one point there were 13 people. At night, she and her sister liked to go out with friends they had made in town, but their aunt gave them an early curfew.

"She was just trying to protect us," Mersiha said. "But we resented it. 'What, are we in jail?'"

Sometimes she would explode, "You're not my mother!"

She would try to find a quiet spot in the house, so she could feel her mother's presence.

"I would ask her, 'Why, mommy? Why is this happening?'"

Telling me this, she closed her eyes. "I miss her now."

During their time apart, Mersiha missed simple things, like her mother touching her hair.

"She used to braid it. To this day"—she touched her short, thick hair—"I don't know how to do my hair."

As Mersiha's 18th birthday neared, her aunt planned a party. This would have been a big event back home.

She wanted to make Mersiha happy. She said, "I know I'm not your mom, but I love you very much."

Her aunt invited about a dozen young people. A friend brought a guitar. They sang songs by Dino Merlin, a Bosnian pop singer, and Azra, a Yugoslav new wave band.

Her aunt brought out her signature birthday cake—a hazelnut sponge cake, studded with gumdrops.

"She asked me to make a wish," Mersiha said. "I wished for my mom. She didn't come."

———

For Halima, 30, the threats were all around her.

As she ran, she was nursing Yusuf, her 1-year-old son. Her husband was carrying their 3-year-old daughter, who was known for being out-spoken, a brat, on his shoulders. Leaving their village of Makalango, in southern Somalia, they were heading to a refugee camp on the Kenyan border.

It was 1992; nearby villages were being terrorized by different factions and clans. One night, the couple awoke to the sound of their neighbors screaming; they were attacked as they slept. Along with about 15 other families, Halima, her husband, and kids started running.

For Halima, the hardships of the run—little food, predatory animals—were aggravated, or even eclipsed, by Atika, her demanding little girl.

"She talked a lot, insulting them," said Sofia, who has heard this story from her mother many times. "'You're letting me starve! You need to stop and feed me!'"

"They'd stop for a few seconds, then she'd hear hyenas. She would cry, 'Pick me up! Get me out of here!'"

To soothe the little girl, her father said, "When we get there, you'll have pasta and rice." These were considered luxury foods, hard to get.

"I can't wait to get my pasta and rice!" she said.

Another time, he snapped, "We'll send you back to Somalia!"

"You'd better not!"

Sophia said appreciatively about Atika, "She was so smart and blunt for her age."

She was heavy to carry: "She peed on my dad's shoulders," Sofia said.

Halima could not stop to pee. She had five other children to keep track of.

Families fanned out ahead and behind her, staggering forward.

Few had shoes. Sofia said, "People had cuts and burns all over their feet."

All that mattered was to keep moving. "You lose your shoe, you are left behind," said Mohamed Ganiso, Halima's nephew, who was then 12 years old.

"Even your mom can't stop for you—she can't wait for you," he added, referring to Halima, who was raising him and his younger brother; their mother had died of malnutrition. Carrying water for the family, Mohamed tried to stay in the front of the group, or in the middle.

In the chaos, some families got separated: "We lost each other," Ahmed Mukonje of Utica said about his young wife, four months pregnant, when they started running toward Kenya in 1993. "I went one way. She went a different way."

"It was really the worst time," he added. There was so much confusion: "If you missed somebody, you thought they got killed." It was only after he got to the United States that he learned his wife was alive, and back in Somalia.

Falling behind because of exhaustion or injury meant death. "That's how the animals get you," Mohamed said.

One of Halima's sisters was so spent, she could no longer walk. She collapsed under a tree.

"Relatives watched as a lion devoured her," Sofia said. "She was just so exhausted she couldn't do it anymore."

There was another tragic event: A young aunt, pregnant, and carrying newborn twin boys—with two other kids trailing after her—felt she was about to collapse. "She didn't have a husband to help her," Sofia said.

Unable to carry the twins anymore, "she left them in the forest."

All the mothers were at the end of their rope: Halima passed out nursing Yusuf. "Some people had to throw water on her," Sofia said. For a moment, Halima thought about leaving her difficult 3-year-old behind. "Everybody had other children, babies to take care of."

Yet Atika was not Halima's most difficult child.

Zahara, 14, was running with her parents.

She had left her husband—her first cousin—behind in the village. "He refused to go," Sofia said about the 16-year-old boy.

Halima had married Zahara off so young, hoping it would protect her from being raped by marauders.

Exhausted—two months pregnant—Zahara could not keep up. Also, she was absorbing every blow: She saw several people attacked by lions. She cried when she saw her aunt leave the twins.

Her parents kept encouraging her, their firstborn child: "We're not leaving you. You're doing a good job. Walk."

At the Utanga refugee camp, outside Mombasa, they all moved into a one-room hut. "At first, the family was dependent on Zahara," Sofia said.

Zahara quickly picked up bits of Swahili, English, Arabic, and Turkana. In the dense, multilingual environment, she was savvy about getting her family what they needed: food, ID cards. She gave birth to Mana; her mother cared for the baby along with her own kids.

Zahara made friends everywhere; she wanted to learn new things. And she was pushy, not afraid to ask for help.

A Kenyan camp official showed her how to plant green and red peppers, okra, and spinach. She and her mother made sambusas—and sold huge buckets of them.

But she was rebellious, much like Sadia. "The apple doesn't fall far from the tree," Sofia said, smiling.

Zahara had always fought with her parents—and started running away from home at an early age.

Halima would be wild with worry: Years later, she would tell relatives, "It was a genocide out there. And she's acting up!"

In the camp, Zahara would often leave the crowded hut and go off on her own. A feeling would come over her—that she needed to get some air.

"My parents couldn't rely on her," Sofia said. They hired two Sudanese men to teach the children English and Swahili.

Then Zahara started disappearing for months: Each time, she returned with a beautiful baby girl: Ralya, then Sadia . . .

46. ON WINGS

THE BABY was late.

Sadia woke up on a Tuesday with one thought: "I got to get the baby out." Her doctor at St. Luke's was planning to induce her that Saturday.

For a couple of months, she could barely drag herself out of bed. But that August morning in 2019, she sprang up as if she had wings on her back. Chol was at work; she drove by herself to Sylvan Beach, a village about 40 minutes away.

She entered the cool water of Oneida Lake, her long dress floating out around her. For two hours she swam, her printed turban like a flower along the water.

Then she drove back to Utica, turning onto Rutger Street, passing her grandmother's house, and then her own house, before reaching Proctor Park. She walked around the long, green field for an hour.

"That didn't work," she said flatly.

Next, she headed to Planet Fitness, which she had recently joined. "I did the balls, the machines, everything." Still no contractions, though she had stomach pains. Then, realizing that she was starving—she went to Fastrac and got a Slurpy and a sub.

That night she and Chol stayed up late watching movies. When she felt waves of pain, they called the hospital. "They said maybe it was the fake contractions," Sadia said. And she managed to fall asleep. Then *boom*—a huge contraction woke her. As she jumped off the bed, her water broke.

For the next 36 hours, she stayed in a bed at St. Luke's, in enormous pain. Her labor was not progressing. Chol—good humored and patient—never left her side.

He shot bits of video: In one, as he strokes Sadia's face, she tries to bite his hand.

"Do I look like meat?" he asks, laughing.

"I feel like I'm dying!"

Rubbing her belly, he asks, teasingly, "Can I slide down?"

Again, she tries to bite him.

Sofia was there. And Sadia's in-laws were constantly in touch.

But Zahara never called.

The first day Sadia was hospitalized, Chol's mother called Zahara. Hurt and angry, she said: *"You know our daughter is in labor!"*

"Nobody told me!" Zahara said. She went to St. Luke's to try to see Sadia. But she was turned away at the reception desk: They told her that no more than two people were allowed in the delivery room at the same time.

Sadia started to run a fever of 101. And the staff readied her for an emergency C-section. Three epidurals did not work, she said.

The baby boy—almost 11 pounds—was finally pulled from her. Afterward, Sadia started crying: "Oh, that's my baby!"

———

Rajab was like a prince. His face was smooth and full-cheeked, his limbs strong and chubby. He latched on to Sadia's breast right away. "He ran to it!" Sadia said. Each night, he slept for 17 hours straight.

Delighted, she hovered over the sleeping baby: "This is my pumpkin. My pumpkin!"

Sadia created a nursery starkly different from the children's bedrooms in her grandmother's house. She had grown up within walls the colors of African fruit—dark plums, lemons, and limes. The floors were covered with dark-patterned old rugs.

In contrast, Rajab's room was light and spare. She and Chol had painted the walls a pale gray, not so different from the Utica sky. White blinds covered the window. A small, smiling elephant peered from one wall. The wooden floors were bare, except for a small rug with the same elephant.

The baby's onesies—about 20—mostly cream colored, with tiny African animals, hung on an open rack.

Chol was hands-on from the start: At the hospital, he cut the umbilical cord and wiped the baby down. At home, he bathed and changed his son. When the baby's pacifier disappeared, he ran out to get another.

Sadia saw him as an equal partner: "He has the same rights I do," she said. "He's an amazing dad."

Sadia did not want anyone caring for Rajab, outside of a tight trio. "I won't let nobody babysit my child, except for my mother-in-law," she said. "It's not a matter of trust. It's about how I want my baby to be treated."

"I want him to be the only person focused on. I don't want curse words and stuff. I don't want you to cook—to do anything but pay attention to my baby."

When her sisters clamored to babysit, Sadia said, "No, I'm good." She did not even want Sofia watching Rajab. She worried she would be distracted by her daughter, Amrah.

"I'm going to be"—Sadia searched for the words—"a helicopter mom," she said, laughing. "A bulldozer mom! Not the basic Somali Bantu mom."

She saw her mother-in-law as a model parent.

Sadia had recently stayed with her in Syracuse for a week. Amal gently showered her daughter-in-law's swollen body. She cooked nutritious meals, made her rest, sent her off to the movies. She encouraged her to lose the weight she had gained.

Sadia worried she would be hit by postpartum depression, like so many of her young aunts and cousins. But even her old depression had vanished.

Her eyes were bright and clear. Her face was bare. She had pulled on a black T-shirt and pants.

"I feel like I'm brand new," Sadia said.

With Rajab, Amal was intuitive and patient: Even in the middle of the night, she jumped up, fed the baby, changed him, and brought him back to Sadia.

"I'm like, 'Ma—you don't have to!'"

Amal hoped the young couple would move close by.

But Sadia was content in Utica: "Syracuse? All that traffic—no!"

Zahara still had not seen her grandson.

She had stopped by the hospital a second time. And she was again turned away, because of the two-visitor rule. But Sadia was suspicious of her mother's intentions. "Fake!" Sadia said. "Just showing up? She knows the rules—she had most of her kids at that hospital!"

Sadia had now been home for two months; her mother still had not called.

Weeks later, I asked Zahara if she had seen Sadia's baby. She was quiet for a full minute. Then she said, sorrowfully, "The child is innocent."

Halima also nursed a sense of great hurt.

Sofia overheard her on the phone, talking with a relative: "Sadia abandoned us. She's content with not having a relationship with her mother and grandmother."

———

Sadia felt her fate had changed: She was no longer the least-favored child, but beloved. "I found my mom and dad."

Amal and Moyluk had expectations; Sadia liked that. "They've already told us they're not going to babysit unless Chol goes back to school," she said, smiling. They expect Sadia to have a career.

So does Chol. "I want you to make something of yourself," he told her. For her own sake and for the baby's. "You never know in life—something could happen to me."

She was touched that Chol had recently bought her a laptop, and also paid for her US citizenship application. She was excited about taking the naturalization exam; Sofia was taking it too.

Ralya had recently become a citizen; Mana became one years ago.

There are 100 questions on the study sheet for the civics part of the test. Examiners choose 10 questions; applicants must answer 6 correctly.

Sadia enjoyed learning how the US government works: "I never really knew anything," she said.

When the baby falls sleep, Sadia puts on her headphones.

As she cooks and straightens up—moving around her light-filled apartment—she listens to the exam tape.

"I'm memorizing it," she said, proudly.

What is the supreme law of the land?
the Constitution
What does the Constitution do?
sets up the government
defines the government
protects basic rights of Americans
The idea of self-government is in the first three words of the Constitution.
What are these words?
We the People

47. THE OPENING

MERSIHA opened her restaurant, Yummilicious Café & Bakery, on Valentine's Day 2020.

Mayor Palmieri—in a dark gray suit and tie—showed up; he had won a third term. A local TV crew was there, along with a crush of family, friends, members of the Bosnian community, and longtime customers.

People seemed genuinely delighted: The café was different from any other Utica restaurant.

Strands of white flowers hung from the outside portico, making the building look like a docked boat. Light streamed in from the large front window. One wall was covered with white silk roses. Dark blue velvet love seats were scattered around the large room.

The blackboard above the bar listed Bosnian specialties, including cevapi and alvar—sausages with roasted peppers—but also European-style dishes, and Utican fare: pizza and chicken riggies.

Mersiha in her chef's smock, her broad face radiant, greeted guests congratulating her: "Thank you! I know, I know—we are so happy!"

Ismar, in his waiter's apron, stood talking and laughing with friends by the pastry display case. Then something happened that Ismar would mull over for weeks.

The mayor appeared—and held out his hand.

Mersiha had just told him that her eldest son—a junior, with an almost 4.0 average at SUNY Poly—was planning to move to the West Coast.

"What are you doing after graduation?" the mayor asked Ismar.

Taken aback, Ismar said, "I want to design computer games—maybe in Seattle or LA."

The mayor looked at him, perplexed: "Why go to the West Coast, when Cree is moving to Utica?"

"Cree's a billion-dollar company," the mayor added. "You have a strong academic background. If you stay here and work for Cree for a few years, it will be a great investment for you."

"We really want you here," the mayor said. He put out his hand. "Are you going to promise me you'll stay?"

Ismar hesitated, then shook his hand.

This encounter stunned him: "The mayor is a charismatic guy—an outstanding guy!" he said afterward.

"I thought he was going to say, 'I heard about your dream,' and encourage me. I didn't expect him to say, 'I have a plan.'"

"It was a kind of promise," Ismar said about their handshake. "I still want to go to the West Coast. But maybe I'll stay here for a while."

Then he added, "I still want to do something big though, like my parents."

Mersiha gathered her family together. As the mayor stood by her side, she cut a red ribbon that was strung across the café.

Then the mayor, looking serious, asked if she would like to say a few words.

She took a deep breath. Ismar and Faris both looked dazed. Ajla, in a cranberry sweatshirt, looked down, shyly. As the camera rolled, Elhan broke away and did a wild jig.

Hajrudin—in a black do-rag and chef's apron—quickly put a restraining hand on his son's shoulder.

"I would like to thank my husband, kids," Mersiha said, slowly. She mentioned other family members, close friends, and colleagues. "And the mayor, of course." She was grateful he had come; she had asked a Bosnian friend at City Hall to do her a favor.

She looked around at the roomful of native Uticans and Bosnian refugees. Many of the Bosnians had arrived as teenagers, just when she did, and now had kids in college. Like her, they had struggled; some had buried parents. At least a dozen had opened small businesses.

With a burst of energy, she said, "Thank you to the city for having us—and giving us the opportunity to give something back to the community."

"We hope you will love us!" ____

Three weeks later, Hajrudin stood in the café, cutting out grocery coupons. It was Sunday, their day off. "If we'd waited one more week to open, we'd have been screwed," he said.

Just before opening, they had run out of cash, having spent $3,000 on food and materials. They owed money on 11 credit cards.

"My sister said if you need any money . . ." Hajrudin's voice trailed off. "We don't want to owe anybody." But he acknowledged they might need to borrow a bit to get through the next few weeks. "We have to be smart."

But the couple were exhilarated by the customer response: Last night, the café was packed. "Fifteen people came in at once!" Mersiha said.

She made 80 cappuccinos. Her pastries—crème puffs, eclairs, baklava, krempita—were wiped out four times. She had to run into the kitchen to bake an extra cake.

Hajrudin was cautious: "It's been better than I thought."

"Much, much!" Mersiha said. Smiling, she read aloud customers' reviews from her cell phone: "Diverse menu . . . delicious pastries, and down-to-earth owners. The Bosnian coffee is the best I've ever had, reminds me of my grandma's."

She turned to her husband: "Now we have to work even harder—to keep up the same quality of food, the cleanliness, the service."

"Chef Ramsaya!" Hajrudin said, referring to Gordon Ramsay, the British chef and TV personality.

"I want everything to be perfect," Mersiha said. "Look at this!" On her cell phone, she showed me photos of two dessert crepes: The first crepe was light gold, perfectly folded, with a drizzle of Nutella; her face lit up at her handiwork. The other was darker, topped by hazelnut squiggles.

"Who made this one—who?" she asked me, pointing to the second photo.

"I like how I did it!" Hajrudin told me. "She has to have her signature on everything."

"I'm all about details," Mersiha said. "I just have a more artistic eye. They say that people born in April are creative."

"And you believe that?" Hajrudin asked, incredulously.

To answer him, Mersiha looked around the café, painted a cool gray. There were only two paintings—abstractions—on the wall. "I know what I'm doing," she said. "I like simplicity. I don't like too much stuff."

Then the carping evaporated: Hajrudin pored over the local grocery ads for bargains. "What do you think we should do for St. Patrick's Day?" he asked; the holiday was two weeks away. "I can do Bosnian Pot—it's like corned beef and cabbage."

"OK!" Mersiha said. "I'll make something green for dessert."

The last few weeks had been an enormous strain. It was not just anxiety about money. The couple and their two eldest boys were working around the clock.

"We've all lost weight," Mersiha said. And it was true: Hajrudin looked almost gaunt. The boys, who relish helping at the café, even as they carry a full load of classes, were also thinner.

But Mersiha was working the hardest—baking most of the night, then running the café with Hajrudin. She was also teaching part time at BOCES.

Her forearms had swollen to twice their normal size. Her hands were puffy. "My fingers are tingling all the time," she said. "They hurt so much I can't feel them."

"They look old," she said, looking at her hands.

But what bothered her most was being away from her two youngest kids. She, Hajrudin, and the older boys did shifts, running home four or five times a day to be with them.

Mersiha took a nap during one visit. When she awoke, Elhan was sitting on the bed, staring at her. "Mommy, what are you doing home?" he asked.

"Things will be better when we can fix up the apartment upstairs," she told me. Then they would all be together.

Yet Mersiha kept taking on more work.

She had recently catered a baby shower for 80 people. But after the event—a big success—it hit her that she had not made any money.

She provided a dessert table with 10 different kinds of pastries, and also decorations, table settings, and goodie bags that contained homemade candy bars and cookies. "I spent $800 on decorations and materials," she said. "I charged $1,000."

Why didn't she charge more?

She glared at Hajrudin. "Because my husband refuses to charge more. If we do, he thinks people will not order."

"He freaked out when I charged $4 for Bosnian coffee," she said, glancing at the café's blackboard menu. "He said cut it down to $2.50. I refused."

Hajrudin looked up from the newspaper.

"He's afraid of what Bosnian people would say," she said. "The 'Special Bosnians.'"

"Who are the 'Special Bosnians'?" I asked.

The 'Special Bosnians' are the ones who judge everyone, she said. They resent another Bosnian's success. "Ninety percent of the community are happy for us. They say it's so good to have a place where they can feel comfortable. They like the prices—very reasonable."

"But some people are jealous," she added. "They want to destroy you."

One of the 'Special Bosnians'—a big-boned man in his fifties—had recently walked into the café. Looking around skeptically, he said, "Your lights are so bright!"

Then he took a chair—and put it near the bar, which they are using as counter space. He sat down: "I want to be served here!"

"We don't have a bar," Mersiha told him.

"Every bar has a bar."

"This isn't a bar!" Mersiha knew his son had opened a bar in Utica that failed. "We don't serve any alcohol."

"I put my chair here—I will sit here and have my coffee. A macchiato!"

Then he looked at the prices. "Listen to me, your coffee is too expensive."

"It's Italian coffee—the best!" Mersiha said. "I'm not changing my coffee!"

———

That Sunday afternoon was like a thousand others in Utica.

The city is at its sleepiest on Sunday. Most stores and restaurants are closed. Few people are out walking. Even the cars going down Genesee sound hushed. The blocks where the new hospital will rise have been razed and roped off. Several old factory buildings stand, waiting to be renovated.

Some downtown streets, torn apart, are also waiting: A new gateway to the city is being created, with a roundabout and a new street—Liberty Street—which is designed to have park benches, bike racks, and dozens of trees.

As daylight fades, the glow from Mersiha's café spills onto the empty parking lot on Rutger Street.

Rutger—once one of the most beautiful blocks in Utica—is a kind of crossroads for Ali, Sadia, and Mersiha.

They have all lived or worked there: Ali began his life with Heidi in a studio apartment. Sadia grew up in her grandmother's big house, then later returned to start her own family. And Mersiha married on Rutger—then came back 20 years later, to gamble everything on a dream.

They have never met. But I have wondered if they ever passed each other—perhaps while walking in Proctor Park, or driving down the broad, leafy street.

Refugees socialize at home. But maybe Mersiha's café will draw in newcomers. On some sunny afternoon, will Sadia, who lives only blocks away, stop by with her baby?

Heidi has already checked out the café's website. When Ali returns to Utica, will the couple drive there one evening, sit on a love seat, and order Bosnian coffee and baklava?

On Rutger Street, these newcomers have fallen in love; battled bedbugs; failed math; dreamed big; felt trapped and fought; been broken and healed.

———

At 5 that afternoon, Mersiha stood up abruptly, "Oh, my God, I have to finish a cake." Hajrudin finished wiping down the tables, then he too disappeared into the kitchen.

Later, Mersiha came out and sat by herself on a love seat. Her swollen left hand covered her face, which was contorted with pain.

Then Hajrudin came out of the kitchen. She immediately brightened.

"Come here, baby! Let's relax!" she called to him.

Wearing a striped polo shirt and a cap, he placed a krempita—three inches of vanilla custard in puff pastry—in front of her, then sat down next to her.

Happily, she ate it. "It's good!"

They discussed the week ahead, her arm around his thin shoulders. Then getting up, she headed toward the kitchen to get a pizza for their kids. Hajrudin said quietly, "I don't know how you handle all this."

48. KARMA

ALI rose from a long nap.

Only 10 minutes later, he was standing by his apartment door. It was a revelation: He was free—to get in the car and drive to T.J.Maxx for shirts. He could go to the Salmon River and fish with friends.

He could hold Heidi.

He could wear clean clothes; at the base, a laundry service threw everybody's clothes together into giant washing machines. "I was not comfortable having my clothes next to others,'" he explained.

"Heidi does laundry three times a day," he added, teasing her.

"I'd rather do laundry than anything else!" Heidi said, laughing.

But Ali was not home for good.

His contract had been extended because of time lost during the political turmoil; he would be home for only two weeks.

It was October 2020: It had been 18 months since his last visit.

"I feel like this is just a dream," he said. "I'll probably wake up in my room in Baghdad and go to work."

Like Rip Van Winkel, Ali returned to a town that was the same—yet profoundly changed. COVID had locked down the small city—along with the rest of the world—and it was slowly reopening.

For Heidi's sake, Ali had tried to appear calm during the months of chaos and his two quarantines at the base. "But sometimes, I couldn't sleep for two days," he said. "You think about a thousand things at once: Heidi—what's going on at home. My mom—she's diabetic, she's sick, she's old."

"You think, what if I get moved somewhere, and it is not a good location for doing the job? What if I get sick?"

Ali wished he had been given some coping techniques: Before leaving Baghdad, he went up to some military personnel. "You are trained to be away from home," he told them. "You are here for a few months, then you go back. I'm a civilian, and I've been away for 18 months!"

They were surprised—and commiserated with him, Ali said.

In two weeks, he will fly down to North Carolina for a medical exam at a government facility. If cleared, he will return to Iraq for another six months, before returning home for good.

At that point, he will have been away for three years.

And yet, when I asked what happens if there is a glitch in his exam, he said, startled: "God forbid!"

"I want things to go normal. I still have things I want to achieve at work."

He remains torn: He longs to be in the United States. But he finds it difficult to walk away from Iraq. A regular life feels elusive.

For fleeting moments, Ali has thought about signing up for another year.

"He feels a pull," Heidi said tightly.

The situation has finally taken its toll on her: When Ali had to cancel a previous visit home, "it really killed me inside," she said. "Since then, my attitude has changed a little bit. I'm not allowing myself to feel 100 percent happy anymore."

"Ali noticed," she said.

"Right now, I want to jump around, be excited. But I'm just kind of flat. I don't want to be that way," she added. "But I can't get crushed again."

She has put up a wall: "If Ali comes back in April, I can pull it down."

———

I asked Ali: Is his desire to fight terrorists linked to his brother's death?

"Yes."

"It's a small thing," he said, referring to his work. He hopes it contributes to the fight against terrorism. But his work does not ease his sense of loss. "No matter what I do, it's not equal to spending one minute with my brother."

"What happened was something big. It affected not just me and my family, but everyone who knew him."

Ali does not like revenge. "But I'm still a Middle Easterner," he said, smiling. "Maybe I can call my work karma or payback for the terrorists. Not just for what they did to my brother, but to everyone."

"The other guys I work with," he added about his team. "I'm hoping they have the same feeling."

Things are a bit better now in Baghdad: The Iraqi government re-opened Tahrir Square, where the protesters demonstrated. There is less violence, and a new prime minister, Mustafa Al-Kadhimi.

"The government is always promising," Ali said, "but unfortunately, nothing gets done."

———

Yet, despite his qualms, Ali *is* going forward—and making plans to come home in April.

Like a soldier, he will be leaving behind intimate bonds and a sense of shared mission. He knows he cannot just slip back into everyday life.

"I'll be honest," he said, "it will be very difficult coming back to Utica."

He does not want to feel lost: "My plan is to occupy myself."

He has saved enough money to buy a house with cash. He hopes that purchasing a house—which could take months—will be absorbing and help him feel restored.

Then he will look for work, contacting the refugee center, clinics, and hospitals. His friend who manages an interpretation service is interested in hiring him as an administrator.

In Baghdad, he started getting ready for civilian life: Sitting in what he calls "my 3×3 can"—a tiny room 3 meters by 3 meters—he studied YouTube videos.

He learned how to make things: Resin tables. Pizza ovens. Fire pits.

"I'm going to make them at home," he told Heidi.

"It's not going to happen!" she said, laughing.

He started learning how to paint, carefully copying abstract scenes with acrylics, using the colors of the ocean.

Heidi covered their dining room table with plastic, so they could paint together. "Ali really pays attention to the videos," Heidi said. "He can mimic them. I get sidetracked and do my own thing."

He also studied videos about how to fix things. "I'm a person who is not handy," he explained. "I just want to understand how things work. American houses are different from other houses."

But he will not try anything ambitious, he added: "I'm not taking away a professional's career!"

He knows what he wants: a small house with a big garage that he can turn into a workshop.

He said firmly, "A new house is a new life."

———

On his third day home, Ali, Heidi, Julia, and her new girlfriend, Allison, whom she met at college, drove out to Green Lake, a small glacial lake outside Syracuse.

It was a bright but very windy fall day. The leaves on the maple trees ringing the lake were still red, yellow, and orange, but fading.

It is Heidi and Ali's special spot: Sometimes they have it to themselves. But that day there were lots of other people; some had brought their dogs. A wedding party posed for photographs.

Julia and Allison, who had recently become a couple, immediately wandered off. They could be seen at a distance—both with long, blonde-brown hair—play fighting in the grass.

"I don't think Ali really noticed," Heidi said, smiling.

Ali still had jet lag, and he and Heidi wandered around the trails by the lake. He marveled at the color: They passed tall, lush evergreens. At the base in Baghdad, everything is gray.

Though he was tired, he walked quickly: He has become incredibly fit. Heidi kept up.

Reserved, Ali has never put into words his gratitude for the love and loyalty Heidi has shown. This does not bother Heidi.

"Ali's way is to say, 'We are a team.'"

They went to the water's edge.

Green Lake is like a lake in a folktale, in which a ring—or a child's golden ball—has been tossed to the bottom.

The lake is aquamarine.

Not from algae. But from the high concentration of minerals that reflect the wavelengths of light, closer to the blue end of the spectrum.

It is unusually deep—almost 200 feet at its lowest point—and meromictic, which means that the cold, dense bottom waters tend to stay separate from the shallower, warmer waters.

Because of this, sediment sinks and collects at the bottom, where it is preserved. Down below, the water is the bluest blue.

Photographers love to shoot the lake's smooth, reflective surface. But Ali brought his new underwater drone—he has been dreaming about testing it there with Heidi.

Ali sent the white drone out over the lake, then under water, maybe 30, 40 feet below.

He and Heidi looked at each other, delighted: Heidi had never been interested. "But this was cool," she said.

Standing shoulder to shoulder—both in sweatshirts and caps—the couple watched the monitor: A big, silvery largemouth bass swam by.

It was hard to see—cloudy. Maybe there were stones and leaf matter.

Then the silvery bass reappeared—and quickly rose through the blue water.

EPILOGUE **WE RALLIED**

IN MARCH 2020, Utica looked like a ghost town: Its parks, stores, bars, restaurants, churches, mosques, zoo, and museum closed. Construction projects—like the Nexus Center—were put on hold.

"We took a deep breath," John Zogby said about the city where he grew up.

In New York City—about 250 miles away—the coronavirus began like a brushfire. In Utica, it started out slow: On March 19, 2020, there were two cases in Oneida County. Almost four months later, there was a seven-day average of 28 cases.

But by January 3, 2021, the seven-day average had jumped to 305 cases, and the hospitals were overloaded.

The mayor and his staff got COVID-19. So did a quarter of the fire department, and many people mentioned in this book—including Dr. Hua, the family doctor, and LuPway Doh, the Karen community leader. They recovered.

Sadia, Mersiha, and Ali did not get sick.

But most of Sadia's family did. Sofia was ill for weeks. Her mother, Halima—who ran a fever of over 105 degrees—was hit hardest.

"My mom was just lying on the floor, facedown," Sofia said. Nobody in the family saw a doctor. "We stayed home and let it pass."

Many refugees who worked in factories were not aware how easily the virus can spread. "So many told me they have the symptoms," Dr. Hua said. "But their employers said, 'Come into work.'"

She warned her patients, "If dad gets sick, the rest of the family gets sick."

"Our refugee population is very resilient," Dr. Hua added. Coming from countries torn apart by war, they are experienced at getting through terrible times.

Many businesses suffered.

"But everybody rallied," said Carmela Caruso, the owner of Caruso's Pastry Shoppe. "It's just what we do." There was a level of loyalty and support.

Uticans kept their gallows humor: "When recessions hit us, we don't have so far to fall," said Marquis Phillips, Utica's director of city initiatives.

The federal government is providing a cushion, he added: The city is receiving $64 million as part of a COVID relief bill, which will be used to support infrastructure projects, improve housing stock, and expand business opportunities for those in disadvantaged communities.

In the spring of 2020, streets across the country flooded with protesters after George Floyd was killed by a Minneapolis police officer. And in Utica, hundreds gathered in Kemble Park in Cornhill and marched downtown to Oneida Square.

"There was absolutely no violence," said Freddie Hamilton, the Black community activist, who lives in Cornhill. "I don't think people were surprised. That's the way we expected it to be."

An enormous Black Lives Matter mural—a kind of patchwork quilt depicting Utica's Black community—went up in Kemble Park. "Police signed the wall—they painted a square," said Mr. Phillips, who is Black, and worked on the project.

Zahara was stunned, hearing about the murder.

"I thought, 'My boy!'" she said. She saw her sons in George Floyd. She worried: "What will happen to my boys? I tell them, please be careful in America."

———

The hospital—which once divided Utica—is rising.

Ten floors of steel girders have gone up. Steve Wynn, the former Las Vegas developer, who was raised in Utica, recently gave a gift of $50 million to the Mohawk Valley Health System, through his family foundation. The hospital was renamed the Wynn Hospital.

The ongoing construction makes people feel optimistic: "There's going to be this large structure downtown," Ms. Callahan, director of The Center, said, marveling. "Every day, it changes."

The door that closed to refugees will reopen. Ms. Callahan, who has worked with refugees for 15 years, expects that in the fiscal year 2022, President Biden will admit about 120,000 newcomers. This fiscal year—as of March 2021—Utica has welcomed only five refugees.

It will not be easy to restart the resettlement program: The Trump administration "essentially stopped the processing," Ms. Callahan said. Refugees cannot simply show up tomorrow: Just checking security can take years. Hundreds of professionals connected to refugee resettlement programs were let go or moved on.

"The program was broken," she added. "It will take a few years to fix."

———

Mersiha's café was only open for a month before lockdown.

There was no time to mourn: Mersiha went to her boss and asked if she could return to her full-time teaching job. "She saved me," Mersiha said.

Her two older boys got jobs as personal shoppers at Walmart. Hajrudin adjusted the café's menu, offering soups and salads for pickup and delivery. They applied for small business grants from the government and were denied—but managed to get a $3,500 bank loan.

"All those deaths," Mersiha said about the winter of 2020. "There was always the fear. But we did right, I think. We kept our masks on, took care of our hands. Nobody got sick."

Things shifted in May: "Ramadan was coming. We started opening the café, little by little."

Customers came from blocks away, and from as far away as Syracuse and Albany. Iraqi, Yemeni, and Somali Bantu refugees stopped by.

That summer, they put six tables outside. "People loved that!"

The couple paid off 10 credit cards. But then they opened two more.

They needed to buy lumber and supplies, so a friend could finish renovating the café's upstairs apartment. Then they will move in and sell their house.

They are anxious to leave their block: Many of their refugee neighbors moved to the suburbs during the pandemic. And in an echo of what happened in the nineties, strangers arrived from other cities and rented from absentee landlords. Recently, there has been drug dealing and a drive-by shooting.

"I hope refugees buy our house!" Mersiha said.

Many Bosnians love Mersiha's café. But the 'Special Bosnians' do not come around.

"I don't care," Mersiha said, laughing. "If I can live without my mother, I can live without them!"

Recently, a woman came in, ordered a cake, then handed Mersiha an envelope. "I didn't even know her," Mersiha recalled, shaking her head.

"Open it when I leave," the woman said.

Mersiha read the card: *I feel so good, seeing you succeed.*

———

Heidi kept meaning to stop by Mersiha's café. But she was busy with work, and worried about Ali.

"I think I have PTSD," Ali said matter-of-factly, on a recent call with me from Baghdad. At night, he sleeps about 30 minutes, then is awake. "I get tired, get grouchy, can't focus."

A year ago, he saw a psychiatrist. It was helpful, he said, but he did not return after the first session. He was afraid he would be reported as unfit and sent home before his contract ended.

His trauma started after his friend Nawres was killed.

Nawres Waleed Hamid was the Iraqi-American translator—identified as an American contractor—killed in a rocket attack in northern Iraq, in December 2019. His death set off an international crisis.

He and Ali were on the same team in Baghdad. But after eight months, Nawres returned home to Sacramento, California, where he lived with his wife and two young sons.

Like Ali, he felt pulled back: He wanted to rejoin his team in Baghdad. But he was sent to Kirkuk, a city in northern Iraq.

"He was hilarious!" Ali said, remembering his friend. "So funny, polite, smart." Nawres loved playing guitar. And though Ali had not played in 15 years, he bought one so they could play together.

"It did not happen. The guitar is sitting under my bed."

Ali is ready to part with Iraq.

"I will miss the food, the people, neighborhoods," he said. But he is exhausted from dealing with a culture devastated by war.

When he began his interpreting job in the Middle East, he felt split down the middle: half American, half Iraqi. "Now I feel 75 percent American, 25 percent Iraqi," he said wryly.

On May 5, 2021, Ali got on a plane and began the long journey back to Utica.

———

Sadia started running after her baby was born. Three, four miles down Rutger Street and through Proctor Park. She passes Mersiha's café, where she has bought pastry.

"The mother and son are nice," she said.

The world beckoned, as it did when she was 15. In December 2020, Sadia and her sister-in-law did something striking for two young refugee women: They took a train to New York City and stayed at a midtown hotel, while Chol took care of Rajab at home.

It was the height of the pandemic; the city was relatively empty. Yet to Sadia, the streets felt jammed. "People push you, and don't say, 'Sorry.'"

As the two young women walked down Madison Avenue—hoping to buy some new clothes—they saw unimaginable wealth.

"They don't have no Walmart!" Sadia said. "All you see are brands— Louis Vuitton, Fendi, Prada." Yet, only two months later, she returned to the city with friends, and a list of museums and inexpensive stores.

Sadia had not seen her mother—now 47 and pregnant with her 14th child—in over two years. She had drifted away from her siblings.

This worried Ralya; she and Sadia were both working at Walmart's bakery.

"Everyone is growing older," Ralya told her sister. "Mom has diabetes and stuff. You need to come and visit the kids. The little ones are forgetting about you little by little."

Sadia stopped by Ralya's to see her siblings. "But my sister is hard-headed," Ralya told me. She would not see their mother.

"Sadia *is* my mom," she added, laughing. "They're the same! They can't forget."

Ralya was pregnant with twins: One night that winter—in her fourth month—she went into labor, and Siddi rushed her to the hospital. The twins, a boy and girl, were stillborn.

Ralya called her family. "You could hear it in her voice," Sadia said about her sister's grief.

Zahara was overwhelmed: *"Nobody will forget, forever,"* she told me.

Every night, the family gathered: the older relatives at Zahara's, the younger ones at Ralya's. They cooked together: chicken with rice, beans, and corn.

One night, Ralya asked Sadia to drop off some soda and water at their mother's house.

Sadia had not been there in years. Yet, walking in the front door—in a blue baati, her arms loaded with bottles—she felt at ease.

Zahara, nine months pregnant, was in the kitchen talking with Siddi's mother, who had eight kids of her own.

"Hi," Sadia said to her mother.

"Hi," Zahara said, brightening. "How is your son? Where is he at?"

They chatted: Sadia told her mother how smart Rajab is: "He knows his A for apple, C for cat."

"How is his hand?" her mother asked. She heard her grandson had fallen and hurt his hand.

"It's good."

But then, anxious about Ralya, Sadia left to check on her.

All anger between mother and daughter had vanished.

"Your child has been away, you're happy to see her," Zahara told me later. "You forget whatever she did. You forgive her."

"It doesn't matter," she added about the past. "You see your child is happy. She's healthy. You pray for her."

For Sadia, too, everything changed in an instant.

In her mother's kitchen—the scene of so many battles—she was at home.

"It was *my mom*," Sadia said. "It just felt normal. Like she was there the whole time. Like she was never gone."

April 6, 2021

ABOUT THE PROCESS

Over a period of eight years—from fall 2013 to spring 2021—I followed Sadia, Mersiha, Ali, and their families. I conducted hundreds of interviews, but mostly observed them at home as they went about their daily lives: chatting, teasing, and arguing with family members; cooking, eating, and cleaning; texting and talking on cell phones.

Occasionally, I attended a family event—a wedding or graduation— or saw them at work or went along on errands. But refugees are in tightly knit families. Home is safety, comfort—everything. And that's where I visited them.

I took notes in longhand, getting down every word. As a journalist, I've done this for 35 years. It feels natural to me, and my subjects quickly get used to my scribbling. The pen and pad seem to fade away. And I— five feet tall, generally sitting in the corner of a couch or on a chair—fade a bit, too.

I found that short stints worked best. I'd drive up to Utica for about a week. My subjects were busy—in the middle of things—yet graciously made time for me, if they could.

If they couldn't see me, I didn't press. I didn't want them to feel imposed upon; this was such a long project. Sometimes, I'd see one of my subjects a couple of times during a trip; sometimes, not for months.

I made about 30 trips to Utica, staying downtown and in nearby Clinton, New York. I did phone interviews from my home outside New York City.

Sometimes I had a specific reason to go: One of my subjects was going through something important, or I had a bunch of scheduled interviews with city officials or firefighters.

But mostly, I just made some calls and headed upstate.

It wasn't always easy to connect: Zahara's family frequently changed cell numbers and often didn't pick up. So sometimes, arriving in Utica, I simply stopped by Zahara's house.

Sadia was the hardest to reach: Like many teenagers, she'd lose her cell phone. Forget to check her messages. Her doorbell didn't work.

Sometimes, she'd seem to disappear. But after a while, she'd get back in touch.

I interviewed about 100 other Uticans: bankers, contractors, factory workers, reporters, restaurant and café owners, bartenders, doctors, hospital administrators, city council members, community activists, people who were unemployed, politicians, professors, funeral directors, veterans, and amateur historians.

A few of them form a kind of chorus within this book.

I had a huge challenge: I lost Ali.

Before leaving for Iraq in 2018, Ali explained he wouldn't be able to communicate with me. If I had a question, Heidi could forward it.

I could have decided to find another subject. But I'd known Ali since 2013, felt very connected—and wanted to keep following him.

It hit me I could continue telling his story through Heidi's eyes. I felt this could work, because Heidi herself—wry, frank, and intensely loyal—is a wonderful subject.

Toward the end of Ali's three years away, he and I started to correspond—and we spoke twice by phone.

For security reasons, his name—and his siblings'—was changed. Also, in the chapter "With Strangers," Maggie, a young Utica woman, takes in Sadia; her name was changed to protect her privacy.

For years, I tried to visit Proctor High School. It has been an important part of young refugees' lives. But its doors are closed to journalists. This may be a response to the controversy about New York State's 2015 lawsuit against the school district for refusing to enroll refugee students over 16.

Then in 2019, a young woman who'd graduated from Proctor heard about my project—and offered to shepherd me in. Through her, I got a glimpse of the school, and connected to Danielle Brain, the remarkable English teacher.

I observed the majority of the scenes depicted in this book as they unfolded.

If I wasn't present, then I interviewed multiple people who were involved, to get an accurate sense of things. And I gathered information, when possible, through articles, videos, and photos.

Hajrudin's war story and the stories told in "On the Run" are oral history.

My subjects have been thinking about and telling these stories within their families for years.

I'd ask the storyteller the same questions, over and over. And I did my best to confirm details with family members and outside sources. But these are memories—and they stand as they were told.

When the manuscript was completed, I hired a fact checker.

I didn't pay my subjects for interviews or their time. And no one ever asked me for money. Once Zahara asked if I could help her get a job; I explained I couldn't. When Sadia was 15, she asked if she could visit me in New York City; I said it wasn't a good idea.

She understood why—to tell the story, you need these boundaries. Sometimes it was a struggle—to not show how *deeply* I cared. These families welcomed me into their homes with generosity and patience: There was so much to admire.

ACKNOWLEDGMENTS

To Sadia, Ali, Mersiha, and your families—my deepest gratitude.

I never stopped being amazed by your good humor, frankness, and courage; I learned so much from each of you.

My special thanks to Sadia, who drew me into this story.

I'm grateful to my agent, Emily Forland, who nurtured this project every step of the way for five years. To my editor, Haley Lynch, who immediately understood the manuscript and gave me her complete support. And to the director of Beacon Press, Helene Atwan, who gave me the time I needed to finish this book.

Also, to Rakia Clark, who originally acquired this book, and to the Beacon team—Janet Vail, Laura Kenney, Susan Lumenello, Louis Roe, Alyssa Hassan, Marcy Barnes, and Sanj Kharbanda—for their patience and skill.

The following people—over many years—gave me their insights:

Shelly Callahan kept me in touch with changes in Utica's refugee population, no matter how busy she was. Dr. Kathryn Stam and Chris Sunderland shared their affection for Utica's young refugees. LuPway Doh shared his worries about the Karen community—and his pride in its history and culture.

John Zogby and Carmela Caruso—through their stories—made the city's past come alive.

I'm also grateful to Mayor Robert Palmieri, Marquis Phillips, Mohamed Ganiso, Sakib Duracak, Fire Chief Scott Ingersoll, Fire Captain Anthony Zumpano, retired Fire Lieutenant Phil Fasolo, Police Chief Mark Williams, Police Captain Bryan Coromato, retired Police Captain Mickey Maunz, Zach Ambrose, Freddie Hamilton, Patrick Johnson, Danielle Brain, Krista Pembroke, Dr. Natalie Hua, Dr. Katherine Warden, Dr. Mark Warfel, Imam Amsel Memic, the Alsayfi family, and Susan and Tim Sweetland.

Kevin Marken and Trinh Truong generously opened doors.

My thanks to the *Observer-Dispatch* reporters, who covered the fires of the 1990s. And to Nancy Ford, the paper's staff photographer: Her marvelous photos of the man with the Panama hat helped me reconstruct the Kanatenah fire.

Erol Balkan and Sharon Rippey of Hamilton College and Jenny McPhee, director of the Center for Applied Liberal Arts continuing education programs at NYU School of Professional Studies, gave me their friendship and support. My thanks to Cullen Thomas, my colleague who read an early draft, and to Linnea Feldman Emison, my fact checker.

Diego Ribadeneira, my editor at the *New York Times*, helped shape my original story about Utica and made it better. Amy Virshup, whom I wrote for when she edited the *Times'* Metropolitan section, has an appreciation for a story's humanism; her editorial voice has stayed with me.

Lisa Palatella—my friend, a film editor—shared her thoughts about story structure during long COVID walks. My friend, Leti Mariotti, discussed these stories with me over coffee for years. Leslye Wood and Vivian Spiegelman lifted my spirits in late night talks.

My thanks to my writing teachers at Kirkland College and Columbia University School of the Arts: Denise Levertov, William Rosenfeld, and Galway Kinnell. My students sustained me as I wrote this book.

I'm so grateful to my parents, Millie and Bill Hartman, for always encouraging me as a young writer. To the inspiring Hartman clan: my brothers, Phil and Jesse; my sister-in-law, Emilie; and Leon, Estefa, Odetta, Camellia, Charlie, and Lulu.

To my grandparents, Charles and Yetta Levenson, Jewish refugees who fled Poland and created a new world in Bensonhurst, Brooklyn.

To my children, Asa and Willa—my joy.

And to my husband, Ben, the carpenter who sat down next to me at the Great Jones Café long ago. His love and encouragement brought this book to life.

NOTES

AUTHOR'S NOTE

x **Utica was not the only struggling city** Julia Preston, "Ailing Midwestern Cities Extend a Welcoming Hand to Immigrants," *New York Times*, October 7, 2013.

x **More than 65 million people** Somini Sengupta, "Record 65 Million People Displaced, UN Says," *New York Times*, June 20, 2016; UNHCR, United Nations Refugee Agency, USA, "Global Trends 2015": https://www.unhcr.org/576408cd7.

x **It was the largest wave** David A. Graham, "Violence Has Forced 60 Million People from Their Homes," *Atlantic*, June 18, 2015.

x **All through 2015** IOM Global Migration Data Analysis Centre, "Over 3,770 Migrants Have Died Trying to Cross the Mediterranean to Europe in 2015," https://missingmigrants.iom.int/over-3770-migrants-have-died-trying-cross -mediterranean-europe-2015.

PART I LANDINGS

Chapter 1 DESIRE

3 **A total of 19 family members** Interview with Zahara, September 18, 2013.

3 **The elegant but run-down house** Recorded deed of Halima's house on Rutger, Office of the Oneida County Clerk, Utica, New York.

3 **It was used as** Zahara, September 18, 2013.

4 **The name Rahama** About the name Rahama: https://www.names.org/n/rahama /about.

4 **Her family** Ethnic groups, tribes, peoples, and clans can all mean the same thing. Information from Daniel J. Van Lehman, visiting scholar, Middle East Studies Center, Portland State University, August 4, 2021.

Chapter 2 FIRE

9 **As white people started fleeing** Interview with Patrick Johnson, March 11, 2021. His family moved to Cornhill in 1960; they were the fourth Black family in the district.

9 **At the height of the crisis** This number refers to overall fires: Interview with Chief Ingersoll, June 6, 2019.

9 **They headed toward streets** Interview with Lieutenant Phil Fasolo, January 28, 2021.

10 **But as Utica's population** According to US census report.

10 **Laughing, he told the interviewer** CBS interview with Mayor Ed Hanna, 1997: https://www.youtube.com/watch?v=a9ftEoFOexI.

10 **A house in Cornhill** Interview with John Zogby, January 21, 2020.

11 **Many moved to North and South Carolina** Zogby, January 21, 2020.

11 **And some owners torched** Chief Ingersoll, June 6, 2019.

11 **In the mid-nineties** "Putting Out the Fire," *TechBeat*, Fall 1998.

11 **Gas thrown down sinks** Interview with Fasolo and Mickey Maunz, retired member of Utica Police Department, Criminal Investigative Unit, March 6, 2020.

11 **There was rarely closure** Scott Wallace, "State Praises Arson Strike Force," *Observer-Dispatch*, March 4, 1998.

11 **The police lost control** *TechBeat*, Fall 1998.

12 **Anyone can walk into** Scott Wallace, " 'City of Strangers,' " *Observer-Dispatch*, February 15, 1998.

12 **Instead of using guns** Rocco La Duca and Chinki Sinha, "Fire Chief: 'Something Is Happening'; Recent Arson Rate Approaches 1990s Levels," *Observer-Dispatch*, July 12, 2008.

12 **One hung on to her leg** Interview with Azira Tabucic, August 14, 2020.

12 **Buffalo lost over half** Ken Belson, "Vacant Houses, Scourge of a Beaten-Down Buffalo," *New York Times*, September 13, 2007.

12 **On virtually every block** Belson, *New York Times*, September 13, 2007.

12 **By 2000, there were vast stretches** Marc J. Masson, "Vacant and Abandoned Housing in Buffalo," Partnership for the Public Good, *Buffalo Brief*, December 2014.

12 **By 1997, the population had declined** Salena Zito, "The Day That Destroyed the Working Class," *New York Post*, September 16, 2017; population graph, Youngstown, Ohio: https://development.ohio.gov/files/research/youngstown.pdf.

12 **It was designed by Richard George** Fiona O'Downey, "Historical Perspective: Olbiston Once a Jewel on 'Genesee Hill,' " *Observer-Dispatch*, June 16, 2019.

12 **In recent decades, it had fallen** Noelle Crombie, "Rebuilding a Neighborhood," *Observer-Dispatch*, March 19, 1994.

13 **Ten fire trucks and 50 firefighters** Fasolo, March 6, 2020.

13 **At 2 a.m. on an icy March morning** Noelle Crombie and Glenn Coin, "Struggle to Survive," *Observer-Dispatch*, March 15, 1994.

13 **Some emergency exit doors** Crombie and Coin, *Observer-Dispatch*, March 15, 1994.

13 **Grover Smith, asleep** Crombie, *Observer-Dispatch*, March 19, 1994.

13 **And the city began to absorb** Crombie, *Observer-Dispatch*, March 19, 1994.

13 **Three were hospitalized** Crombie and Coin, *Observer-Dispatch*, March 15, 1994.

Chapter 9 IN BLOOM

From 2013 to 2021, Shelly Callahan—in numerous interviews—kept me in touch with changes in the refugee community. Sakib Duracak and Mohamed Ganiso did the same, regarding their respective communities. Their insights informed this chapter and others. I'm also grateful to Catherine L. Besteman, professor of anthropology at Colby College, for her thoughtful responses to my fact checker's questions about the Somali Bantus.

36 **By 2019, more than 4,000** A summary of the waves of refugees resettled by the Mohawk Valley Resource Center for Refugees: https://www.thecenterutica.org/about/our-history/.

36 **Newcomers are given** Interview with Shelly Callahan, January 13, 2021.

36 **Chobani estimates** Interview with John Kell, media lead at the Chobani factory in New Berlin, March 5, 2021.

36 **The city tore down** La Duca and Sinha, *Observer-Dispatch*, July 12, 2008.

37 **Russians, who escaped religious** Interview with Shelly Callahan, March 5, 2021.

38 **In recent years, the Somali Bantus** Interview with Daniel J. Van Lehman, July 27, 2021.

39 **That year, the unemployment rate** New York State Department of Labor Statistics for Mohawk Valley region, December 2019.

39 **More than half of Utica's Somali Bantus** Interview with Mohamed Ganiso, October 19, 2019.

39 **Dozens of their children** Interview with Dr. Kathryn Stam, February 18, 2021.

39 **They made broom handles** Henry J. Cookinham, *History of Oneida County, New York: From 1700 to the Present Time*, vol. 1, pt. 2 (Chicago: S. J. Clarke Publishing, 1912), 443–53.

39 **The city was dubbed** Peter Eisenstadt, editor in chief, *Encyclopedia of New York State* (Syracuse, NY: Syracuse University Press, 2005), 1626.

39 **Women mostly worked in the woolen mills** George Perazich and W. T. Stone, *Economic Effect of Textile Mill Closings, Selected Communities in Middle Atlantic States* (Washington, DC: US Dept. of Commerce, 1963).

39 **Utica knitting company** Cookinham, *History of Oneida County.*

39 **By 1940, there were** Lebanese and Syrian Americans; info from Utica College Ethnic Heritage Studies Center: https://www.utica.edu/academic/institutes/ethnic/lebanese.cfm.

39 **Almost a quarter of the city's population** *Steber's Utica City Directory* (New York: R. L. Polk & Co., 1940–1941), 1.

40 **Picking up the slack** Perazich and Stone, *Economic Effect of Textile Mill Closings.*

Chapter 12 SHADOW

48 **The government began deporting** "Red Cross Criticizes Iran and Iraq," *New York Times*, May 12, 1983.

PART II MY UTICA

Chapter 14 THE STRIKE FORCE

I am grateful to Lieutenant Phil Fasolo, Deputy Chief Peter Caruso, and Captain Mickey Maunz—original members of the Utica Strike Force—for sharing their memories in an interview on March 6, 2020.

59 **A team of 16** Text from Phil Fasolo, March 9, 2021; Scott Wallace, "May the Force Be with You," *Observer-Dispatch*, February 15, 1998.

59 **It was a large-scale** *TechBeat*, Fall 1998; interview with Phil Fasolo, January 28, 2021.

60 **They had access** Fasolo, January 28, 2021.

60 **The Strike Force was also given** *TechBeat*, Fall 1998.

60 **If the fire marshal** Scott Wallace, "On the Trail of an Arsonist," *Observer-Dispatch*, February 15, 1998; Fasolo, January 28, 2021.

60 **Investigators were able to track** Scott Wallace, "Among the Bag of High Tech Tricks," *Observer-Dispatch*, February 15, 1998.

60 **US Marshals, working with** *TechBeat*, Fall 1998.

60 **The Strike Force got guilty pleas** La Duca and Sinha, *Observer-Dispatch*, July 12, 2008.

60 **Arson was cut in half.** *TechBeat*, Fall 1998.

61 **They covered walls with tapestries** Interviews with Captain Zumpano, Chief Ingersoll, and Dr. Stam, from 2019 to 2020.

62 **But they had not been able** Keshia Clukey, "Months after Adrean Terrace Fire, 4-Year-Old Making Recovery," *Observer-Dispatch*, July 6, 2013.

62 **Minutes later, Mr. De Carlo** Video of rescue: https://www.youtube.com/watch?v=OZcoVplNKfQ.

63 **These flat, cast-iron elements** Interview with Joe Puleo, Utica firefighter, March 4, 2020.

63 **The refugee center received** Alexander Gerould, "Officials Address Stove Fires at MHA Apartments," *Observer-Dispatch*, December 8, 2014.

63 **The citywide number of fires** Puleo, March 4, 2020.

63 **There are only two African Americans** Interview with Captain Zumpano, March 4, 2021.

63 **So far, they are too young** Interview with Stephanie Heiland of Pathways to Justice Careers, March 10, 2021.

Chapter 16 CONFESSIONS OF A TEACHER

68 **About 80 percent of the student** New York State Department of Education data, school year 2017–2018, https://data.nysed.gov/enrollment.php?year=2018&instid=800000041259.

69 **There are programs that offer help** Info about Young Scholars Liberty Partnerships Program: https://www.utica.edu/academic/yslpp/aboutus.cfm.

70 **AIS—Academic Intervention Services** Info about Academic Intervention Services: https://www.uticaschools.org/Page/3651.

70 **These programs, like the newcomer program** Alissa Scott, "Utica Schools
Sued Over Refugee Students," *New York Times*, April 23, 2015.

70 **And they did not provide** Interview with Deborah L. Wilson-Allam, executive
director of international education at Utica College, February 15, 2021.

70 **This was a violation** New York State's complaint against the Utica school
district: https://ag.ny.gov/pdfs/Utica_City_School_District_Complaint.pdf;
Benjamin Mueller, "New York State Accuses Utica School District of Bias
Against Refugees," *New York Times*, November 17, 2015.

71 **It sent him back** Polly Kreisman, "Teenager from Guatemala Denied Access to
Mamaroneck High School," *The Loop*, May 6, 2016, https://larchmontloop.com
/teenager-from-guatemala-denied-school-in-mamaroneck/.

71 **McCaskey High School** ACLU of Pennsylvania filed a federal lawsuit against
the district of Lancaster: https://www.aclupa.org/en/cases/issa-v-school
-district-lancaster#:~:text=The%20ACLU%20of%20Pennsylvania%2C%20the
,or%20diverting%20them%20to%20an.

71 **In 2015, the NYCLU had filed** Info about lawsuits against Lancaster, Mamaroneck, and Utica school districts: https://www.aclupa.org/en/cases/issa-v
-school-district-lancaster; https://www.nyclu.org/en/press-releases/school
-district-cannot-refuse-admit-immigrant-student-state-orders; https://www
.aclu.org/press-releases/nyclu-lscny-sue-utica-school-district-illegally-denying
-refugee-youth-education.

71 **By doing so, "the District** New York State: https://ag.ny.gov/pdfs/Utica_City
_School_District_Complaint.pdf.

71 **Ms. Wilson-Allam said that in 2014** Info about Utica settlement with NYCLU:
https://www.nyclu.org/en/press-releases/settlement-ensures-refugee-children
-can-go-high-school-utica.

72 **Notices are now posted around Utica** David W. Chen, "Utica Settles State
Claim Alleging Biased Enrollment for Refugee Students," *New York Times*,
July 21, 2016; Elizabeth A. Harris, "Utica Settles Lawsuit Over Refugees' Access
to High School," *New York Times*, May 19, 2016.

72 **The city spends $17,128 per student** Info about school district funding in
central New York. Utica is at the bottom: https://www.syracuse.com/schools
/2020/06/what-school-districts-spend-the-most-and-least-per-student-in
-central-new-york.html.

73 **The graduation rate of those enrolled** Proctor High School graduation rate
data as of August 2019: https://data.nysed.gov/gradrate.php?year=2019&instid
=800000041259.

73 **Kevin Marken, the Utica director** Interview with Kevin Marken, director of
On Point for College, July 2, 2021. Info about On Point for College: https://www
.onpointforcollege.org/.

73 **The college also offers** Interview with Dr. Randall J. VanWagoner, January 8,
2021.

Chapter 18 THE BAN

79 **In the 2016 presidential election** Oneida County election results for the 2016 presidential election: https://www.nytimes.com/elections/2016/results/new-york.

79 **The county has voted for** Info about voting patterns in central New York: https://www.localsyr.com/news/local-news/cny-rural-counties-that-backed-obama-are-now-solidly-trump-country/.

79 **But in 2016, East Utica** Data about how Utica's different districts voted: https://results.enr.clarityelections.com/NY/Oneida/64645/181949/Web01/en/summary.html.

80 **After five years in the country** Info about refugee status: https://www.hias.org/refugee-does-refugee-status-expire; info about refugees becoming citizens: https://www.rescue.org/article/how-immigrants-and-refugees-become-us-citizens.

Chapter 21 COMING HOME

93 **On a spring night in 2019** 911 Oneida County Media Summary Report, June 14, 2019.

93 **It is not unusual** Interview with Mark Williams, Utica's chief of police, June 6, 2019.

93 **In 2018, there were 37** Appendix: *New York Opioid Annual Report 2020*, New York State Department of Health, p. 28: https://health.ny.gov/statistics/opioid/data/pdf/2020_annual_report_appendix.pdf#page=28.

93 **While the crisis affects families** Williams, June 6, 2019; interview with Dr. Natalie Hua, July 28, 2021.

Chapter 23 LOFTS

99 **An outsider might be skeptical** Utica's population in 2000 and 2006: https://www.biggestuscities.com/city/utica-new-york#:~:text=What%20is%20the%20current%20population,largest%20city%20in%20the%20US.

99 **Residents' real per capita income** Utica's real per capita income compared to national per capita income: https://www.google.com/search?q=individual+income+utica+2006&sxsrf=ALeKko2ZUnGiEtoMsrxBsvKZ6_ZVNVQd7Q%3A1622664081180&ei=keO3YI2pCo2v5NoPiZWWoA4&oq=in.

99 **She saw a market for 108** Interview with Laurie Volk, November 25, 2020; I viewed slides from Volk's downtown Utica PowerPoint presentation.

102 **The region's economic problems** Jesse McKinley, "Cuomo's 'Buffalo Billion': Is New York Getting Its Money's Worth?" *New York Times*, July 2, 2018; McKinley, "Cuomo Struggles to Maintain Momentum in Upstate Employment," *New York Times*, November 6, 2015.

102 **Utica started to see a windfall** Dan Guzewich, "State Ups Investment in Utica Aud to $10.5 M," *Rome Daily Sentinel*, September 29, 2017.

102 **The new project—a power electronics** Jesse McKinley, "General Electric

Comes Back to Utica, and Brings Jobs Along with It," *New York Times*, August 20, 2015.

102 **The governor announced that AMS** Dan Guzewich, "Double Dose of Good News 2000 Jobs and $2 Billion Investment in Pair of Projects," *Rome Sentinel*, August 20, 2015.

Chapter 24 MERSIHA LEAPS

104 **Alain E. Kaloyeros, the president** Vivian Yee, "How Cuomo's Signature Economic Growth Project Fell Apart in Utica," *New York Times*, December 27, 2016.

104 **A modern glass and steel building** Interview with Bob Scholefield, executive vice president of facilities and real estate at Mohawk Valley Health System, and Darlene Stromstad, president/CEO of Mohawk Valley Health System, June 14, 2019.

109 **"Everybody here have insurance,"** Info about refugee health insurance: https://www.acf.hhs.gov/orr/programs/refugees/health.

Chapter 25 BOMB THREAT

110 **When Mr. Omerovic, a Bosnian-American** Jolene Cleaver, "Utica College Student Arrested After Campus Threat," *Observer-Dispatch*, March 7, 2018.

Chapter 31 THE KEY

128 **The song commemorates the World War I** Lyrics to "March on the Drina," and description of the Battle of Cer: https://accordeonworld.weebly.com /drinamarch.html.

Chapter 32 WHO WILL HELP YOU?

133 **NATO launched Operation Deliberate Force** Stephen Engelberg and Tim Weiner, "Massacre in Bosnia; Srebrenica: The Days of Slaughter," *New York Times*, October 29, 1995. Description of Operation Deliberate Force: https:// www.globalsecurity.org/military/ops/deliberate_force.htm. "Bosnia's Srebrenica Massacre 25 Years On—In Pictures," BBC, July 11, 2020, https://www.bbc.com /news/world-europe-53346759.

134 **His brother returned to his military unit** Info about the town of Ključ in the aftermath of war: https://www.refworld.org/docid/3ae6ab317b.html.

137 **My head was bigger** Video of Hajrudin the day he was released from the camp: https://youtu.be/G9g1OsBkpBQ. He appears at 13:19; his name is called. He is the second-to-last man in the line of prisoners.

137 **The agreement was signed on** Bill Clinton, "Dayton Accords, International Agreement," https://www.britannica.com/event/Dayton-Accords.

139 **The rumor was they had taken** Anja Vladisavljevic, "Croatia Contests Ruling Sparing War Criminals from Compensation Payments," *Balkan Insight*, May 27, 2019.

PART III, NEW AMERICANS

Chapter 33 THEY DON'T TALK ABOUT IT

146 **It will not be easy** Interview with Dr. Hua, February 26, 2021.

146 **In East Utica and Cornhill** Reuters analyzed childhood blood lead testing data in different neighborhoods in 34 states. "Looking for Lead," https://www .reuters.com/investigates/graphics/lead-water/en/.

146 **Most of the city's housing stock** "Looking for Lead," https://www.reuters.com /investigates/graphics/lead-water/en/.

146 **Later, if they have a snack** Interview with John Adams of Cornell Cooperative Extension, Green and Healthy Homes Initiative, March 11, 2021.

146 **The traditional yellow face paint** Interview with Dr. Warfel, February 17, 2021.

146 **If a child has elevated blood lead** Interview with John Adams, March 11, 2021.

147 **There is reason to be hopeful** Samantha Madison, "Utica Awarded $3.5 Million for Lead Removal," *Observer-Dispatch*, December 12, 2018.

147 **In 2016, that dropped to** Oneida County data about high lead levels in children under 6 from New York State Department of Health: https:// webbi1.health.ny.gov/SASStoredProcess/guest?_program=/EBI/PHIG/apps /chir_dashboard/chir_dashboard&p=ctr&ind_id=Cg28&cos=30.

Chapter 37 THE MAYOR'S SWEEP

167 **Between 2014 and 2018, the city** Utica losing 1,300 residents between 2014 and 2018: https://worldpopulationreview.com/us-cities/utica-ny-population.

167 **This will be the lowest number** The United States plans to cut the refugee program: https://www.pewresearch.org/fact-tank/2019/10/07/key-facts-about -refugees-to-the-u-s/.

167 **Refugees helped boost southeastern Michigan** Niraj Warikoo, "Study: Refugees Added Up to $295 Million to Southeast Michigan Economy in 2016," *Detroit Free Press*, October 17, 2017.

167 **The automotive industry and construction** Trevor Bach, "Will a Refugee Shortage Affect Detroit's Famed Comeback?," *U.S. News & World Report*, February 28, 2019.

168 **The facility is supposed to be** "Cree Aims to Start Operations in Marcy in 14 Months," *Rome Daily Sentinel*, February 11, 2020.

168 **Many in Utica's Black community** Utica's Black community is about 15 percent of the city's population: https://datausa.io/profile/geo/utica-ny/.

168 **They were marginalized from the start.** James S. Pula, ed., *Ethnic Utica* (Utica, NY: Ethnic Heritage Studies Center at Utica College, 2002), 26, 27, 29.

168 **They knew how to avoid** Pula, *Ethnic Utica*, 23, 29.

169 **It is now predominately working class** In an interview on March 13, 2020, Freddie Hamilton, a Cornhill resident and activist, estimated that about a third of the neighborhood is composed of refugees.

Chapter 39 THE VISIT

177 **Saddam was being tried, along with** John F. Burns, "Combative Saddam Back in Court," *New York Times*, November 29, 2005.

178 **The trial was adjourned until November** Burns, "Defiant Hussein, Lashing Out at U.S., Goes on Trial," *New York Times*, October 20, 2005.

Chapter 43 SIX MONTHS

190 **And police had used tear gas** Falih Hassan and Alissa J. Rubin, "Facing a 'Shortage of Everything,' Iraqis Protest Corruption," *New York Times*, October 3, 2019.

190 **During the first few days of protest** Alissa J. Rubin, "Iraqi Security Forces Kill Dozens in Week of Protest," *New York Times*, October 6, 2019.

Chapter 44 HIS TEXT

193 **They also wanted a new constitution** Alissa J. Rubin, "Pressure Grows on Iraq's Prime Minister to Quit as Protests Clog Streets," *New York Times*, October 31, 2019.

193 **A few days later, Mahdi offered** Alissa J. Rubin, "Iraqi Antigovernment Protests Grow, Part Battle Lines and Carnival," *New York Times*, October 28, 2019.

193 **Iran had been supporting powerful** Alissa J. Rubin, "A New Slogan Ignites Iraqis, 'Iran Get Out,'" *New York Times*, November 5, 2019.

193 **He was an Iraqi immigrant** Tim Arango and Neil MacFarquhar, "His Death Rattled World and Shook His U.S. City," *New York Times*, January 19, 2020.

193 **In retaliation, the United States** Julian E. Barnes, "U.S. Launches Airstrikes on Iranian-Backed Forces in Iraq and Syria," *New York Times*, December 29, 2019.

193 **There were calls for the American** Alissa J. Rubin and Ben Hubbard, "Strikes by U.S. Renew Anger Among Iraqis," *New York Times*, December 31, 2019.

194 **They shattered security cameras** Falih Hassan, Ben Hubbard, and Alissa J. Rubin, "Iraqi Protesters Attack Embassy After U.S. Strike," *New York Times*, January 1, 2020.

194 **Across the region—and in America** Michael Crowley, Falih Hassan, and Eric Schmitt, "U.S. Strike in Iraq Kills Qassim Suleimani, Commander of Iranian Forces," *New York Times*, January 2, 2020.

194 **The next day, tens of thousands** Alissa J. Rubin, Ben Hubbard, and Falih Hassan, "Cries of 'Revenge Is Coming' at Funerals for 2 Slain Commanders," *New York Times*, January 5, 2020.

194 **And the American-led coalition suspended** Alissa J. Rubin, Ben Hubbard, Farnaz Fassihi, and Steven Erlanger, "Standoff Builds as Iran Drops Nuclear Limits," *New York Times*, January 6, 2020.

194 **In some parts of the world, there was** Mark Mazzetti, Eric Schmitt, Lara Jakes, and Thomas Gibbons-Neff, "3 Hours from Alert to Attacks: Inside the Race to Protect U.S. Forces from Iran Strikes," *New York Times*, January 8, 2020.

Chapter 48 KARMA

220 **Down below, the water is the bluest blue** K. M. Stewart, K. F. Walker, and
G. E. Likens, "Meromictic Lakes," *Encyclopedia of Inland Waters* (Amsterdam:
Elsevier/Academic Press, 2009), 589–602. Another source: Information about
Green Lake posted around the trails of Green Lake State Park.

EPILOGUE WE RALLIED

221 **Construction projects—like the Nexus** Interview with Marquis Phillips,
April 30, 2021.

221 **But by January 3, 2021, the seven-day** "Oneida County, New York, Coronavirus Cases and Deaths," *USAFACTS,* updated May 1, 2021: https://usafacts
.org/visualizations/coronavirus-covid-19-spread-map/state/new-york/county
/oneida-county; interview with Dr. Hua, April 30, 2021.

222 **The hospital was renamed** Amy Roth Neff, "MVHS Hits Jackpot with
$50 Million Gift from Developer Steve Wynn's Family Foundation," March 5,
2021: https://www.uticaod.com/story/news/2021/03/04/casino-developer
-steve-wynns-family-foundation-gives-mvhs-50-million/6911146002/.

222 **This fiscal year—as of March 2021** Interview with Shelly Callahan, March 10,
2021.

224 **But after eight months, Nawres returned** Arango and MacFarquhar,
New York Times, January 19, 2020; interview with Ali, March 24, 2021.

224 **But he was sent to Kirkuk** Interview with Ali, March 24, 2021

INDEX

25–26; work for ABC News in Iraq, 122–23

Sarhan, Saif: description of, 5, 122; kidnapping of, 123–24; move to Syria, 123; work for ABC News in Iraq, 122

Schneiderman, Eric T., 70

Sofia (Sadia's cousin): account of family's escape from Somalia, 202–5; American-style behavior in, 94; attends Sadia's baby shower, 183, 184; blocking Sadia on Facebook, 46; compares Sadia to Zahara, 204; COVID-19 infection, 221; employment at nursing home, 95; failure of marriage, 94, 95; friendship with Sadia, 15; lead poisoning in Amrah, 147; move back home, 153; move to apartment with Sadia, 95–97; move to grandmother's house, 94–95; relationship with Amrah's father, 95–96; relationship with mother, 153

Somali Bantu refugees: adaptation to life in Utica, 38; cultural practices contributing to home fires, 61–62; divorce among, 41; family disagreements among, 46–47; home purchases by, 118; importance of children to, 19; polygamy among, 119–20; role of leaders in community, 143; view of dating, 18; view of Zahara, 15; wedding celebrations of, 41. *See also by name*

Special Bosnians, 213–14, 223

Stam, Kathryn: on cultural practices contributing to home fires, 61, 64; on importance of children in Somali Bantu families, 19; on lead poisoning, 146; on polygamy in Somali Bantu families, 119; on reception of Somali Bantu in Utica, 38

Strike Force, formation of, 59–60

students: older, high school education of, 70–72; outcomes of, 73;

psychological support for trauma in, 72–73; teaching challenges, 68–69, 74

Suleimani, Qassim, 194–95

Sunderland, Chris, 80

Syrian immigrants, 39

teachers, challenges facing, 68–69, 74

textile mills, in Utica, 39

Thomas, Brian, 99–100, 102, 105

traditional medicine, 147

trauma: in Bosnian refugees, 137–40; in Iraqi refugees, 49, 224; in Karen refugees, 143–45, 150–51; psychological support for, 72–73, 148–49; in Somali Bantu refugees, 202–4

travel ban on Muslims, 79–82

Trump, Donald: election of, 79; Muslim travel ban, 79–82; number of refugees admitted under, 83–84

Utica, New York: arrival of refugee groups in, 35–39; arson in, 9, 11–14; Black Lives Matter protests in, 222; COVID-19 pandemic in, 221–22; crime issues in, 93; cultural practices contributing to home fires, 61–63; development plans for, 166–68, 169; Harbor Point Project in, 166, 169–70; immigrant history of, 39–40; lead poisoning in, 146–47; loft development in, 99–101; new hospital in, 104–5, 222; opioid crisis in, 93; population decline in, 9–11, 167–68; revival of, 99–103; Strike Force, formation of, 59–60

Utica school district, lawsuit against, 71–72

Valastro, Buddy, 33

VanWagoner, Randall J., 72

Vietnamese refugees, 37

Volk, Laurie, 99–100